OECD Green Growth Studies

Urban Green Growth in Dynamic Asia

OECD
BETTER POLICIES FOR BETTER LIVES

This work is published under the responsibility of the Secretary-General of the OECD. The opinions expressed and arguments employed herein do not necessarily reflect the official views of OECD member countries.

This document and any map included herein are without prejudice to the status of or sovereignty over any territory, to the delimitation of international frontiers and boundaries and to the name of any territory, city or area.

Please cite this publication as:
OECD (2016), *Urban Green Growth in Dynamic Asia*, OECD Green Growth Studies, OECD Publishing, Paris.
http://dx.doi.org/10.1787/9789264266360-en

ISBN 978-92-64-26635-3 (print)
ISBN 978-92-64-26636-0 (PDF)

Series: OECD Green Growth Studies
ISSN 2222-9515 (print)
ISSN 2222-9523 (online)

The statistical data for Israel are supplied by and under the responsibility of the relevant Israeli authorities. The use of such data by the OECD is without prejudice to the status of the Golan Heights, East Jerusalem and Israeli settlements in the West Bank under the terms of international law.

Corrigenda to OECD publications may be found on line at: *www.oecd.org/about/publishing/corrigenda.htm*.

Foreword

The Urban Green Growth in Dynamic Asia project explores how to promote green growth in cities in Asia, examining policies and governance practices that encourage environmental sustainability and competitiveness in a rapidly expanding economy. The main aim is to assist Southeast Asian cities in decoupling economic growth from environmental stress and to promote a long-term trajectory of sustained growth.

This synthesis report presents the results of case studies along with practical policy recommendations, reflecting the local contexts of Southeast Asia. While Southeast Asian cities are affected by a range of economic, infrastructure, environmental and social challenges, ongoing rapid development offers opportunities to shift towards greener growth models. The concept of urban green growth can be a powerful vector of sustainable development, by emphasising the existence and potential of enhancing both economic and environmental performance.

This report indicates that there are many unexplored areas for advancing green growth, especially in land use and transportation, solid waste, water resource management, energy, buildings, and green industries and services. However, it highlights that the window of opportunity for Southeast Asia to switch to a sustainable model of growth is fast closing, and that it should act now to reduce the environmental externalities associated with its rapid economic and urban growth. Inaction now could not only hinder economic and social progress but reduce quality of life. Land use is the most important policy area that can underpin other sectoral opportunities, generating synergies to advance green growth.

This report contributes both to the OECD Green Growth Strategy and to the OECD Strategy on Development, as well as to ongoing discussions on the role of cities in tackling the urgent challenges of climate change. The project is part of the OECD Green Cities Programme, launched in 2010, which has conducted four metropolitan case studies (Paris, Chicago, Stockholm and Kitakyushu), two national case studies (the People's Republic of China and Korea) and produced a synthesis report, *Green Growth in Cities* (2013).

The analysis is based on a "focused comparison" strategy of case study research. This entailed asking the same questions to the different case study cities in order to discern similarities and draw general lessons. Although the analysis focuses on Asian cities, the lessons for promoting green growth will also be relevant for other OECD member countries and cities.

The report was prepared by the Directorate for Public Governance and Territorial Development. The Directorate's mission is to help governments at all levels design and implement strategic, evidence-based and innovative policies to strengthen public governance; respond effectively to diverse and disruptive economic, social and environmental challenges; and to deliver on governments' commitments to citizens.

This publication benefited from guidance from the OECD Regional Development Policy Committee and its Working Party on Urban Policy, as well as the support of the local teams and city governments. It draws on data provided by the local team and the *OECD Metropolitan Database*. The analytical approach draws on *Urban Green Growth in Dynamic Asia: A Conceptual Framework* (2014). The expertise and experience of OECD member countries provided relevant international benchmarks and policy examples.

Acknowledgements

This publication was led and co-ordinated by Tadashi Matsumoto (Project Manager, Urban Green Growth/Knowledge Sharing) under the direction of Joaquim Oliveira Martins (Head of the Regional Development Policy Division). Loïc Daudey (Consultant, Green Growth/Knowledge Sharing in Southeast Asia) drafted Chapters 1 and 3, while Tadashi Matsumoto and Kwame Boye Frimpong (Consultant, Green Growth in Southeast Asia) drafted Chapter 2. The report benefited from comments and inputs from colleagues at the OECD: Karen Maguire, William Tompson, Martin Abbott, Christian Pollock, Chris McDonald, Hidekatsu Asada, Peter Borkey and Miza Razali. Pilar Philip, Joanne Dudon and Jennifer Allain prepared the manuscript for publication.

Our thanks go to the local teams of the five case study cities in Southeast Asia that provided comments and inputs to the report: Bandung (Indonesia), Iskandar Malaysia (Malaysia), Metro Cebu (the Philippines), Bangkok (Thailand) and Hai Phong (Viet Nam). The OECD Secretariat would like to thank in particular: Boyd Dionysius Joeman and Sharifah Shahidah Syed Ahmad (Iskandar Regional Development Authority), Province of Cebu; Evelyn Nacario Castro and Jackie Amazona Clavin (Metro Cebu Development and Coordinating Board-Research Program and Organization Development/Ramon Aboitiz Foundation, Inc. Eduardo Aboitiz Development Studies Center); Suwanna Jungrungrueng, Wullaya Wattanarat, Termsiri Chongpoonphol, Jarupong Pengglieng and Nuanphan Phawawes (Bangkok Metropolitan Administration); Vu Hoang Cuong and Le Thi Hanh (City of Hai Phong). The publication also benefited from valuable inputs from the five case study reports and the Knowledge-Sharing Platform on Urban Green Growth in Dynamic Asia, in particular from the Knowledge Sharing Workshops held in Bangkok (6-7 August 2014), Iskandar Malaysia (5-6 November 2014), Bandung (6-7 May 2015), Hai Phong (25-27 June 2015) and Cebu (9-10 December 2015).

The OECD Secretariat would like to acknowledge gratefully the financial support of the government of Japan.

Table of contents

Tables

Figures

Boxes

Acronyms and abbreviations

3Rs	Reduce, reuse and recycle
ASEAN	Association of Southeast Asian Nations
BMA	Bandung Metropolitan Area
BMR	Bangkok Metropolitan Region
BOD	Biochemical oxygen demand
BRT	Bus rapid transit
CO_2	Carbon dioxide
CSO	Civil society organisation
FDI	Foreign direct investment
FUA	Functional urban area
GDP	Gross domestic product
GHG	Greenhouse gas
GIS	Geographic Information System
GRP	Gross regional product
GW	Gigawatts
ICT	Information and communications technology
IMER	Iskandar Malaysia Economic Region
KPI	Key performance indicator
KSA	Knowledge Sharing Alliance
kW	Kilowatt
LGUs	Local government units
LRT	Light-rail transit
MCDA	Metro Cebu Development Authority
MCDCB	Metro Cebu Development Co-ordinating Board
MSW	Municipal solid waste
NRW	Non-revenue water
ODA	Official development assistance
ODF	Official development finance

OOF	Other official flows
PM	Particulate matter
PPP	Public-private partnership
PPP	Purchasing power parity
RE	Renewable energy
SME	Small and medium-sized enterprise
TEU	Twenty-foot equivalent unit
TOD	Transit-oriented development
toe	Tonnes of oil equivalent
WHO	World Health Organization

Executive summary

Urban green growth policies pursue economic development while reducing either negative environmental externalities (for example, air pollution and carbon dioxide emissions) or the consumption of natural resources and environmental assets, including water, energy and undeveloped land, through urban activities. Therefore, cities must be central to green growth efforts as they not only play a critical role in stimulating national growth, but also generate negative environmental externalities.

Successful urban green growth outcomes will require different models, taking into account local policy contexts. Southeast Asia is currently experiencing rapid growth in its economy and urban population. The level of urbanisation of the ASEAN-5 (Association of Southeast Asian Nations) countries increased from 29.5% in 1980 to 51.4% in 2015, and is expected to reach 67.7% in 2050. Gross domestic product per capita increased from USD 8 500 in 1985 to USD 24 800 in 2015, mainly driven by foreign direct investment in the manufacturing industry. However, this positive growth is marred by poor environmental performance and widening social disparities. The results of the case studies produced for this report indicate that rapid growth has created a number of environmental and infrastructure challenges for cities, including uncontrolled urban sprawl and loss of natural assets such as mangroves, air pollution from industries and urban transport, rising greenhouse gas emissions owing to increasing energy consumption, rising amounts of municipal solid waste, as well as water stress and pollution. Exposure and vulnerability to natural disasters, primarily floods, typhoons, hurricanes and earthquakes, have also increased. The annual number of disasters in Southeast Asia has risen dramatically, from 13 in 1970 to 41 in 2014. The frequency and impact of such disasters are expected to increase in the future, as a result of a combination of climate change effects (such as sea-level rise), urbanisation and socio-economic change.

These trends clearly differ from most OECD country experiences. It is important that Southeast Asia shift its growth model not only to promote economic growth, but also to preserve natural assets and environmental services, and promote social development. Any development model that is not based on green growth runs the risk of leaving Southeast Asia ill-equipped to pursue long-term economic, environmental and social prosperity.

Seizing untapped potential: Assessment of green growth policies

Strong opportunities for urban green growth exist in land use and transport, solid waste, water resource management, energy, buildings, and green industries and services, many of which are untapped. However, the window of opportunity for Southeast Asia to switch to a sustainable model of growth is fast closing, and it should act now to reduce the environmental externalities associated with its rapid economic and urban growth. Overall, land use and energy demonstrate the most important policy areas, since they can support other sectoral opportunities.

Several key strategies for effective urban green growth can be identified. Sustainable urban transport policies need to be put much higher on the green growth agenda, and be better co-ordinated with land-use planning (e.g. through transit-oriented development). Policies to reduce the quantity of urban waste and to increase the capacity of waste treatment should go in hand-in-hand. The "3Rs" (reduce, reuse and recycle) principle must be embedded into municipal solid waste strategies. City governments can promote energy and resource efficiency through regulations to ensure that buildings meet a minimum stringent green standard. An equally important measure to nudge industries into being more environmentally friendly and efficient is green labelling, for which public awareness seems low.

Beyond sectoral policies for green growth, strong needs for policy complementarities have been identified in the case studies and show high potential to support green growth objectives. Such synergies can maximise policy outcomes and reduce trade-offs, in particular. For instance, waste-to-energy technology can support waste treatment efforts while easing the pressure on energy supply systems. Disaster risk management, likewise, requires close policy co-ordination between all of the aforementioned opportunity areas. The case study cities also shed light on additional policy objectives – in particular inclusiveness – that are essential and therefore complementary elements for urban green growth in Southeast Asia.

Demand-side policies and the use of pricing mechanisms offer stronger potential to support green growth measures. Shifting tax burdens to encourage environmental performance or penalise negative environmental externalities would have high impact in Southeast Asian cities. Taxes, fees and charges, backed by adequate information on consequences of action can efficiently encourage consumers to behave in a more sustainable manner. For instance, progressive tariff structures and charges on groundwater extraction can help to optimise consumption.

Innovation, quality infrastructure investment and human resource development are catalysts for the long-term growth of Southeast Asian cities and can support green growth objectives. It is important that long-term planning decisions for infrastructure in the coming years is not sacrificed for short-term expediencies given the huge demand.

Good governance for urban green growth in Southeast Asia

Decentralisation trends in Southeast Asia since the 1990s have progressively transferred some responsibilities from central to local governments, which increased the need for vertical policy co-ordination. Such co-ordination is not always effective, due to a lack of policy frameworks at both national and local levels and of co-ordination mechanisms in some sectors. For example, many cities have not adopted master plans for energy and have failed to implement national guidelines in many sectors. National governments need to recognise the role cities can play in each green growth opportunity area and promote collaborative action vertically as well as across municipalities. Many metropolitan areas in Southeast Asia are characterised by a lack of formal and informal collaboration among local governments, despite a critical need for such co-ordination. The OECD's "functional urban areas" (FUA) concept could be applied to Southeast Asian countries in order to seek the most appropriate scale of action.

Financing urban green growth is one of the most critical green growth implementation levers. Although local revenues have increased in many Southeast Asian cities, they have not kept pace with the needs created by economic and urban growth, and the new functions devolved by decentralisation reforms. Local governments should improve the efficiency of tax collection and raise revenues from fees and charges, which are still underdeveloped. Conditions for private investment should also be enhanced, in particular public-private partnerships (PPPs). National governments should design capacity-building and technical assistance programmes to help subnational governments design PPPs. Moreover, international development aid should be more targeted to cities. Among environment-related official development finance (ODF) committed in ASEAN-5 countries, around 37.2% can be clearly identified as targeting cities in 2002-14, with no significant evolution of such proportion over time. Secondary cities only received very small amounts in comparison to capital cities, and the impact of existing projects on urban green growth is sometimes limited.

There is also a significant lack of data to monitor and evaluate cities' green growth performance over time, in particular at the metropolitan scale. This creates difficulties for policy makers to put green growth on their agenda based on evidence-based analysis and to adequately communicate with citizens and other stakeholders to gain support. National and subnational governments should build capacities to produce such data and monitor their performance.

Chapter 1.

The urgent need to make growth in Southeast Asian cities green

This chapter examines urbanisation and economic growth trends in Southeast Asian cities, and the associated infrastructure, environmental and social challenges. An emphasis is placed on cities of the ASEAN-5 region comprising Indonesia, Malaysia, the Philippines, Thailand and Viet Nam. The identification of the main characteristics and development patterns of cities in this region points to the urgent need to green Southeast Asian cities' dynamic economic growth. After briefly introducing the topic, the chapter discusses urbanisation and economic development trends of Southeast Asian cities. It then moves on to discuss infrastructure and environmental challenges and social challenges and their economic and environmental repercussions. It closes with a short conclusion.

Key findings

- Southeast Asia has experienced a dynamic urbanisation process that will continue in the coming decades. The combined urbanisation level of ASEAN-5 (Association of Southeast Asian Nations) countries increased from 29.5% in 1980 to 51.4% in 2015, and is expected to reach 67.7% in 2050. The aggregated urban population of these five countries increased from 79 million in 1980 to 271 million in 2015, and is forecasted to reach 452 million in 2050. Most of the population growth is happening in small and medium-sized cities. Around 67.7% of the urban population of the countries lived in cities with fewer than 500 000 inhabitants in 2015, against 8.6% in cities with more than 10 million inhabitants.

- In parallel, Southeast Asian economies have significantly expanded: gross domestic product (GDP) per capita in the ASEAN-5 region increased from around USD 8 500 in 1985 to around USD 24 800 in 2015. Cities are the main hubs of such economic growth, although high discrepancies in wealth are observable between the largest and secondary cities. Economic growth is mostly based on competitive labour and production costs, and supported by rising amounts of foreign direct investment (FDI). The growth in maritime trade also illustrates the economic dynamism of Southeast Asian market economies: container throughput in the ASEAN-5 region increased from 15.7 million TEUs (twenty-foot equivalent units) in 2000 to 54 million TEUs in 2014. While the manufacturing industry has been growing fast, the tertiary sector has been growing even faster and the economic structure of cities is increasingly dominated by services.

- Public services have not been able to keep up with the pace of urbanisation and economic growth, leading to great infrastructure and environmental challenges. The sprawl of many cities has been accompanied by fast motorisation. In Bangkok City, the motorisation rate increased from 1.2 to 2 vehicles per inhabitant between 2005 and 2013. The dramatic increase in the stock of motorised vehicles is leading to severe congestion in many cities, and to concentrations of particulate matter far above the World Health Organization's air quality standards. Another challenge is fast-rising amounts of solid waste generated by its residents. In Bandung Metropolitan Area, this amount increased from 4 320 tonnes per day in 2006 to 7 661 tonnes per day in 2014, or an increase from 180 to 320 kg per capita per year in just eight years. Such fast increasing quantities of solid waste have posed great challenges to local governments in collecting, handling and treating such waste. Waste collection services often do not reach all residents and landfills remain the preferred treatment method. Many Southeast Asian cities have also experienced increasing water demand and situations of water stress and scarcity, aggravated by the poor coverage and quality of water supply infrastructure. Water sanitation infrastructure is also sub-optimal and has not kept up with the pace of urbanisation, and the quality of water streams and bodies is often under established quality standards. In many Southeast Asia cities, informal services and infrastructure have compensated for the absence of formal structures.

- Southeast Asian cities are increasingly contributing to global greenhouse gas (GHG) emissions. The urban energy consumption has been increasing fast and is set to increase still significantly in the coming decades. In addition, fossil fuels remain the privileged source of energy. Energy-related emissions in Hai Phong accounted for 13.2 million tonnes of CO_2 in 2010 and are expected to increase to 49.6 million tonnes CO_2 in 2020. In parallel, a critical characteristic of Southeast Asian cities is their high vulnerability to the impacts of climate changes. The annual number of natural disasters in Southeast Asia increased from 13 in 1970 to 41 in 2014, resulting in a surge of both economic damages and the number of persons affected. Floods, typhoons, hurricanes and earthquakes are the most frequent types of disasters occurring in the region, sometimes bearing severe human and economic losses. The frequency and impacts of such disasters are expected to increase in the future, as a result of a combination of climate change impacts (such as sea-level rise), urbanisation and socio-economic changes.

Key findings (*continued*)

- Social challenges of Southeast Asian cities may also have long-term economic and environmental repercussions. A general trend towards the reduction of poverty is observable, but urban inequalities are rising: the Gini coefficient in the main Indonesian cities has increased at a faster rate than in Indonesia overall since 2008. In addition, cities in all countries of the region still host significant numbers of slum dwellers with poor access to urban services such as solid waste collection and high vulnerability to natural disasters. Many of these urban populations are "off the radar" and in informal employment.
- While Southeast Asian cities are affected by a range of economic, infrastructure, environmental and social challenges, the ongoing development process nonetheless still offers "windows of opportunities" to shift towards cleaner growth models. Such momentum must be seized immediately by national and local governments to avoid the consequences of business-as-usual development pathways. The concept of urban green growth in this regard can be a powerful vector of sustainable development in Southeast Asian cities, by emphasising the existence and potential of co-benefits between economic and environmental performance. The concept, however, needs to be adapted to the local context: due to the low unemployment rates, high economic growth and infrastructure gaps of Southeast Asian cities, this report demonstrates a stronger need to green Southeast Asian cities' growth rather than expanding the green economy sector, as promoted for OECD cities.

Introduction

What is green growth? What is urban green growth?

The concept of green growth has attracted much interest from governments at all levels as a potential means of stimulating growth and responding to environmental challenges. Responding to a call from its member countries, in 2011 the OECD developed a green growth strategy, *Towards Green Growth* (OECD, 2011). This defines green growth as "fostering economic growth and development while ensuring that natural assets continue to provide the resources and environmental services on which our well-being relies. To do this, it must catalyse investment and innovation which will underpin sustained growth and give rise to new economic opportunities" (OECD, 2011).

Policy makers' interest in green growth has led to a call for more information on the policies which can actually bring about green growth in cities. In this regard, the OECD defines urban green growth as fostering economic growth and development through urban activities that reduce negative environmental externalities and the impact on natural resources and environmental services (OECD, 2013). What is "green" about this growth is how it is stimulated: through urban activities (including policies and programmes) that reduce either: 1) negative environmental externalities, such as air pollution and CO_2 emissions; or 2) the consumption of natural resources and environmental services, including water, energy and undeveloped land. These effects are in part the result of more readily identifiable interactions at the urban level among economic efficiency and environmental objectives. By focusing on growth, this definition recognises that polices to reduce environmental impact can only be sustained over the long term if they generate wealth (OECD, 2013).

Fostering urban green growth is critical because cities play disproportionately large roles in the economic and environmental performance of countries. They are critical drivers of national growth. Just 2% of OECD regions, mainly the largest OECD urban areas, generate roughly one-third of all GDP growth in the OECD. In both the People's Republic of China (hereafter "China") and India, the five largest cities' economies contribute approximately 15% of national GDP – roughly three times their share of the population. In parallel, cities are experiencing explosive urban growth. By the end of the century, the global urbanisation level is projected to rise to around 85%, out of a world population of about 10 billion. This will reinforce cities' weight in the world economy, but this also implies tremendous economic, social and environmental challenges, as there will be 5 billion new urban dwellers to accommodate in the years ahead. Cities already contribute disproportionately to energy consumption, and thus to climate change. They account for an estimated 67% of global energy use and 71% of global energy-related CO_2 emissions. They also concentrate other environmental issues such as air and water pollution, land and water consumption, and solid waste generation.

Meanwhile, cities have the potential to foster green growth in their respective countries. This can be explained by the weight of cities in national economic and environmental performance, as mentioned previously, and also because they are opportune levels of action. Cities are indeed responsible for a significant share of national infrastructure investments – 58.8% in the OECD area. Policy complementarities are also more easily identifiable at the local level. Coherent policy packages can help mitigate the trade-offs among environmental, growth and equity priorities: a properly designed policy package would address the costs of reducing environmental impact in a co-ordinated way and have less impact on the most vulnerable people. It is easier on a local scale to identify environmental and economic policies that are complementary, as activities related to environmental protection and economic development are more integrated at the local level than at the national level. The fact that they are closer to citizens' needs, have better knowledge of local conditions, and can test and refine innovative ideas locally also creates conditions for successful policies (OECD, 2010).

Urban Green Growth in Dynamic Asia: Project outline

Launched in 2010, the OECD Green Cities Programme aims to assess the impact of urban sustainability and green growth policies on urban and national performance across a range of geographic, economic and national regulatory contexts, through case studies in key OECD and non-OECD cities. The aim of the programme is to better understand the concept of green growth in cities; the potential of urban policies for urban and national green growth; and to inform national, subnational and municipal governments as they seek to address economic and environmental challenges by pursuing green growth. Four city-level studies were carried out in 2011 and 2012: Stockholm (Sweden), Kitakyushu (Japan), Chicago (United States) and Paris/Île-de-France (France). These publications are part of the OECD Green Growth Studies series and feed into the synthesis report *Green Growth in Cities* (OECD, 2013). The findings presented in the current volume and in the companion case studies point to many promising links between urban green growth and outcomes such as job creation, attractiveness, innovation and entrepreneurship, and increased land values (Box 1.1).

Box 1.1. *Green Growth in Cities*: Main findings

Green Growth in Cities (OECD, 2013) outlines some of the high priority urban policies for green growth, as well as the national policies needed to complement and support these local policies. The report is illustrated with examples from six urban green growth case studies: four at the city level (Paris, Chicago, Stockholm and Kitakyushu) and two national studies (China and Korea). For example, the city-level case studies provide urban leaders with new insights on how environmental policies can contribute to different types of growth:

- Job creation: the right urban sustainability policies can include retrofitting the existing building stock for improved energy efficiency. For example, the Chicago Tri-State Metropolitan area has built a regional specialty in green building design and retrofitting. In 2010 it gave 45 000 people green jobs, 36% of which were in the green building sector.
- Attracting firms and workers: efficient transport systems, in particular good public transport networks, help cities lure investors. The private sector in the Paris/Île-de-France region has long recognised this, and firms that benefit from proximity to the transport system contribute to its financing.
- Innovation and entrepreneurship: cities can foster the growth of the green technology sector by creating green regional clusters that build on existing industries, services, research and innovation. Kitakyushu has built an impressive recycling cluster, the Eco-Town, which recycles hundreds of tonnes of industrial waste every day, while producing energy for residential and commercial neighbourhoods.
- Increasing the value of urban land: redevelopment, infill and eco-districts can enhance land values while increasing density and reducing residents' environmental impact. Following the success of its Hammarby Sjöstad eco-district, Stockholm is now working with the private sector to develop the Stockholm Royal Seaport eco-district. Buildings there will use less energy than others in Stockholm and the new district will have an advanced smart grid and district heating.

Box 1.1. ***Green Growth in Cities*: Main findings** (*continued*)

The report presents the role of national governments. They can enhance cities' capacity to promote green growth by:

- providing financial and technical support, clear targets, and monitoring mechanisms
- setting price signals and standards (for example, through carbon taxes or other pricing mechanisms)
- reviewing national policies' impact on local incentives, to identify and remove perverse incentives
- encouraging infrastructure investment in line with sustainable development and green goals.

The report observes that local governments lack financial resources for investing in urban green infrastructure, so that efforts to diversify revenue bases become an important strategy for cities. Mobilising private finance is also important to fill the funding gap for many urban green infrastructure projects.

Source: OECD (2013), *Green Growth in Cities*, http://dx.doi.org/10.1787/9789264195325-en.

Outside the OECD area, emerging Asian economies (China, India and Southeast Asia) have experienced fast urbanisation and economic growth and their cities have faced profound transformations affecting the economy, the society and the environment. The speed of growth, the lower level of development compared to OECD cities and some other specific features of cities of the region, such as their high exposure to climate change impacts, call for an urban green growth model different from the ones examined in *Green Growth in Cities* (OECD, 2013), one which takes into account the specific circumstances of Southeast Asian cities. Such a model offers an opportunity to assess the extent to which OECD best practices are relevant to dynamic Asian cities and at the same time to identify policies and approaches in Asia that can inform urban policy making in OECD countries and cities.

The OECD project Urban Green Growth in Dynamic Asia thus aims to explore ways to achieve green growth in fast-growing cities in Southeast Asia, in particular. More specifically, it examines ways to promote greening and competitiveness in a fast-growing economy, to improve environmental performance in cities and urban quality of life, and to increase the institutional capacity to achieve green growth. While the project addresses green growth in Southeast Asian cities, it will also benefit all OECD member countries and cities, as it provides "food for thought" for their own green growth policies by learning from the diverse contexts in Southeast Asian cities. The expertise and experiences of OECD member countries will also play a leading role in providing relevant international benchmarks. The project is articulated around the following elements:

- A conceptual framework sets out the analytical framework that is used to assess policies for urban green growth in fast-growing cities of Southeast Asia, in particular for the city case studies (Matsumoto and Daudey, 2014).
- Case studies of five cities in Southeast Asia (Bangkok, Thailand; Hai Phong, Viet Nam; Bandung, Indonesia; Metro Cebu, the Philippines; and Iskandar Malaysia, Malaysia), carried out between 2014 and 2016, included: 1) an analysis of their key socio-economic, infrastructure and environmental challenges; 2) an assessment of policies in six opportunity areas for green growth (land use and

transport, energy, housing and buildings, water, solid waste, and green goods and services); 3) a special chapter to discuss an urban green growth policy topic particularly relevant to the case study; and 4) identification of governance strategies to foster urban green growth. A detailed profile of each case study city, based on these studies, is provided in Annex A.

- Knowledge-sharing activities, organised between 2013 and 2016, aimed to facilitate knowledge sharing and mutual learning not only among cities in Asia but also with national governments, OECD cities and institutions for development co-operation. Since 2013, a series of conferences and peer learning workshops in the five case study cities were conducted under the framework of the Knowledge-Sharing Platform on Urban Green Growth in Dynamic Asia, created specifically for the project. The platform is supported by the OECD Knowledge Sharing Alliance (KSA). Annex B provides more information about the objectives and outcomes of the platform, and the events organised within its framework.

This report summarises the findings of the project. It consists of three chapters: Chapter 1 provides an analysis of socio-economic, infrastructure and environmental conditions of Southeast Asian cities. Chapter 2 discusses way to seize untapped opportunities for urban green growth. Finally, Chapter 3 proposes ways of ensuring good governance for urban green growth.

The growth of Southeast Asian cities and their role in national economic development

Fast urbanisation and growth of cities in Southeast Asia will continue in the coming decades

In recent decades, Southeast Asia[1] has experienced one of the most dynamic urbanisation processes in the world. Within the Southeast Asian region, the ASEAN-5 countries – Indonesia, Malaysia, the Philippines, Thailand and Viet Nam – are major drivers of such trends. Their combined urbanisation level increased from 29.5% in 1980 to 51.4% in 2015, and is expected to reach 67.7% in 2050 (UN DESA, 2014). In comparison, high-income countries[2] have already reached high levels of urbanisation and their growth is moderate: overall, their level of urbanisation increased from 71.8% in 1980 to 80.4% in 2015, and is expected to reach 86.7% in 2050 (UN DESA, 2014). The absolute number of urban dwellers is also rising at an impressive rate. The aggregated urban population of these five countries increased from 79 million in 1980 to 271 million in 2015, and is forecasted to reach 452 million in 2050 (Table 1.1 and Figure 1.1). In this regard, cities of the ASEAN-5 region concentrate most of the population growth, with an increase of 472% from 1980 to 2050, against less than 2% for rural populations and 122% at the country level over the same period.

Table 1.1. **Urbanisation level and urban population in ASEAN-5 and high-income countries**

1980-2030

Region	Urbanisation level (%)			Urban population (millions)			1980-2050 annual growth rate of urban population (%)
	1980	2015	2050	1980	2015	2050	
ASEAN-5	29.5	51.4	67.7	79	271	452	2.5
High-income countries	71.8	80.4	86.7	749	1 043	1 213	0.7

Source: Based on UN DESA (2014), *World Urbanisation Prospects: The 2014 Revision*, https://esa.un.org/unpd/wup/Publications/Files/WUP2014-Report.pdf.

Figure 1.1. **Urban versus rural population growth in ASEAN-5 (aggregated)**

1950-2050

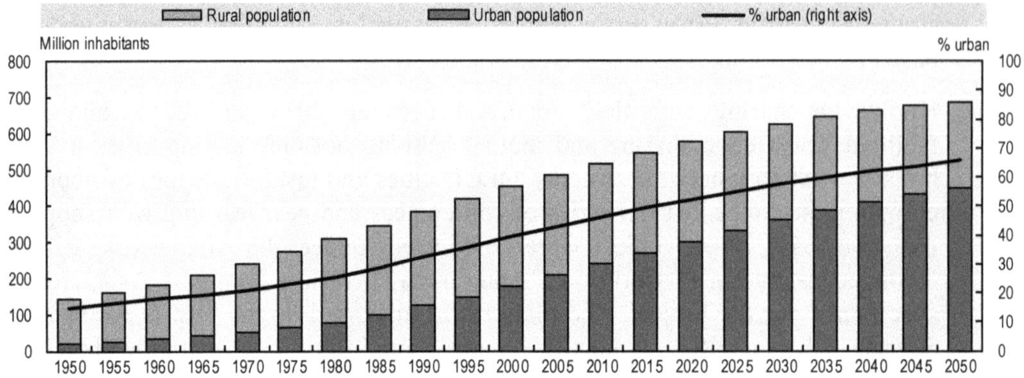

Source: UN DESA (2014), *World Urbanisation Prospects: The 2014 Revision*, https://esa.un.org/unpd/wup/Publications/Files/WUP2014-Report.pdf.

Some significant disparities in the urbanisation trends of the ASEAN-5 countries are observable, however. While Malaysia and Indonesia have experienced fast urbanisation since the 1950s, their levels of urbanisation are unequal (74.7% in 2015 in Malaysia against 53.7% in Indonesia). The Philippines, in particular, is following a unique trajectory, with a declining urbanisation level since 1990, down from 48.6% to 44.3% in 2015, but is expected to take up again to reach 56.3% in 2050 (Figure 1.2). This is mainly explained by a continuous increase in rural populations in parallel, contrary to the other ASEAN-5 countries where rural populations have significantly fallen.[3] In other words, despite decreases in urbanisation level in the Philippines between 1990 and 2015, the number of urban dwellers nonetheless increased from 30.1 million to 45.2 million, and is forecasted to reach 48.9 million in 2020 (UN DESA, 2014).

Figure 1.2. **Urbanisation level in ASEAN-5 countries**

1950-2050

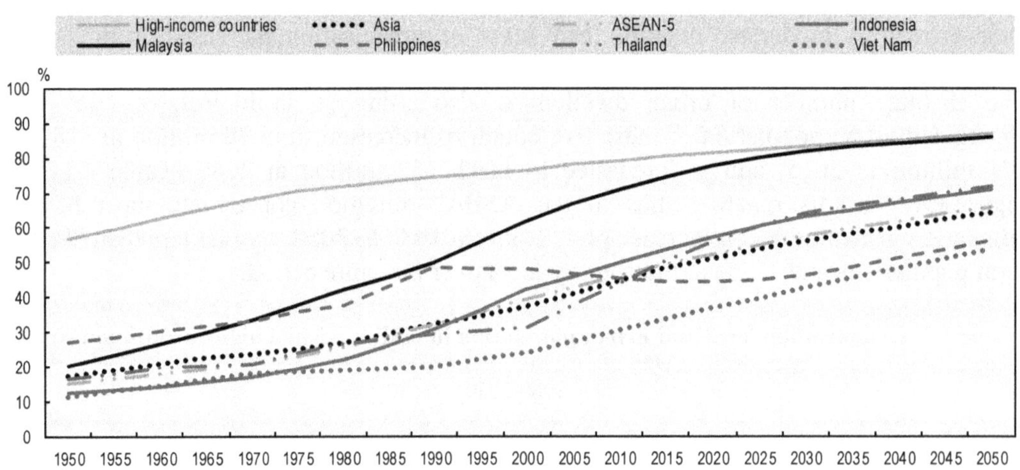

Source: UN DESA (2014), *World Urbanisation Prospects: The 2014 Revision*, https://esa.un.org/unpd/wup/Publications/Files/WUP2014-Report.pdf.

Major cities of the ASEAN-5 region are critical drivers of such trends. From 1990 to 2015, the population of the four largest cities of each country has grown faster than their respective country overall, Indonesia being the only exception. The faster growth rate of cities compared to national averages is forecasted to be even more pronounced between 2015 and 2030, including in Indonesia. Amongst these cities, Samut Prakan and Chon Buri (both located in the south-eastern vicinity of Bangkok City) and Can Tho (located in the western vicinity of Ho Chi Minh City) are expected to experience the fastest annual growth rates of the region between 2015 and 2030, at respectively 3.7%, 2.9% and 3.3%. The three largest cities – Jakarta, Manila and Bangkok – are expected to grow more moderately at respective rates of 2%, 1.7% and 1.5% (Table 1.2).

Table 1.2. **Population increase in major ASEAN-5 cities**

1990-2030

	Population in 2015 (millions)	Projected population in 2030 (millions)	Annual increase 2015-30 (%)
Indonesia	255.709	293.482	0.9
Jakarta	10.323	13.812	2
Surabaya	2.853	3.760	1.9
Bandung	2.544	3.433	2
Medan	2.204	2.955	2
Malaysia	30.651	36.846	1.2
Kuala Lumpur	6.837	9.423	2.2
Johor Bahru	0.912	1.249	2.1
Ipoh	0.737	0.998	2
Kuching	0.560	0.755	2
Philippines	101.803	127.797	1.5
Manila	12.946	16.756	1.7
Metro Cebu	1.772	2.480	2.3
Davao City	1.630	2.216	2.1
Zamboanga	0.936	1.313	2.3
Thailand	67.401	67.554	0
Bangkok City	9.270	11.528	1.5
Samut Prakan	1.814	3.139	3.7
Udon Thani	0.526	0.772	2.6
Chon Buri	0.518	0.796	2.9
Viet Nam	93.387	101.830	0.6
Ho Chi Minh City	7.298	10.200	2.3
Ha Noi	3.629	5.498	2.8
Can Tho	1.175	1.902	3.3
Hai Phong	0.952	1.569	2.6

Note: Population in 2015 are projections based on UN DESA (2014).

Source: UN DESA (2014), *World Urbanisation Prospects: The 2014 Revision*, https://esa.un.org/unpd/wup/Publications/Files/WUP2014-Report.pdf.

The five case study cities of the Urban Green Growth in Dynamic Asia project have also experienced significant population growth rates. The populations of the Bangkok Metropolitan Region (BMR), Thailand and the Bandung Metropolitan Area (BMA), Indonesia – the two largest metropolitan areas among the case studies – increased from 9.4 million to 10.6 million, and from 6.6 million to 8.6 million, respectively, from 2000 to 2015. The total population of Metro Cebu, the Philippines and Iskandar Malaysia, Malaysia is much lower, but the recorded growth much faster, at around 2.6% a year from 2000 to 2015 for the former, and 3.7% a year from 2005 to 2015 for the latter (against

0.8% and 1.8% for the BMR and BMA, respectively). In the cases of the BMR, the BMA and Metro Cebu, the growth has been much faster in the suburban areas than in the core city. The population of Hai Phong City has increased at an annual rate of around 1.4%, from 1.7 million to 1.96 million inhabitants between 2000 and 2010. This, however, includes rural populations of Hai Phong City Province which accounted for 53% of the total 1.9 million inhabitants in 2015 (OECD, 2016a). Taken alone, populations of the urban districts increased at an annual rate of 6% between 2000 and 2010, from 0.6 million to 1.1 million inhabitants (Figure 1.3).

Figure 1.3. **Population growth and annual urban growth in the five case study cities**

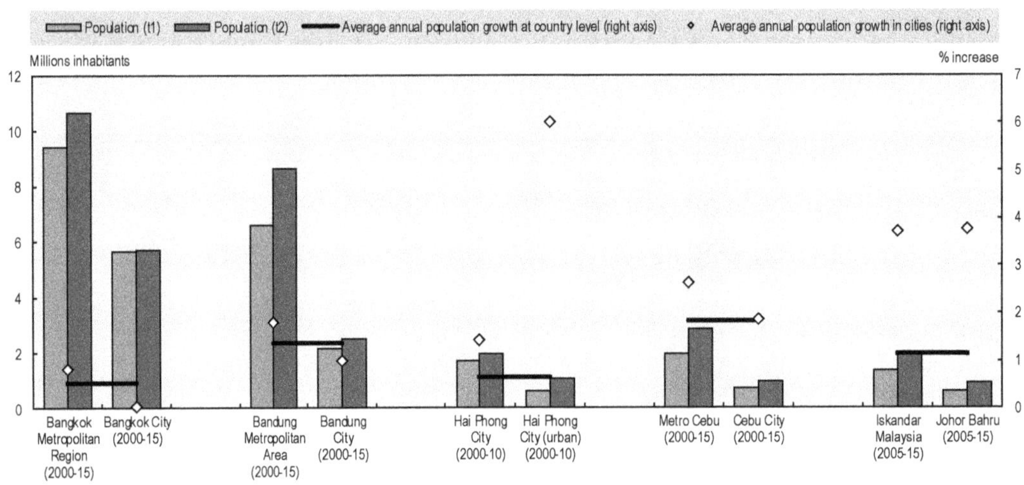

Sources: OECD (2015a), *Green Growth in Bangkok, Thailand*, http://dx.doi.org/10.1787/9789264237087-en; OECD (2016a), *Green Growth in Hai Phong, Viet Nam*, forthcoming, http://dx.doi.org/10.1787/9789264260207-en; OECD (2016d), *Green Growth in Bandung, Indonesia*, http://dx.doi.org/10.1787/9789264264113-en; OECD (2016e), *Green Growth in Cebu, the Philippines*, forthcoming; OECD (2016c), *Green Growth in Iskandar Malaysia, Malaysia*, forthcoming.

Cities in the ASEAN-5 countries are predominantly small in size. Around 67.7% of the urban population of the countries lived in cities with fewer than 500 000 inhabitants in 2015, against 8.6% in cities with more than 10 million inhabitants. Currently, ASEAN-5 countries host only two cities with more than 10 million inhabitants: Jakarta and Manila.[4] The share of urban dwellers living in cities under 500 000 inhabitants has, however, been decreasing, from 69.2% of the urban population in 2000 to 67.11% in 2015. Cities with more than 10 million inhabitants will, on the contrary, account for 14.5% of the total urban population then – in particular because Bangkok City and Ho Chi Minh City will be counted as such. In comparison, cities with fewer than 500 000 inhabitants accounted for a much lower share of the total urban population in China (43%), India (47%), North America (35%), and Latin America and the Caribbean (47%) in 2015. The profile of ASEAN-5 cities is more comparable to Europe, where cities with fewer than 500 000 inhabitants accounted for 66% of the total urban population in 2015 (Figure 1.4).

Cities are drivers of robust economic growth in Southeast Asia

ASEAN-5 countries have also experienced strong economic growth: overall, GDP per capita increased from around USD 8 500 in 1985 to around USD 24 800 in 2015, despite economic crises that hit the Asian economy in 1997 and in 2008. In Indonesia,

Malaysia, the Philippines, Thailand and Viet Nam, GDP per capita at constant 2010 USD increased at annual rates comprised between 3% and 6% between 2000 and 2015. In comparison, GDP per capita in OECD countries increased at an annual rate of 0.9% over the same period. Economic growth has, however, been more dynamic in other emerging Asian countries, in particular Cambodia, China, India, and Lao People's Democratic Republic (Table 1.3). The income level of ASEAN-5 countries has not only increased at the same time as urbanisation, but a catching up of GDP per capita relative to the United States is also observed, showing the high correlation between both processes. The only exception is the Philippines, where the gap with the United States increased over this period, in particular when the urbanisation level decreased, as explained previously. The catching up rates of these countries have, however, been less rapid than Korea's, whose GDP per capita ratio relative to the United States surged from 0.17 in 1980 to 0.62 in 2013 (Figure 1.5).

Figure 1.4. **Share of cities by size class in ASEAN-5, People's Republic of China, India, Europe, North America, and Latin America and the Caribbean**

2000-30

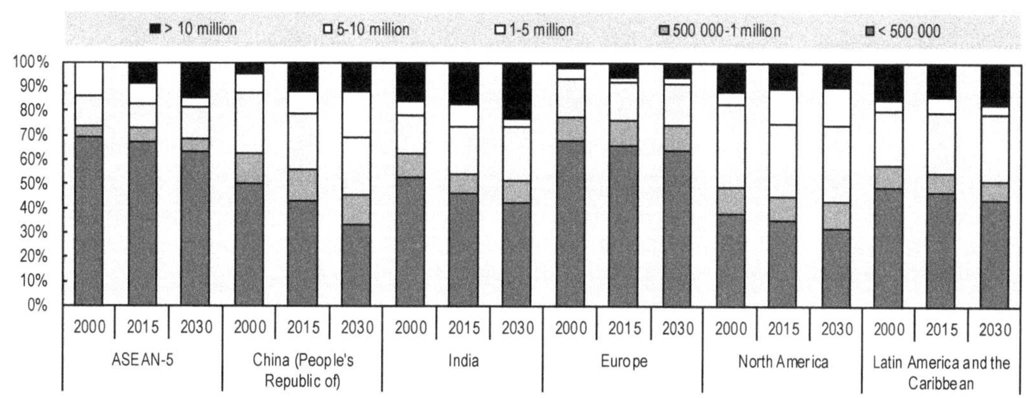

Source: UN DESA (2014), *World Urbanisation Prospects: The 2014 Revision*, https://esa.un.org/unpd/wup/Publications/Files/WUP2014-Report.pdf.

Figure 1.5. **Urbanisation level and GDP per capita ratio relative to the United States in ASEAN-5, Japan and Korea**

1980-2013

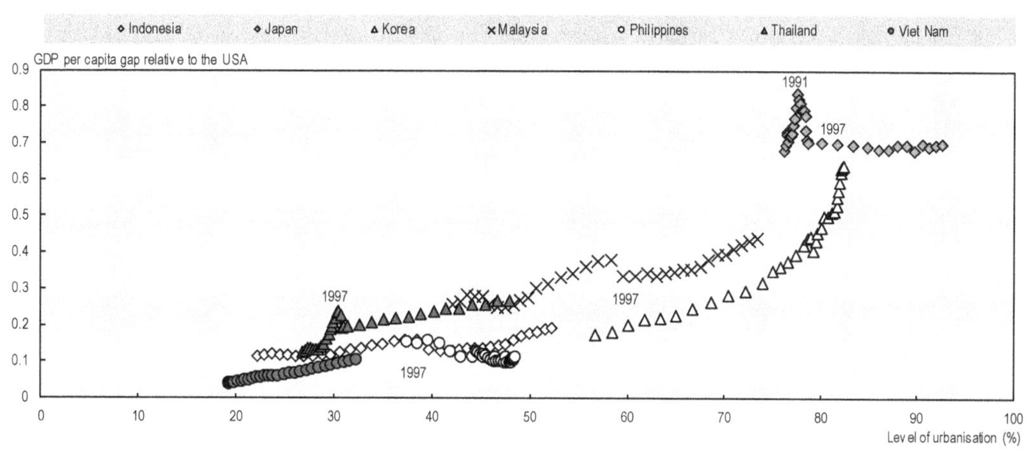

Source: World Development Indicators.

Table 1.3. **Real GDP per capita growth of ASEAN, People's Republic of China, India and OECD countries**

Annual percentage change, Constant 2010 USD

Country	2000-05	2005-10	2010-15	2000-15	GDP per capita in 2015 (PPP)
ASEAN-5					
Indonesia	3.3	4.4	4.2	4	11 035.1
Malaysia	2.7	2.7	3.7	3	26 891.4
Philippines	2.5	3.3	4.2	3.3	7 358.8
Thailand	4.4	3.5	2.5	3.4	16 305.5
Viet Nam	5.6	5.2	4.8	5.2	6 022.6
Other ASEAN countries					
Brunei Darussalam	0.2	-1	-1.5	-0.8	70 817.0
Cambodia	7.4	5.1	5.5	6	3 483.3
Lao PDR	4.7	6.2	6	5.6	5 675.5
Singapore	3.7	3.1	2.2	3	85 208.8
China and India					
China (People's Republic of)	9.1	10.7	7.3	9	14 238.7
India	5	6.5	5.4	5.6	6 088.6
OECD countries	1.4	0.3	0.9	0.9	39 765.0

Source: World Development Indicators.

Economic growth of major cities of the ASEAN-5 falls in line with these country-level trends: the annual average GDP growth of some of the largest cities of the region, at different periods of time between 2000 and 2015, is systematically comprised between 3% and 7% (Figure 1.6). Cities also concentrate wealth: in Southeast Asia, cities accounted for 48% of GDP in 2007, more than double their share of the population (21%). In comparison, OECD 275 metropolitan areas (defined as urban agglomerations of more than 500 000 inhabitants) account for 55% of combined total national GDP and their share of the total population was similar (around half of the population) (OECD, 2015b).

Figure 1.6. **Annual growth of gross regional product per capita in major ASEAN-5 cities**

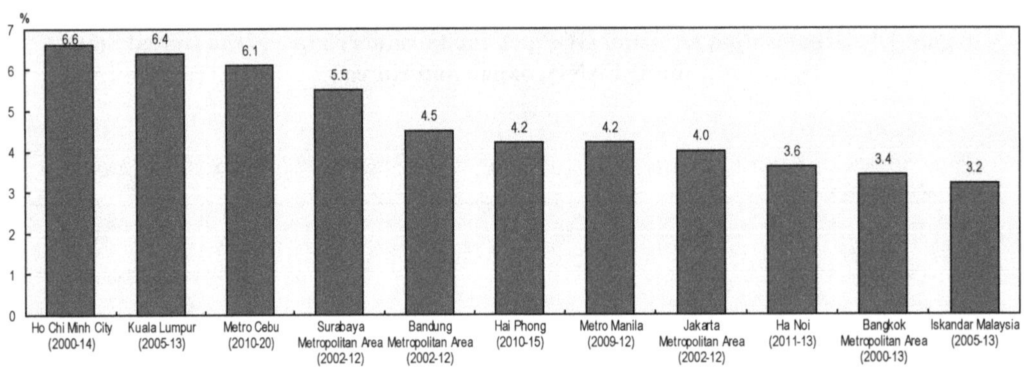

Note: Gross regional product per capita is expressed in constant prices. Bangkok, Metro Cebu, Metro Manila, Surabaya, Jakarta and Bandung values are based on 2000 constant prices; Iskandar Malaysia and Kuala Lumpur values are based on 2005 constant prices. Ho Chi Minh City, Ha Noi and Hai Phong are based on 2010 constant prices.

Sources: OECD (2015a), *Green Growth in Bangkok, Thailand,* http://dx.doi.org/10.1787/9789264237087-en; OECD (2016a), *Green Growth in Hai Phong, Viet Nam,* forthcoming, http://dx.doi.org/10.1787/9789264260207-en; OECD (2016d), *Green Growth in Bandung, Indonesia,* http://dx.doi.org/10.1787/9789264264113-en; OECD (2016e), *Green Growth in Cebu, the Philippines,* forthcoming; OECD (2016c), *Green Growth in Iskandar Malaysia, Malaysia,* forthcoming.

The economic growth of Southeast Asian cities that has accompanied fast urbanisation in the past decades has been experienced by all countries overall, but hides wide disparities in the wealth of ASEAN nations. While all ASEAN-5 countries are classified as middle-income countries, the required estimated time to become high-income countries varies significantly from one country to another: for instance, in the best-case scenario it is estimated that Malaysia will reach the status of high-income country in 2021, while Viet Nam will only reach this status in 2054. It is estimated that Thailand, Indonesia and the Philippines will become high-income countries in 2035, 2043 and 2048, respectively (OECD, 2016b). These disparities are both observable across countries and across cities of different countries: GDP per capita in Malaysia is more than four times that in Viet Nam, for instance. Dwellers of major cities tend to be richer than the average person in their country: GDP per capita in the case study cities is systematically higher than GDP per capita in their respective countries. Generally speaking, high discrepancies are also observable between the capital cities and other cities (Figure 1.7).

Figure 1.7. **GDP per capita in ASEAN-5 countries and selected major cities**

USD, PPP, current international prices

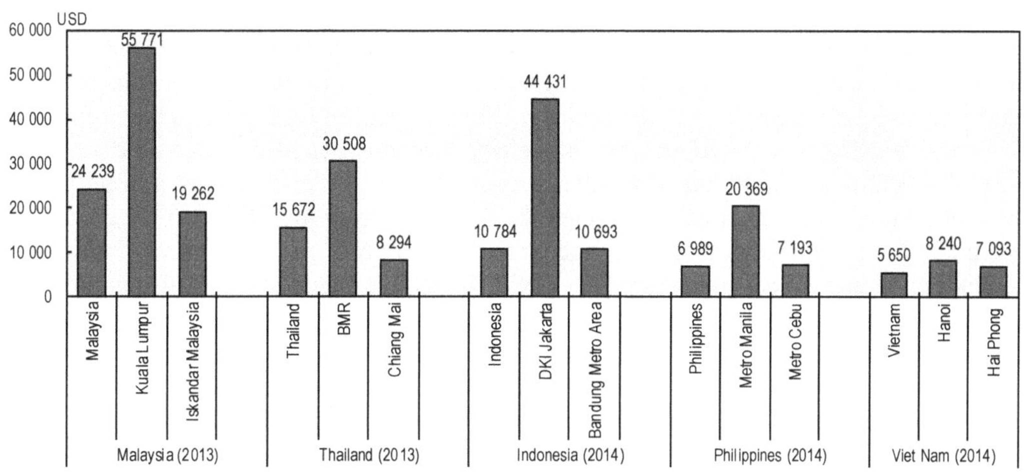

Source: OECD (2015a), *Green Growth in Bangkok, Thailand*, http://dx.doi.org/10.1787/9789264237087-en; OECD (2016a), *Green Growth in Hai Phong, Viet Nam*, forthcoming, http://dx.doi.org/10.1787/9789264260207-en; OECD (2016d), *Green Growth in Bandung, Indonesia*, http://dx.doi.org/10.1787/9789264264113-en; OECD (2016e), *Green Growth in Cebu, the Philippines*, forthcoming; OECD (2016c), *Green Growth in Iskandar Malaysia, Malaysia*, forthcoming.

Growth supported by surging foreign direct investment and maritime trade

Dynamic economic growth of Southeast Asian cities is strongly driven by rising amounts of foreign direct investment (FDI). The growth has been particularly dramatic over the past 15 years: from 2000 to 2015, FDI inflows in the ASEAN-5 region increased almost tenfold, from USD 5.4 billion to USD 52 billion. Indonesia was the top recipient country in 2015, with more than USD 15 billion of FDI (Figure 1.8). In terms of FDI expressed as a percentage of GDP, Indonesia has, however, been the least performing of the ASEAN-5 countries, with an annual GDP contribution of FDI at about 2.2% on average from 2000 to 2015, against 5.3% in Viet Nam and 3.3% in Malaysia – the top two recipients according to this classification. Thailand illustrates irregular ups and downs in recent years, partly due to a flood in 2011 and political turmoil in 2014.

Figure 1.8. **Foreign direct investment inflows in ASEAN-5 countries**

2000-15

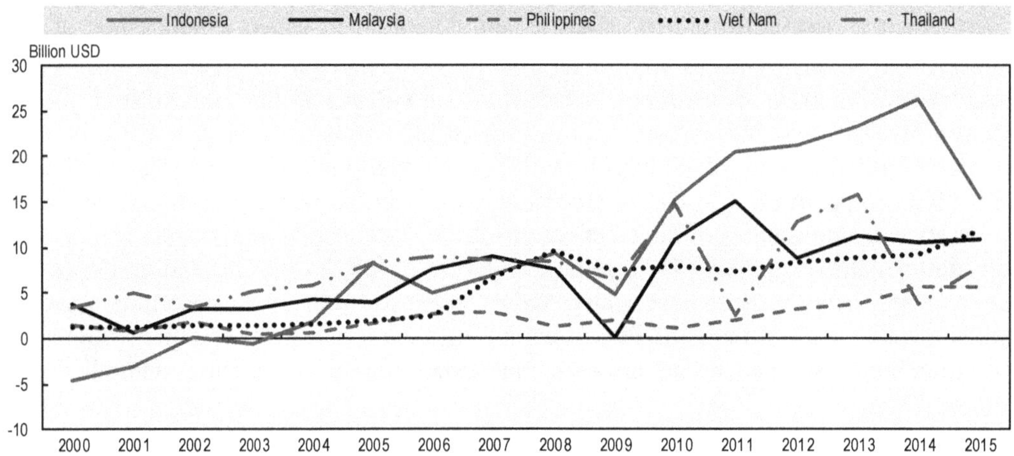

Source: World Development Indicators.

FDI has mostly supported the growth of the manufacturing industry at the country level. Between 2003 and 2014, around 57% of greenfield investment[5] targeted manufacturing in Malaysia, 54% in Indonesia, 53% in Thailand, 50% in Viet Nam and 42% in the Philippines (Figure 1.9). The weight of the manufacturing economy is also observable in many ASEAN-5 cities: in Hai Phong, for instance, around 69% of FDI projects – accounting for 68% of total investment capital – targeted the industry sector in 2015 (OECD, 2016a). In Iskandar Malaysia, manufacturing accounted for 35.6% of cumulative investment (including domestic investment) in 2013 (OECD, 2016c), and in the city of Bangkok, the number of establishments, of employees, and the value of gross output in the electronics, food processing, metalworking and textile industries all increased significantly between 1997 and 2007 (OECD, 2015a). The growth of the service sector, however, tends to be even more pronounced in ASEAN-5 cities (see below for more details).

Figure 1.9. **Greenfield investments by sector in ASEAN-5 countries, 2003-14**

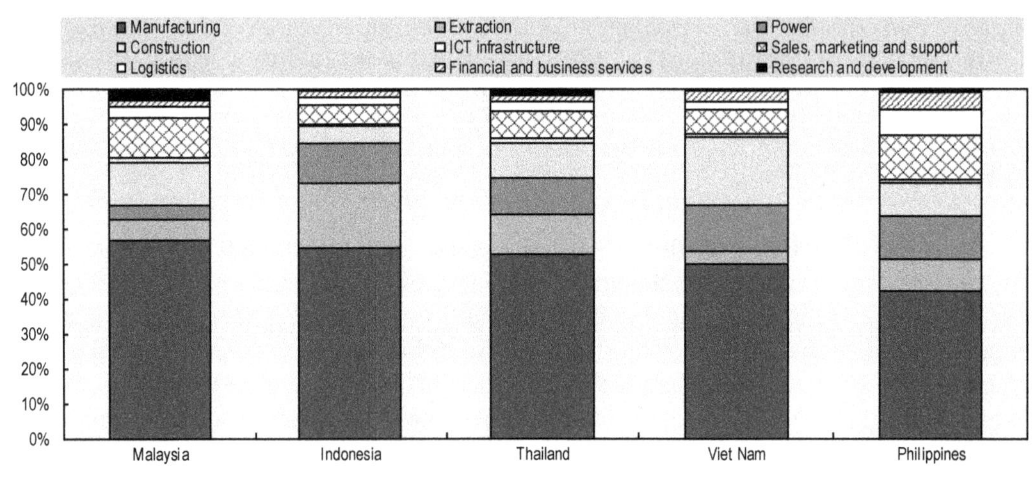

Source: OECD (2016b), *Economic Outlook for Southeast Asia, China and India 2016: Enhancing Regional Ties*, http://dx.doi.org/10.1787/saeo-2016-en.

The economic growth and FDI attractiveness of cities in Southeast Asia is supported by its cheap labour force, and its young population should continue to fuel the economy in the coming decades. In Bandung Metropolitan Area, Iskandar Malaysia and Metro Cebu, the population aged 15-64 is 67%, 69% and 65%, respectively. In comparison, the average of the 290 largest OECD metropolitan areas is 81%. This is mainly due to the abundant youth population (under 15) in Southeast Asia: in Bandung Metropolitan Area and Iskandar Malaysia for instance, the youth population accounts for 29% and 27% of the population, against 17.9% in the 290 OECD metropolitan areas (OECD Metro Explorer). The growth is also accompanied by declining unemployment rates: in Bandung Metropolitan Area, it declined from 16% to 8.5% of the workforce from 2004 to 2014 (OECD, 2016d).

The increasing centrality of Asia's port activity is linked to its economic growth: in 1972, approximately 40% of all world port activity took place in Europe, 20% in North America and 20% in Asia. These shares had dramatically changed by 2009, when more than half of world port activity took place in Asia, around a fifth in Europe and a tenth in North America (OECD, 2014). At a lower scale, the Southeast Asian region illustrates this growth in port activity: according to UNCTAD Maritime Transport, the total fleet in Southeast Asia increased from 58 280 in 2002 to 150 337 in 2014. The number of container ships has increased from 5 630 to 22 069 (Maritime Insights, 2014). Container throughput has therefore increased dramatically in the region, and in 2013, the ASEAN-10 countries[6] accounted for 13.5% of the world's total container throughput. ASEAN-5 countries, in particular, are major contributors: container throughput increased from 15.7 million TEUs in 2000 to 59 million TEUs in 2014 in the region. Container throughput is particularly high in Malaysia owing to the presence of trans-shipment ports[7] (Figure 1.10).

Figure 1.10. **Container throughout in ASEAN-5 countries**

2000-14

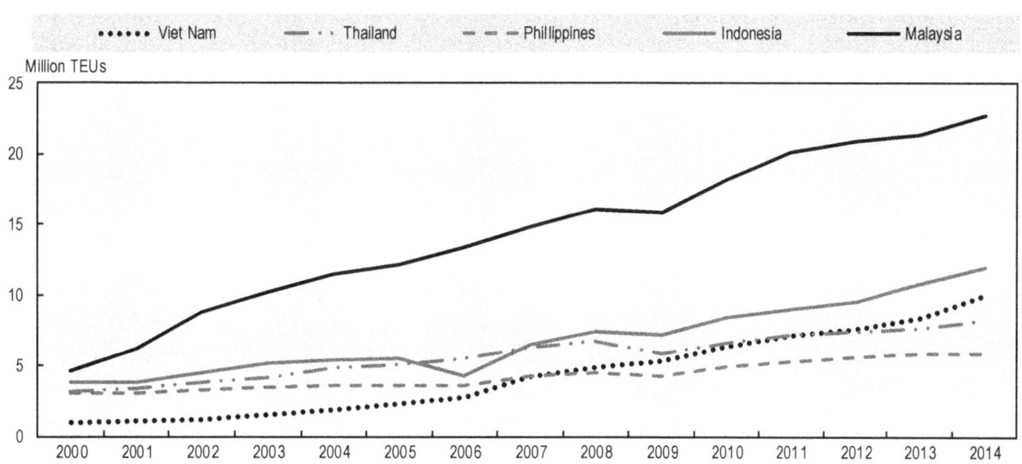

Source: World Bank (2016a), "Container port traffic (TEU: 20 foot equivalent units)", World Development Indicators, http://data.worldbank.org/indicator/IS.SHP.GOOD.TU/countries; and Viet Nam Seaports Association (2000-14), "Summary of throughput", www.vpa.org.vn/english/information/info_static2000.htm.

Port activities are concentrated in cities where such increasing trade volumes are therefore directly observable. At the image of Viet Nam, container throughput in Hai Phong (the second busiest seaport of Viet Nam after Ho Chi Minh City) increased more than tenfold from 2000 to 2014 from 0.2 million to 2.5 million TEUs. Cargo throughput,[8] over the same period, increased from 8 million tonnes to 41 million tonnes (OECD, 2016a). Hai Phong was one of the fastest growing major container ports in Southeast Asia between 2005 and 2013 (total growth of 305%), along with Cebu (390%) and Iloilo City (387%) (the Philippines), Ho Chi Minh City (Viet Nam) (201%) and Tanjung Pelepas in Iskandar Malaysia (105%). Iskandar Malaysia hosts two of the ten most important ASEAN-5 ports in terms of tonnage (Tanjung Pelepas and Pasir Gudang). Despite such growth, these ports, and even the largest port of the region (Port Klang in Malaysia) are still far from Singapore, one of the world leaders, in terms of total cargo volumes: Singapore's container volumes reached 33.9 million TEUs in 2014, against 10.9 million TEUs in Port Klang (Figure 1.11). This shows the potential of ports in the region to grow, but also their different nature from Singapore's port, which is the major trans-shipment hub in the region.

Figure 1.11. **Volumes in the main Southeast Asian container ports**

2014

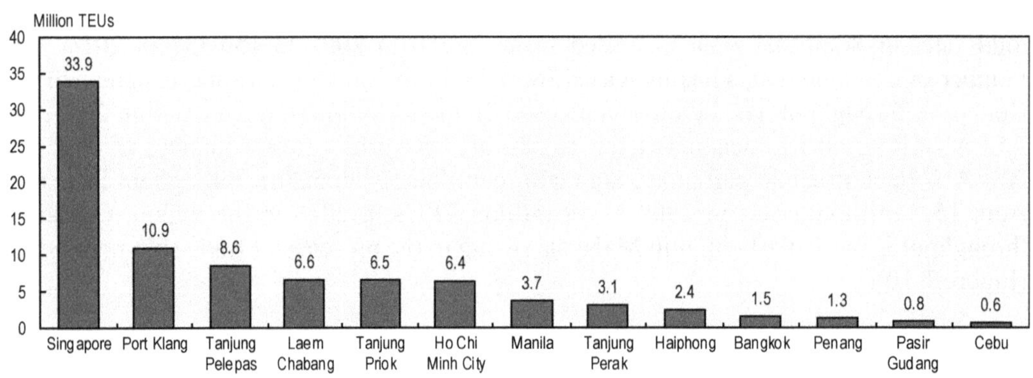

Note: Volumes for Cebu refer to 2013.

Source: International Transport Forum/OECD collection data.

At the city level, the tertiary sector is dominant and its share of GDP tends to increase in the five case study cities: in Iskandar Malaysia for instance, the tertiary sector increased from 50% to 55% of GDP between 2005 and 2013; in Bandung City, it increased from 61% to 69% from 2002 to 2012, while the secondary sector decreased from 39% to 31% (Figure 1.12).

The "green" economy sector remains very weak or inexistent in ASEAN-5 cities. There are no available data on the size of this sector in terms of GDP, employment and innovation, which tends to suggest that this is still an under-developed portion of the economy. In the OECD area, the development of environment-related technologies increased from 6.7% of the total technologies developed in 2000 to 10.8% in 2012. Likewise, gross value added of the environmental goods and services sector[9] in the European Union increased from 1.6% of total GDP of EU members in 2000 to 2.1% in 2011 (OECD, 2014). Such accounting could be used by ASEAN countries to track the performance of the green economy sector. However, due to the low unemployment rates, high economic growth and infrastructure gaps of Southeast Asian cities, this report will demonstrate a stronger need to green Southeast Asian cities' growth rather than promoting growth in the green economy sector (see the end of this chapter).

Figure 1.12. **GDP by sector in Hai Phong, Bangkok, Bandung and Iskandar Malaysia**

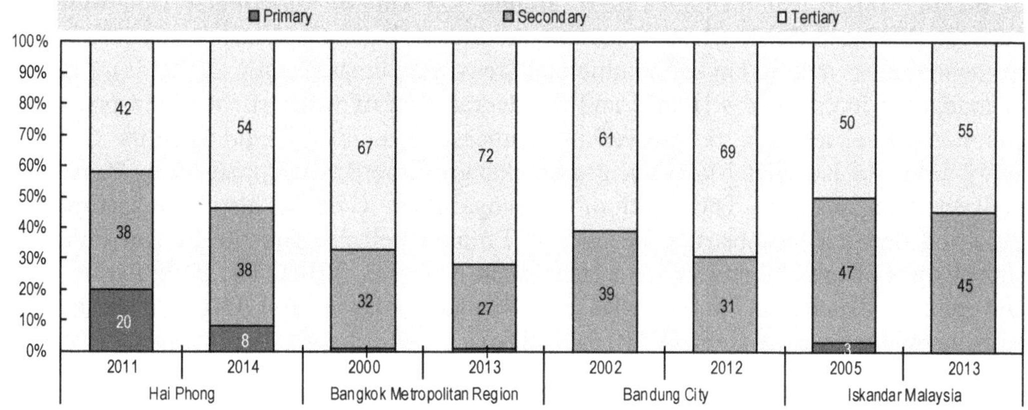

Source: Case study reports.

Infrastructure and environmental challenges of fast urbanisation and economic growth

Southeast Asian cities are struggling to manage the pace of the population growth rate and although economic growth has also been observed, the case of Korea suggests that more benefits could be reaped from the urbanisation process. The provision of public service, in particular urban infrastructure, has not kept up with the speed of urbanisation, leading to a range of challenges which will have long-term economic and environmental consequences if not addressed urgently. These challenges are particularly acute in the transport and land-use sectors, in solid waste and water management, and in regard to climate change risks (greenhouse gas emissions from rising energy consumption, and vulnerability to the impacts of climate changes).

Urban sprawl and motorisation have led to losses of natural assets and high levels of air pollution

Urban sprawl is one of the most visible consequences of fast urbanisation in Southeast Asia. In Iskandar Malaysia,[10] urban areas increased by 53.5% between 2000 and 2010 (an annual growth rate of 6.7%), from around 271 km^2 to 416 km^2. In Hai Phong's urban agglomeration, urban areas expanded by 23.5% over the same period (an annual growth rate of 1.1%), from around 161 km^2 to 179 km^2. In Metro Cebu, they expanded by 31.3% (an annual growth rate of 2.7%), from 122 km^2 to 160 km^2. Much of the urban expansion has taken place in peri-urban areas (Figure 1.13). Because of the significant population growth, densities have also risen in parallel, from 3 026 pop/km^2 to 3 115 pop/km^2 in Iskandar Malaysia's urban areas, from 5 066 pop/km^2 to 6 144 pop/km^2 in Hai Phong's urban agglomeration (from 4 521 pop/km^2 to 5 662 pop/km^2 in the entire Hai Phong City jurisdiction), and from 8 248 pop/km^2 to 9 442 pop/km^2 in Metro Cebu's urban areas. This demonstrates a complex challenge for Southeast Asian cities in minimising the negative impacts of urban sprawl while accommodating the increasing population and economic activities, as explained below and in Chapter 2.

A frequent consequence of the expansion of built-up areas in Southeast Asian cities is the loss or degradation of natural assets. This is especially due to expansion of settlements and economic activities in sensitive environments (e.g. settlements along the coastline and rivers; port activities). In the Bangkok Metropolitan Region (excluding the Provinces of Samut Sakhon and Samut Prakan), around 553 km^2 of agricultural land were lost between 2000 and 2010, while in parallel around 46 km^2 of industrial areas, 41 km^2 of residential areas and 69 km^2 of commercial areas were created (OECD, 2015a). The loss of mangrove forests and wetlands and the degradation of water streams and bodies are common consequences also observed in Southeast Asia cities, including in the five case study cities. In Iskandar Malaysia, coastal mangrove forests declined by 6.6% (9 km^2) between 2005 and 2012. The mouth of the Sungai Pulai River has also been narrowed by 50% and dredged to construct the port of Tanjung Pelepas, and the Sungai Pulai site shows signs of lower recovery rates (Khazanah Nasional, 2014). The pollution of rivers and economic activities in estuaries of Iskandar Malaysia and Hai Phong has also endangered biodiversity (OECD, 2016a; 2016c).

Figure 1.13. **Built-up area expansion in Hai Phong, Iskandar Malaysia and Metro Cebu**

2000-10

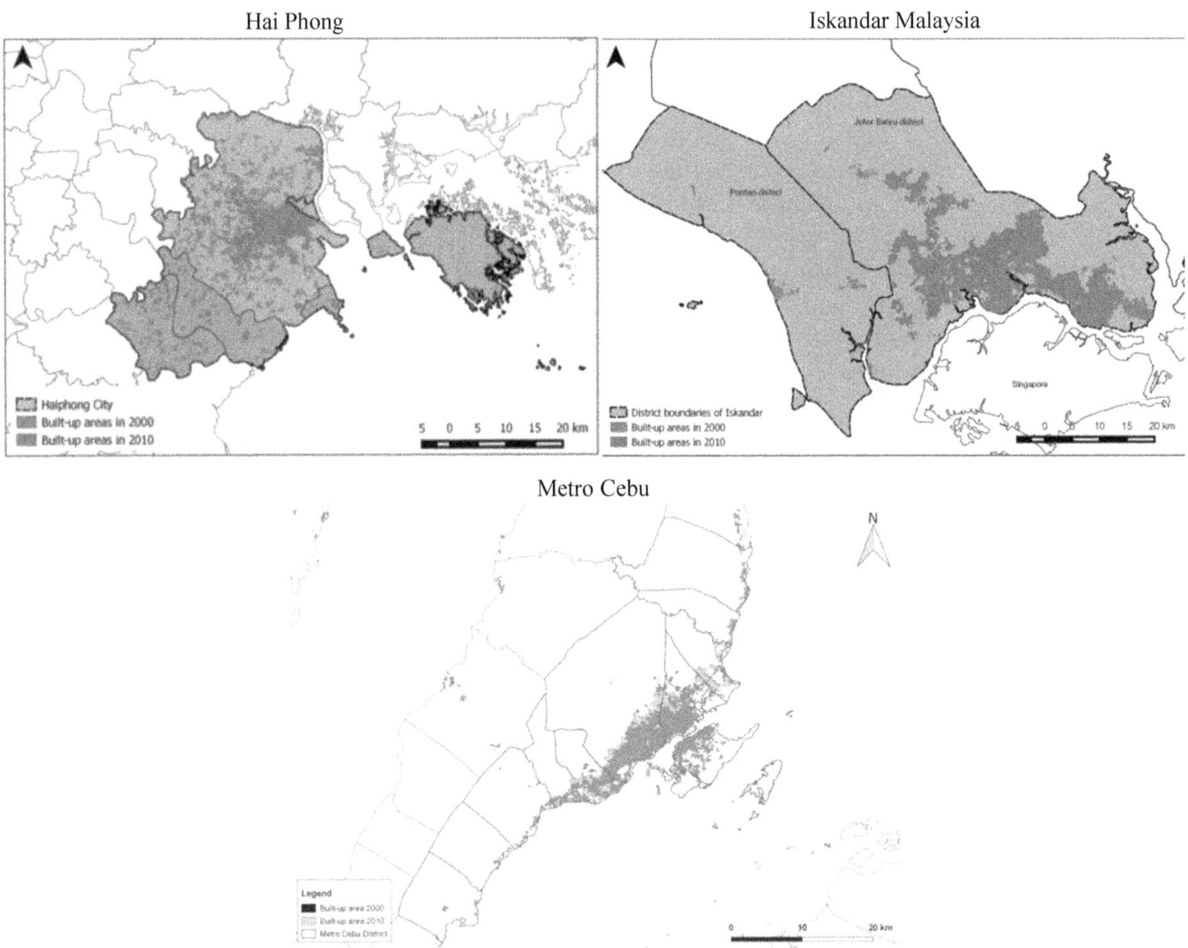

Source: Case study reports.

Population growth and urban sprawl are also partly responsible for fast motorisation of Southeast Asian cities. In Bangkok City, the number of motorcycles and four-wheeled vehicles increased from around 6.7 million in 2005 to around 11.1 million in 2013. Over the same period, the number of motorcycles and four-wheeled vehicles increased from around 0.8 million to around 2.9 million in Bandung City. The motorisation rate also increased in Bangkok, from around 1.2 vehicles per inhabitant in 2005 to around 2 vehicles per inhabitant in 2013, and from around 0.4 to 1.1 vehicles per inhabitant in Bandung City (Figure 1.14). This tends to show the impact of economic and income growth on the urban populations. While growth in the stock of motor vehicles and in the motorisation rate has also been experienced in OECD countries, this is being experienced at a much faster rate in Southeast Asia, relative to the increase in GDP per capita. This is especially true for motorcycles (Figure 1.15).

Figure 1.14. **Number of private vehicles registered in Bangkok City and Bandung City**

2005-13

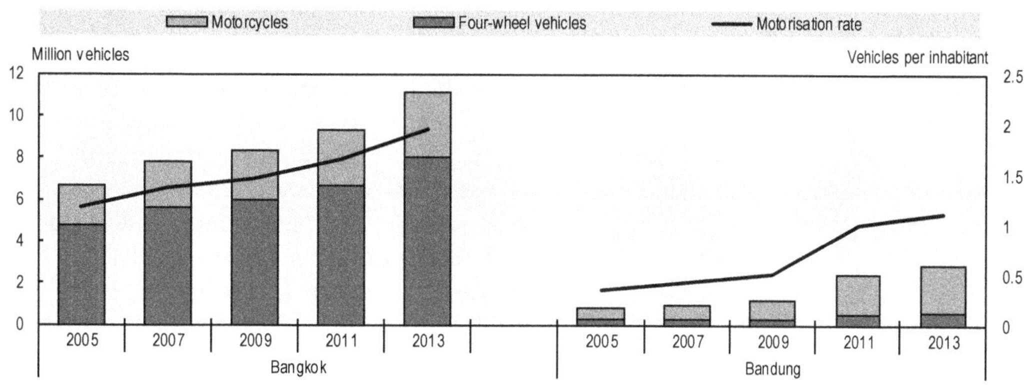

Sources: OECD (2015a), *Green Growth in Bangkok, Thailand,* http://dx.doi.org/10.1787/9789264237087-en; OECD (2016d), *Green Growth in Bandung, Indonesia,* http://dx.doi.org/10.1787/9789264264113-en.

Figure 1.15. **Motorcycle ownership relative to economic growth in selected Asian countries**

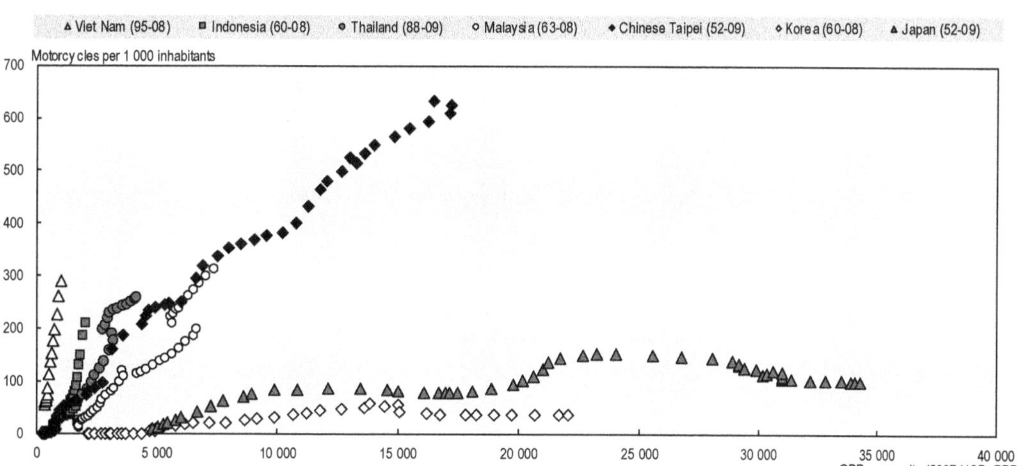

Source: Tuan, V.A. (2011), "Dynamic interactions between private passenger car and motorcycle ownership in Asia: A cross-country analysis", http://dx.doi.org/10.11175/easts.9.541.

In parallel to rising motorisation rates, Southeast Asian cities have largely failed to provide efficient and wide public transport coverage. The modal split of public transport in Iskandar Malaysia was estimated at around 15% in 2010 and is expected to fall to 10% by 2030 if nothing is done to improve the public transport system (OECD, 2016c). The modal share of public transport in Bandung City was at 24% in 2014; in the Bangkok Metropolitan Region (BMR), it was at 43% but is expected to decline to 41% by 2037 despite current extension of the urban railway network (OECD, 2015a). In parallel, many Southeast Asian cities have seen the development of a large system of informal transport to compensate for the lack of public transport. Such informal transport is particularly useful to the urban populations to commute across municipalities, as existing public transport networks tend to only cover areas within a single jurisdiction (UN HABITAT and UN ESCAP, 2015). The absence of efficient and wide public transport is also due to urban sprawl and the lack of compactness of cities, especially new urban areas, which is an obstacle to the sustainability of large public transport systems. In Singapore, the modal share of public transport is at around 64% and is supported by a rather compact urban environment.

The dramatic increase in the stock of motorised vehicles is leading to severe congestion in many Southeast Asian cities, which is holding back both economic development and quality of life. Traffic is indeed often cited as a major concern by urban dwellers. Another common factor of urban congestion in this region is the street layouts: a city like Bangkok, for instance, has a good network of freeways, but the number of arterial roads is still insufficient. Many of the existing *soi* (side streets) are dead-end streets, unlike the street grids of such cities as Barcelona or New York (Figure 1.16). This compels drivers to use main roads, which are heavily congested (Dissanayake, 2012). The historic infrastructure is thus a critical factor in the inefficiency of the transport networks.

Figure 1.16. **Street network in a district of Bangkok City**

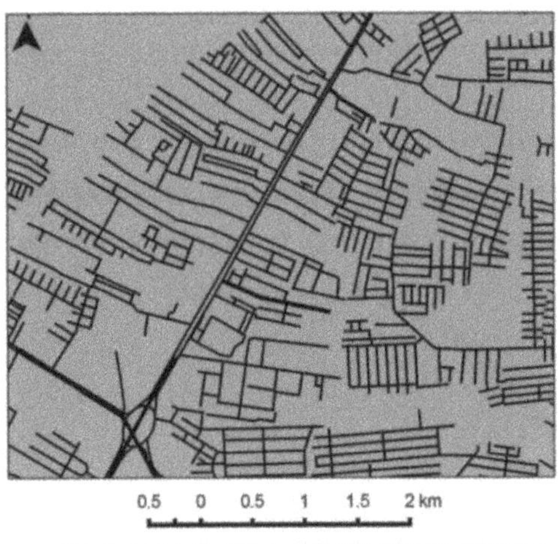

Source: Own elaboration based on OpenStreetMap (n.d.), www.openstreetmap.org/#map=5/51.500/-0.100.

A direct environmental (and public health) consequence of sprawl, motorisation and congestion is high levels of air pollution. Indeed, all major cities of the ASEAN-5 region show concentrations of particulate matter (PM_{10} and $PM_{2.5}$) above the World Health Organization's (WHO) standards. In Bandung City, for instance, an annual average PM_{10} concentration of 59 $\mu g/m^3$ and an annual average $PM_{2.5}$ concentration of 33 $\mu g/m^3$ were recorded in 2014, while the WHO standards are set at 20 $\mu g/m^3$ and 10 $\mu g/m^3$, respectively (Figure 1.17). The type of fuels used in vehicles is also responsible for such concentrations of air pollutants in Southeast Asian cities, although ASEAN-5 countries are progressively upgrading fuel standards.

Figure 1.17. **Annual average concentration of PM_{10} and $PM_{2.5}$ in major cities of ASEAN-5**

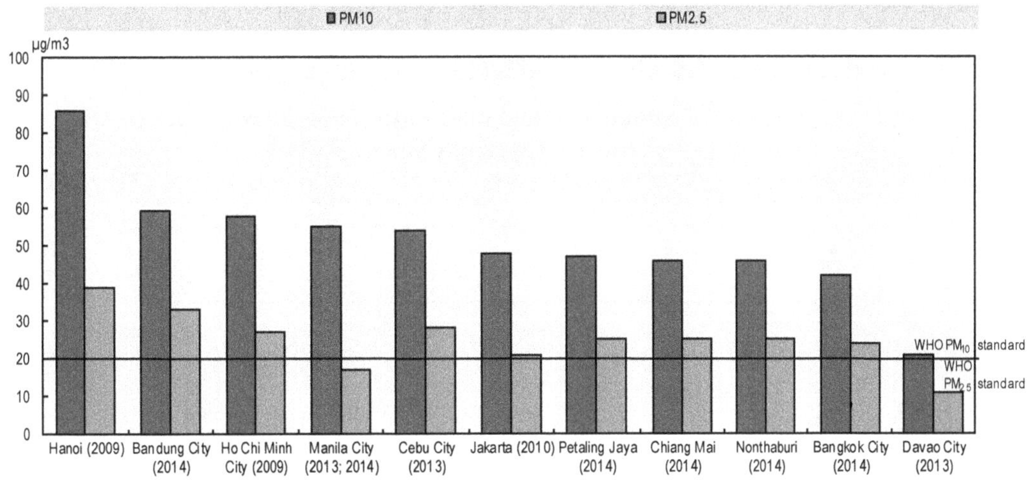

Source: World Health Organisation (2016 and 2014), *Ambient (Outdoor) Air Pollution in Cities Database*, www.who.int/phe/health_topics/outdoorair/databases/cities/en.

Southeast Asian cities face increasing amounts of solid waste and unsustainable treatment methods

The growth of Southeast Asian cities is accompanied by fast rising amounts of solid waste generated by its residents. In Bangkok City, the amounts of municipal solid waste generated daily increased from 8 291 tonnes per day in 2005 to 9 993 tonnes per day in 2013 (21% increase); in Bandung Metropolitan Area, it increased from 4 320 tonnes per day in 2006 to 7 661 tonnes per day in 2014 (77% increase). These trends are set to continue in the near future: the amount of municipal solid waste generated in Hai Phong is expected to increase from 1 348 tonnes per day in 2010 to 3 054 tonnes per day in 2025; in Iskandar Malaysia, it is expected to increase from 1 836 to 4 322 tonnes per day over the same period. The growth in solid waste amounts generated is not only the consequence of sheer population growth in these cities, but also a consequence of the fact that societies are growing richer: indeed, solid waste generation per capita has systematically increased in all of the five case study cities; in Bangkok City, for instance, per capita solid waste generation grew from 535 kg per year in 2005 to 641 kg per year in 2013, far above the OECD average of 556 kg per year which has remained steady since 2000 (Figure 1.18). Amounts of industrial and hazardous solid waste are also increasing in parallel. In Bangkok City, the annual amount of toxic waste collected increased from 4 593 tonnes in 2002 to 9 866 tonnes in 2012 (OECD, 2015a).

Such fast increasing quantities of solid waste generated has posed great challenges to local governments in collecting, handling and treating such waste. Waste collection services often do not reach all residents, especially slum dwellers, and non-collected waste creates health, well-being and environmental hazards. Waste generated in slums is often discharged openly in rivers and canals, as these urban populations tend to settle along their shores. This is contributing to high levels of pollution in water streams and bodies but also vulnerability to floods, as shown in the next sections. Another issue frequently met in Southeast Asian cities is the method employed to dispose of and treat municipal solid waste. Landfills are the preferred treatment method in most of these cities, such as Bangkok City (87% of total waste), Bandung City (69%), Hai Phong (85%)

and Metro Cebu (65%). Recycling is absent or only accounts for a minor share of treatment methods. In comparison, a city such as Seoul only disposes around 14% of its municipal solid waste to landfills, and privileges composting (33.1%) recycling (33.7%), and incineration and energy recovery activities (23.5%) (Figure 1.19).

Figure 1.18. **Evolution of amounts of total solid waste and solid waste per capita in the five case study cities**

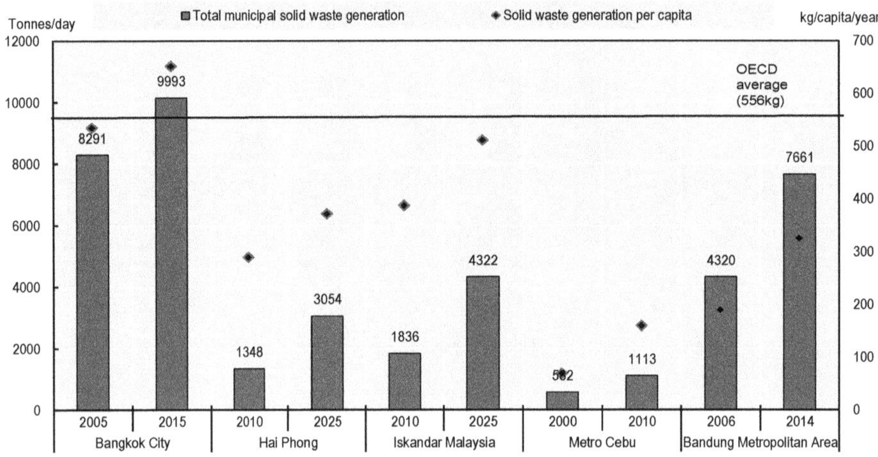

Sources: OECD (2015a), *Green Growth in Bangkok, Thailand*, http://dx.doi.org/10.1787/9789264237087-en; OECD (2016a), *Green Growth in Hai Phong, Viet Nam*, forthcoming, http://dx.doi.org/10.1787/9789264260207-en; OECD (2016d), *Green Growth in Bandung, Indonesia*, http://dx.doi.org/10.1787/9789264264113-en; OECD (2016e), *Green Growth in Cebu, the Philippines*, forthcoming; OECD (2016c), *Green Growth in Iskandar Malaysia, Malaysia*, forthcoming; UNEP (2009), "Technology for waste management/infrastructure – Cebu (Philippines)".

Figure 1.19. **Treatment of collected municipal solid waste in Seoul, Paris, Bangkok, Bandung, Hai Phong and Metro Cebu**

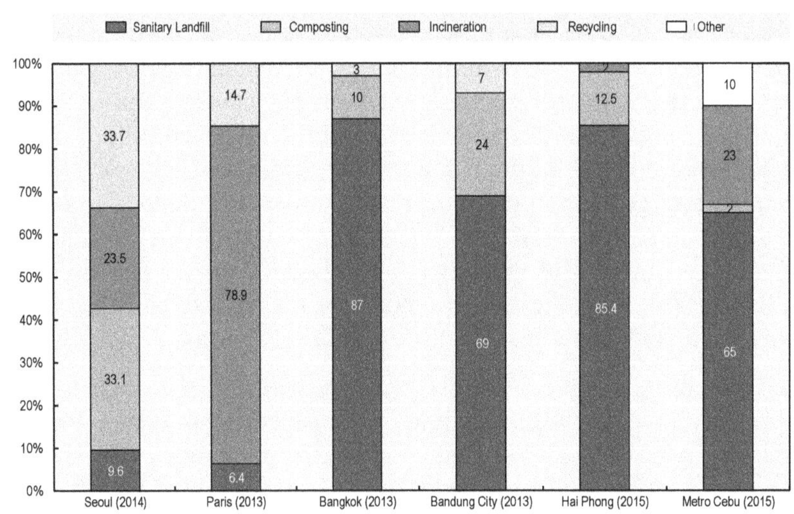

Sources: Seoul Government Statistics (2015), http://stat.seoul.go.kr/octagonweb/jsp/WWS7/WWSDS7100.jsp; City of Paris (2013), *Rapport Annuel sur le Prix et la Qualité du Service Public de Gestion des Déchets à Paris*; OECD (2013b), *Green Growth in Stockholm, Sweden*, http://dx.doi.org/10.1787/9789264195158-en; OECD (2015a), *Green Growth in Bangkok, Thailand*, http://dx.doi.org/10.1787/9789264237087-en; OECD (2016a), *Green Growth in Hai Phong, Viet Nam*, forthcoming, http://dx.doi.org/10.1787/9789264260207-en; OECD (2016d), *Green Growth in Bandung, Indonesia*, http://dx.doi.org/10.1787/9789264264113-en; OECD (2016e), *Green Growth in Cebu, the Philippines*, forthcoming.

Southeast Asian cities' fast growth has increased pressure on water resources

The management of water resources and wastewater is another critical infrastructure, environmental and social challenge that Southeast Asian cities are more and more urgently confronted by, as a consequence of population and economic growth. Water security – defined by the OECD as the management of scarcity, floods, pollution and freshwater ecosystem resilience – is indeed a high concern in most of these cities. This is a complex issue presenting a range of sub-challenges. First of all, many Southeast Asian cities have experienced increasing water demand: in Bangkok City, water consumption increased from 1.2 million m^3/day in 2007 to 1.4 million m^3/day in 2015 (Metropolitan Waterworks Authority, 2015). In Metro Cebu, water demand is expected to more than triple from around 228 000 m^3/day in 2013 to around 796 000 m^3/day in 2050 (OECD, 2016e). In Bandung Metropolitan Area, water demand is expected to increase from 440 000 m^3/day in 2010 to 795 000 m^3/day in 2018. Per capita water consumption in these cities is also increasing as the population becomes richer (Figure 1.20). In parallel, the lack of abundant water resources in some cities is leading to situations of water stress and scarcity. Many cities struggle to meet water demand as a consequence: in Bandung Metropolitan Area, only 75% of water demand was met in 2010 (ADB, 2011). In Metro Cebu, episodes of water scarcity are frequent and pose severe well-being and health risks. High groundwater extraction has also led to land subsidence (Bangkok) or salt intrusion in coastal cities (Metro Cebu).

Figure 1.20. **Evolution of total and per capita water consumption in Bangkok City, Metro Cebu and Bandung Metropolitan Area**

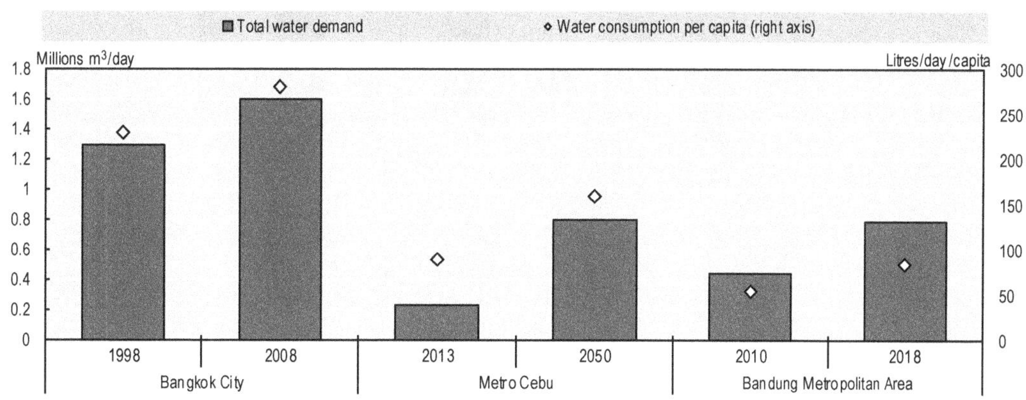

Note: Bangkok here refers to the area serviced by the Metropolitan Waterworks Authority: Bangkok City, Samut Prakan and Nonthaburi provinces.

Sources: ADB (2011), "Republic of Indonesia: Preparing the integrated Citarum Water Resources Management Investment Program periodic financing request 2", https://www.adb.org/sites/default/files/project-document/74867/37049-062-ino-tar.pdf; OECD (2015a), *Green Growth in Bangkok, Thailand*, http://dx.doi.org/10.1787/9789264237087-en; JICA and MCDCB (2015), *The Roadmap Study for Sustainable Urban Development in Metro Cebu.*

The pressure on water resources and the economic and social stakes around water in Southeast Asian cities are accentuated by the poor coverage and quality of water supply infrastructure. In the Metro Cebu Water District – a sub-area of Metro Cebu managed by a franchise water corporation – only 56% of the population is connected to a pipe water network. At the scale of Metro Cebu, in terms of volume, only 12.5% of drinking water and 49.9% of water used for other purposes than drinking is supplied through pipe connections. In Bandung Metropolitan Area, only 48.2% of urban areas are connected to a pipe network; the figure drops to 8.9% of households in peri-urban areas. Public taps, wells (public, households, neighbour), bottled water, rain and freshwater tend to be complementary (and less sustainable) sources of water supply in Southeast Asian cities. In addition, the quality of pipe infrastructure is sub-optimal: non-revenue water (NRW)[11] is generally high in many cities of the region: in Bandung City and Iskandar Malaysia, 38% and 25% of water is lost between production and distribution, respectively. In comparison, only 5% of water produced was lost before distribution in Singapore in 2014. Significant efforts have, however, been undertaken in Southeast Asian cities to improve the pipe network and reduce the NRW: in Hai Phong for instance, the NRW declined from 70% in 1993 to 14% in 2013; in Bangkok City, it declined from 42% in 1998 to 27% in 2012 (Figure 1.21).

Figure 1.21. **Evolution of non-revenue water in Bangkok, Metro Cebu, Hai Phong, Bandung, Iskandar Malaysia and Singapore**

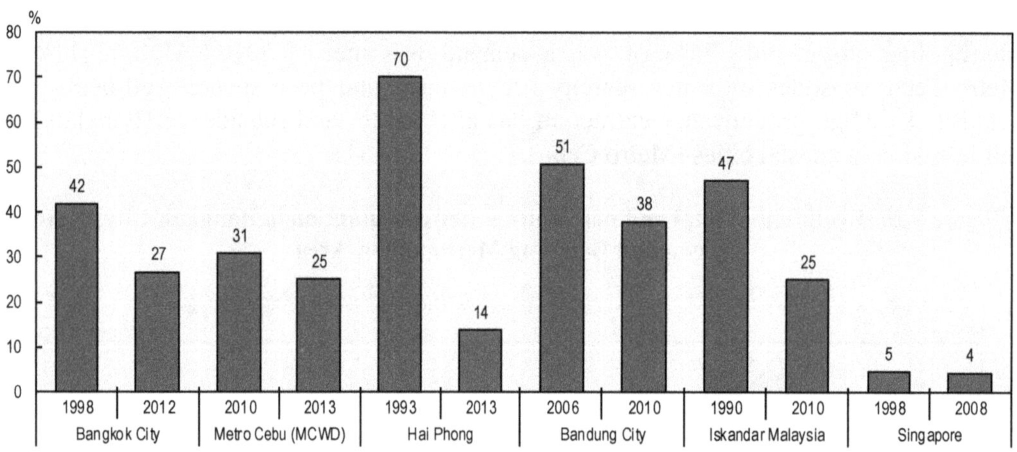

Source: OECD (2015a), *Green Growth in Bangkok, Thailand*, http://dx.doi.org/10.1787/9789264237087-en; OECD (2016a), *Green Growth in Hai Phong, Viet Nam*, forthcoming, http://dx.doi.org/10.1787/9789264260207-en; OECD (2016d), *Green Growth in Bandung, Indonesia*, http://dx.doi.org/10.1787/9789264264113-en; OECD (2016e), *Green Growth in Cebu, the Philippines*, forthcoming; OECD (2016c), *Green Growth in Iskandar Malaysia, Malaysia*, forthcoming.

Water sanitation infrastructure is also sub-optimal and has not kept up with the pace of urbanisation. Currently, there is no centralised sewerage system and no wastewater treatment plant[12] in Metro Cebu. Only 3.4% of households evacuate black water (i.e. wastewater with human wastes) through sewers, while 86% is evacuated into septic tanks and 10% through drainage and therefore having no treatment. Only 7% of grey water (i.e. wastewater without human wastes) is evacuated through sewerage, most being evacuated through drainage with no treatment (80%) or into septic tanks (13%). In addition, most wastewater discharged into septic tanks is not effectively processed and infiltrates the soil and groundwater, because many septic tanks have not been desludged and are in poor conditions (OECD, 2016e). In Bangkok City, only 46% of wastewater is treated, although this represents a significant improvement since 2000 when only 2% was treated (OECD, 2015a). The growth in the number of industries has also raised the issue of industrial wastewater treatment in many Southeast Asian cities.

Untreated wastewater is generally discharged into the ground, drainage systems, rivers, canals or the sea, damaging precious ecosystems. In particular, the quality of surface water in rivers and canals, measured by the amount of biochemical oxygen demand (BOD), is a serious environmental problem. In Bangkok City, 70% of the 296 monitoring stations in the Chao Phraya River and canals indicate that water is moderately polluted (4-15 mg/L) and 17% indicate that water is severely polluted (15-30 mg/L). BOD is as high as 30-50 mg/L in the densest areas in the centre of the city (OECD, 2015a). In Cebu, the BOD in the Butuanon River was recently measured at 70 mg/L (OECD, 2016e), and in Iskandar Malaysia, at 62 mg/L in the Segget River (OECD, 2016c). In Hai Phong, the BOD value in the Cam Ca River was at 4.8 mg/L in 2009 but still has not met the national standards (OECD, 2016a). The poor surface water quality is a serious threat to human health and eco-systems. Moreover, it will damage rivers, beaches and natural coasts, which are important local assets for the tourism industry.

Climate change risks are increasingly prominent in Southeast Asian cities

Southeast Asian cities are characterised by rising energy consumption and greenhouse gas emissions

Energy demand in Southeast Asia increased by 50% between 2000 and 2013, and is expected to increase by 80% between 2013 and 2040, to around 1 070 Mtoe (IEA, 2015). The power sector, in particular, is a driving factor of such growth: electricity demand in the region is expected to triple from 2013 to 2040, from 789 TWh to 2 212 TWh. Similar trends are observable in cities. In Bangkok Metropolitan Area,[13] electricity consumption increased from 35 600 GWH in 2002 to 35 645 GWh in 2015, mainly in the residential and commercial sectors. In Hai Phong, electricity consumption is expected to increase from 3 120 GWh in 2013 to 9 030 GWh in 2020, mainly in the industry sector, due to its particular weight in Hai Phong's economy. In both cities, per capita electricity consumption is increasing in parallel: from 4 600 KWh/capita/year in 2002 to 5 900 KWh/capita/year in 2013 in Bangkok; and from 3 100 KWh/capita/year in 2013 to 7 200 KWh/capita/year in 2020 in Hai Phong (Figure 1.22). Indonesia, the Philippines and Viet Nam are the top three countries, among the ASEAN-10 region, with the highest increase in electricity demand from 2009 to 2030, with respectively an estimated additional 993 TWh, 472 TWh and 347 TWh (Table 1.4).

Figure 1.22. **Energy power consumption in Hai Phong (projections) and Bangkok, by sector of the economy**

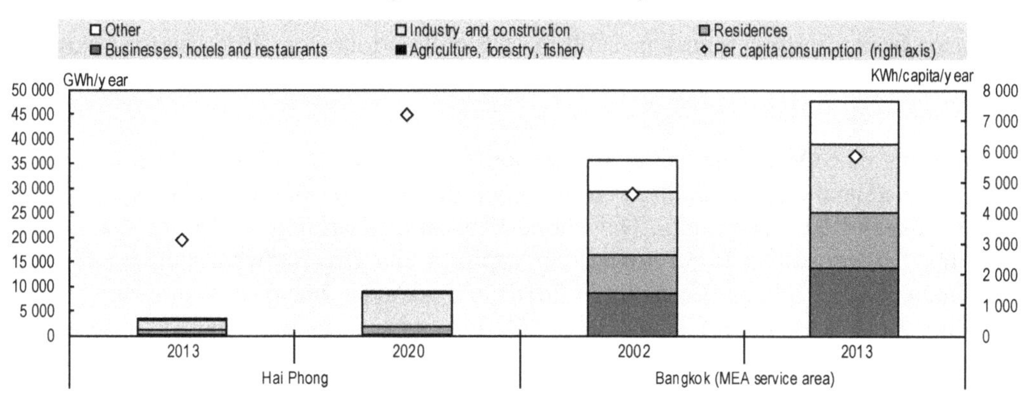

Source: Case study reports.

Table 1.4. **Projected increase in electricity demand in ASEAN countries by 2030**

Country	Per capita electricity demand (kWh/capita)	Population in 2030 (million)	Total electricity demand (TWh)	Electricity demand increase from 2009 (TWh)
Brunei Darussalam	8 652	0.4	3.7	0.3
Cambodia	4 000	17.2	68.7	66.8
Indonesia	4 000	284.2	1 136.7	993.0
Lao PDR	4 000	7.6	30.2	27.8
Malaysia	4 000	33.8	135.0	26.2
Myanmar	4 000	67.8	271.4	265.8
Philippines	4 000	132.5	530.0	471.9
Singapore	7 789	5.8	45.2	6.0
Thailand	4 000	71.5	285.9	151.1
Viet Nam	4 000	107.0	428.1	346.9
ASEAN total	4 033	727.2	2 935.0	2 355.9

Sources: Population projections are based on projections of population growth rates for 2009-30 by Fouré, J., A. Bénassy-Quéré and L. Fontagné (2012), "The great shift: Macroeconomic projections for the world economy at the 2050 horizon",. Population data in 2009 are from the International Database of the US Census Bureau, https://www.census.gov/population/international/data/idb/region.php.

At the country level, fossil fuels remain the privileged source of energy. In Thailand, fossil fuels accounted for 76.2% of final energy consumption in 2013, against 10.9% for alternative and renewable energy, 10.7% for traditional renewable energy, 0.6% for large hydropower and 1.5% for imported hydropower (OECD, 2015a). In Indonesia, fossil fuels accounted for 88% of power generation in 2013, against 8% for hydropower, 4% for geothermal and 2% for other renewables (OECD, 2016d). Overall, fossil fuels account for 74% of primary energy demand in Southeast Asia in 2013; this share will increase to 78% in 2040 (IEA, 2015).

The reliance on fossil fuels and increasing energy consumption in Southeast Asian cities has resulted in rising greenhouse gas emissions, in particular carbon dioxide (CO_2). In Viet Nam, carbon emissions at the country level increased from 103.8 million tonnes in 1994 to 246.8 million tonnes in 2010, and are projected to reach 760.5 million tonnes in 2030. Most of the increase is borne by the energy sector whose emissions increased from 25.6 to 141.1 million tonnes between 1994 and 2010, and are projected to reach 648.5 million tonnes in 2030 (Figure 1.23). Similarly, energy-related emissions in Hai Phong accounted for 13.2 million tonnes of CO_2 (76.9% of total CO_2 emissions) in 2010 and are expected to increase to 49.6 million tonnes CO_2 (79.2% of total CO_2 emission) in 2020 in a business-as-usual scenario (City of Kitakyushu and City of Hai Phong, 2015). In Johor Bahru and Pasir Gudang (Iskandar Malaysia), energy-related CO_2 emissions increased from 5 million tonnes in 2000 to 18.5 million tonnes in 2012, and are expected to increase to 38.6 million tonnes in 2025, in a business-as-usual scenario (Gouldson et al., 2012).

In terms of CO_2 emissions per capita, some disparities are observable across urban areas. While Bandung City emitted around 2.3 million tonnes of CO_2 in 2013, equivalent to 0.8 tonnes of CO_2 per capita, Hai Phong City emitted around 17.2 million tonnes of CO_2 in 2010, equivalent to 8.7 tonnes per capita. Cebu City shows a similar profile as Bandung City (2.1 tonnes per capita in 2010) and Iskandar Malaysia a similar profile as Hai Phong (11.8 tonnes per capita in 2015). In comparison, the average (unweighted) CO_2 emissions per capita in 290 OECD metropolitan areas are of 9.6 tonnes per capita per year (OECD Metro Explorer) (Figure 1.24). The discrepancies observed between the Asian cities mentioned previously are correlated to the choice of city limits. The

Figure 1.23. **CO_2 emissions by sector in Viet Nam**

1994-30

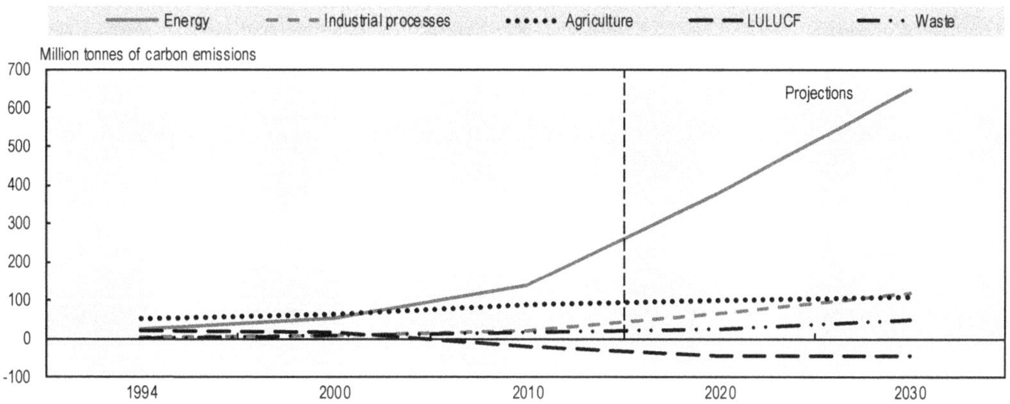

Note: LULUCF refers to "land use, land-use change and forestry".

Source: Viet Nam Ministry of Natural Resources and Environment (2014), *The Initial Biennial Updated Report of Viet Nam to the United Nations Framework Convention on Climate Change*, http://unfccc.int/resource/docs/natc/vnmbur1.pdf.

administrative limits of Hai Phong and Iskandar Malaysia, for instance, include significant amounts of peri-urban and rural areas where industries are located, whereas both Bandung City and Cebu City correspond to the urban centres of their respective metropolitan areas and are more service-oriented. This can explain the significant differences between Hai Phong and Iskandar Malaysia on the one side, and Bandung City and Cebu City on the other. Indeed, industries (both in terms of energy consumption and industrial processes), are the major sources of CO_2 emissions in Hai Phong and Iskandar Malaysia (79.2% and 44.1% of total CO_2 emissions, respectively), while in Bandung City and Cebu City, the transport sector is the primary source of CO_2 emissions (60.5% and 40% of total emissions, respectively) (Figure 1.25). Careful interpretation of data on CO_2 emissions is therefore necessary, because of these differences in territorial limits.

Figure 1.24. **Per capita CO_2 emissions in selected ASEAN-5 cities and OECD metropolitan areas**

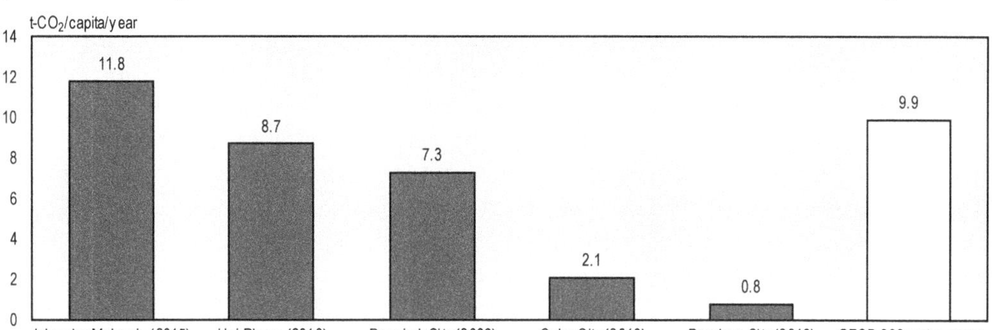

Sources: OECD (2015a), *Green Growth in Bangkok, Thailand*, http://dx.doi.org/10.1787/9789264237087-en; OECD (2016a), *Green Growth in Hai Phong, Viet Nam*, forthcoming, http://dx.doi.org/10.1787/9789264260207-en; OECD (2016d), *Green Growth in Bandung, Indonesia*, http://dx.doi.org/10.1787/9789264264113-en; OECD (2016e), *Green Growth in Cebu, the Philippines*, forthcoming; OECD (2016c), *Green Growth in Iskandar Malaysia, Malaysia*, forthcoming; C40Cities (2014), "C40 GHG emissions 2014", webpage, www.c40.org/research/open_data/1; UN DESA (2014), *World Urbanisation Prospects: The 2014 Revision*, https://esa.un.org/unpd/wup/Publications/Files/WUP2014-Report.pdf.

Figure 1.25. **CO_2 emissions by sector in Bangkok, Bandung, Hai Phong, Iskandar Malaysia and Cebu**

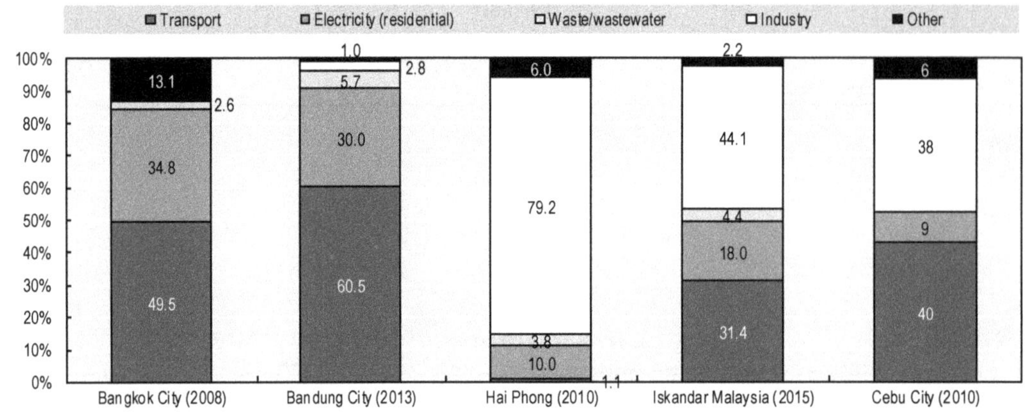

Sources: OECD (2015a), *Green Growth in Bangkok, Thailand,* http://dx.doi.org/10.1787/9789264237087-en; OECD (2016a), *Green Growth in Hai Phong, Viet Nam,* forthcoming, http://dx.doi.org/10.1787/9789264260207-en; OECD (2016d), *Green Growth in Bandung, Indonesia,* http://dx.doi.org/10.1787/9789264264113-en; OECD (2016e), *Green Growth in Cebu, the Philippines,* forthcoming; OECD (2016c), *Green Growth in Iskandar Malaysia, Malaysia*, forthcoming; C40Cities (2014), "C40 GHG emissions 2014", webpage, www.c40.org/research/open_data/1; UN DESA (2014), *World Urbanisation Prospects: The 2014 Revision,* https://esa.un.org/unpd/wup/Publications/Files/WUP2014-Report.pdf.

Southeast Asian cities face high disaster risks from floods and typhoons

While both population and economies grow, a critical characteristic of Southeast Asian cities is the high risk of natural disasters they face, and their vulnerability to the impacts of climate changes. Floods, typhoons, hurricanes and earthquakes are the most frequent types of disasters occurring in the region. The annual number of natural disasters in Southeast Asia increased from 13 in 1970 to 41 in 2014, with a peak at 66 disasters in 2011. During this period, the human impact and economic losses due to these disasters have progressively increased to reach alarming levels (Figure 1.26). The Philippines, Thailand and Viet Nam have some of the worst combination of water-related hazards and water-related resilience in the Asia-Pacific region (Figure 1.27). In 2011, a major flood hit the Bangkok Metropolitan Region and caused economic damages estimated at USD 23.9 billion (THB 296 billion) in Bangkok City alone, and at USD 113.6 billion (THB 1 405 billion) in the entire country (at purchasing power parity values). Eight hundred fifteen persons were reported dead and 13.6 million affected by the disaster (ADB, 2013). In the Philippines, typhoon Haiyan/Yolanda caused estimated damages at USD 5 billion (at purchasing power parity values) and around 6 300 human losses (NDRRMC, 2014). While Hai Phong, Bandung, Metro Cebu and Iskandar Malaysia have not been affected by disasters of such intensity, they are nonetheless routinely faced with seasonal floods, and even typhoons in the case of Hai Phong.

The frequency and impacts of such disasters are expected to increase in the future, as a result of a combination of climate change impacts (such as sea-level rise), urbanisation and socio-economic changes. Southeast Asia is characterised by a high concentration of exposed population and assets. One study estimated that in a scenario taking into account climate change impacts, subsidence[14] and socio-economic changes, 15 cities from Asia, including 4 from the ASEAN-5 region, would be amongst the top 20 cities with the highest population exposed to floods by 2070 (Ho Chi Minh, 9.2 million persons; Bangkok, 5.1 million persons; Hai Phong, 4.7 million persons; and Jakarta, 2.2 million persons). These four cities would also be amongst the top 20 cities experiencing the highest proportional increase in exposed population by 2070. The same study estimated that Bangkok and Ho Chi Minh City would be amongst the top 20 cities with the most exposed assets to floods in 2070, according to the same scenario (USD 1.1 billion and USD 0.7 billion, respectively). Hai Phong, Bangkok and Ho Chi Minh City would be amongst the top 20 cities in terms of proportional increase in exposed assets (Hanson et al., 2011).

Figure 1.26. **Evolution of the number of people affected by natural disasters in Southeast Asia and economic losses**

1970-2014

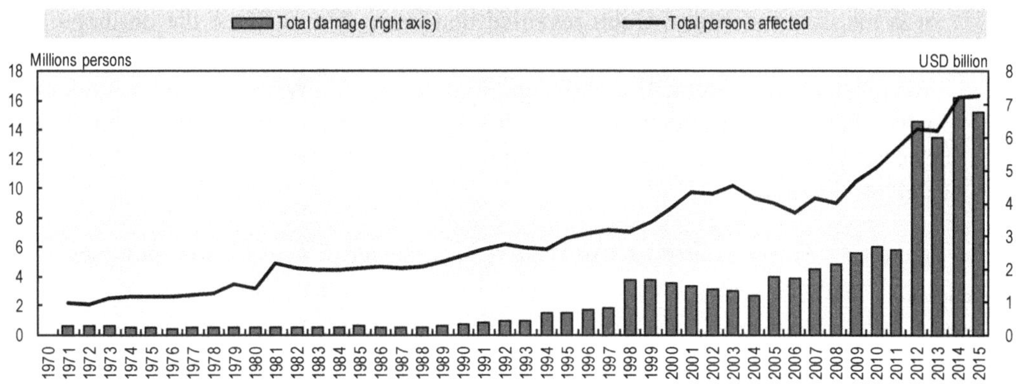

Notes: Total damage and total persons affected are smoothed calculations. Total persons affected include persons requiring immediate assistance during a period of emergency, i.e. requiring basic survival needs such as food, water, shelter, sanitation and immediate medical assistance. It also includes homeless and injured people as a consequence of the disaster. It does not include people who died from the disaster. Total deaths over the period 1970-2015 have not followed the same rising patterns as total damage and total persons affected. In 2004 (tsunami) and 2008 (Cyclone Nargis), however, high human losses were recorded.

Source: Guha-Sapir, D., R. Below and P. Hoyois (2016), *EM-DAT: The CRED/OFDA International Disaster Database*, www.emdat.be.

A combination of multiple factors explains the high risk of natural disasters faced by many Southeast Asian cities. Some of them are directly linked to fast urbanisation and economic growth processes occurring in these countries and presented previously:

- Southeast Asian cities face a strong probability of climatic and geological events, in particular due to the monsoon season that occurs in all Southeast Asian countries. The average annual rainfall in Bangkok over the period 1991-2013 was 1 710.6 mm (it was 2 257.5 mm in 2011, when the flood that severely hit Thailand occurred). In comparison, the average annual rainfall in France is 867 mm. There is also an increasing body of scientific evidence that the intensity of extreme weather events such as cyclones is rising as a consequence of climate deregulations. In north-eastern Viet Nam, entire major cities such as Hai Phong and Ninh Binh may be exposed to storm surges by 2050 (OECD, 2016a).
- Southeast Asian cities must cope with an increasing exposure of urban populations, in particular to floods. Some cities such as Bangkok (less than 2 metres above sea level) and coastal cities are low-lying and more prone to floods. However, a critical factor of exposure is settlement patterns in Southeast Asian cities. In Bangkok, Bandung and Metro Cebu, for instance, many informal settlers live along the shore of rivers and canals, in zones which are therefore

more likely to be flooded. Sprawling urban development has also often resulted in the destruction of natural habitats that used to play a critical role in absorbing runoff and protecting cities from flood disasters.

- Southeast Asian cities show increasing vulnerability – i.e. the propensity or predisposition to be adversely affected (IPCC, 2012) – to natural disasters. Urban infrastructures are, for instance, often deficient to ensure the resilience of cities. In many of them, drainage facilities are lacking or not working properly: in the Metro Cebu area, it is estimated that around 42.6% of households do not have drainage systems in their neighbourhood, and around 21% of households with drainage facilities have reported them in bad or very bad conditions. Drainage that was inspected in Metro Cebu revealed that more than 50% of the drainage lines are either silted or clogged by garbage – a situation often encountered in Southeast Asian cities (including Bangkok and Bandung). Many assets and residents (in particular the urban poor) also lack insurance or other safety-net mechanisms or access to resilient urban infrastructure and are therefore highly vulnerable to natural disasters.

Figure 1.27. **Water-related hazard relative to resilience in Asia-Pacific countries**

FIGURE 18

Water-Related Hazard Relative to Resilience

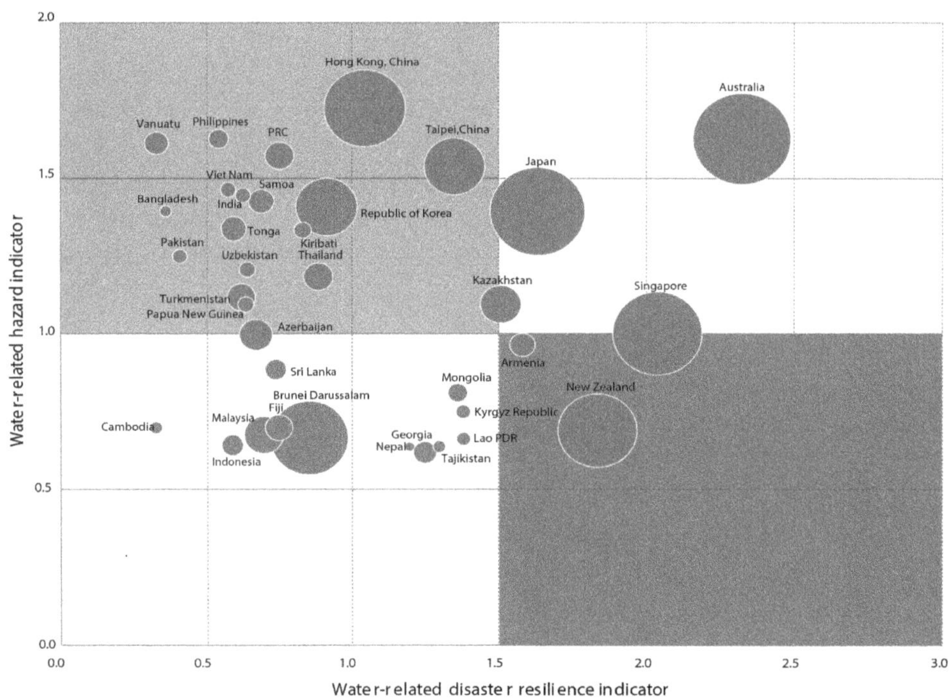

Note: Resilience is calculated as a function of exposure, vulnerability and capacity.

Source: ADB (2013), *Asian Water Development Outlook 2013, Measuring Water Security in Asia and the Pacific*, https://www.adb.org/sites/default/files/publication/30190/asian-water-development-outlook-2013.pdf.

Social challenges of Southeast Asian cities may have long-term economic and environmental repercussions

Despite reductions in poverty, rising urban inequalities and slums remain urgent social challenges in Southeast Asian cities

A general trend towards the reduction of poverty is observable in Southeast Asian cities. Overall, the share of urban population living under the poverty line has substantially decreased in the region: it fell from 19.4% to 8.3% in Indonesia between 1999 and 2014, from 22.3% to 9% in Thailand between 2000 and 2012, and from 35.2% to 12% in Viet Nam from 2002 to 2013 (Figure 1.28). In Hai Phong, the percentage of poor households decreased from 6.6% in 2010 to 1.5% in 2015 (OECD, 2016a). In Bandung City, the percentage of persons living under the poverty line decreased from 9.7% to 8% between 2005 and 2012 (OECD, 2016d).

Figure 1.28. **Share of urban population living under the poverty line in Southeast Asian countries**

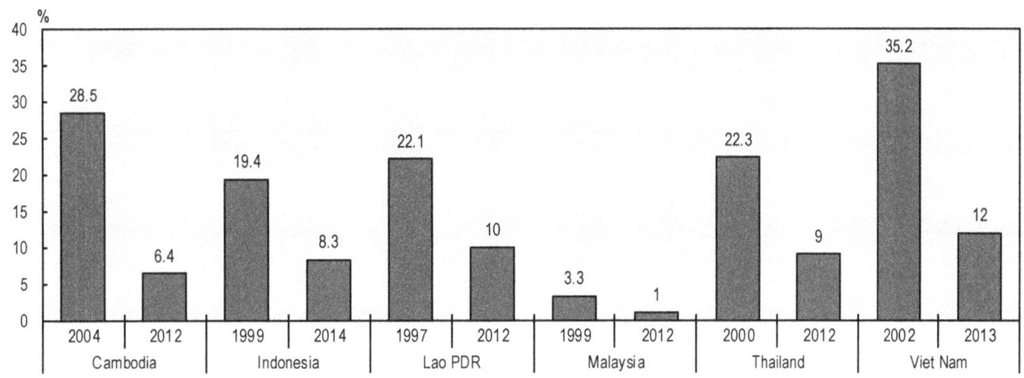

Source: United Nations (2016a), "Millennium Development Goals Indicators", , http://mdgs.un.org/unsd/mdg/Data.aspx.

Southeast Asian cities nonetheless face high social challenges that have direct consequences on their environmental performance and may undermine long-term economic growth if not addressed urgently. They are characterised by high levels of urban inequalities that have been increasing in the recent years: in Bandung Metropolitan Area, the Gini coefficient increased from 0.3 in 2008 to 0.4 in 2014; in Jakarta City, it increased from 0.33 to 0.43; and in Surabaya City, it increased from 0.32 to 0.39. While this trend is observable in the entire country (the Gini coefficient in Indonesia increased from 0.35 to 0.41 over the same period), it seems to be more dramatic in cities: the percentage increase in the Gini coefficient has been higher in Bandung Metropolitan Area (35%), Jakarta City (30%), Surabaya City (22%) and Yogyakarta (19%) than in Indonesia overall (17%) (Figure 1.29). Rising income disparities are critical obstacles for economic growth, and threaten the inclusive development of Southeast Asian cities in the long term.

In addition, despite reductions in poverty (as mentioned previously) and in the share of the population living in slums in Southeast Asia (from 50% in 1990 to 31% in 2010), the absolute number of urban dwellers living in slums has remained steady or slightly increased in cities of the region, due to population growth. The United Nations system defines slums as characterised by the absence of basic services, such as improved drinking water and adequate sanitation, along with insecure tenure, non-durable housing and overcrowding (UN HABITAT and UN ESCAP, 2015). In Indonesia, the number of urban slum dwellers slightly increased from around 28 million in 1990 to 29 million in 2014; in Thailand, it increased from 5.5 million in 2005 to 8.3 million in 2014 (Figure 1.30). In Bangkok City, 2 051 slums hosting around 2.1 million persons were identified in 2013 (BMA, 2014). This accounts for almost one-quarter of the capital city's total population, including non-registered inhabitants. Bandung City counts an estimated 120 000 persons living in slums.

Figure 1.29. **Gini co-efficient in selected cities and areas of Indonesia**

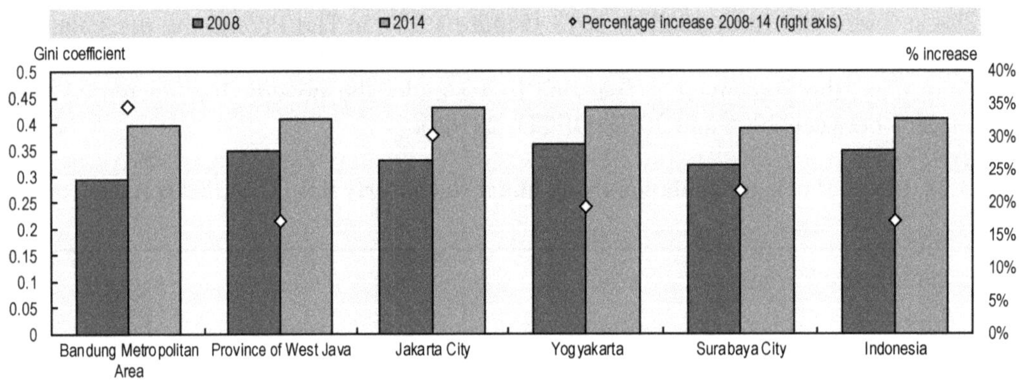

Sources: Badan Pusat Statistik,(2016) / Central Bureau of Statistics, Gini Ratio Menurut Kabupaten/Kota Tahun 2008 – 2014 / Gini Ratio By Regency / City Year 2008 - 2014, Available at https://nganjukkab.bps.go.id/linkTabelStatis/view/id/45 (Accessed 07 November, 2016).

Figure 1.30. **Urban slum populations in Indonesia, the Philippines, Thailand and Viet Nam**

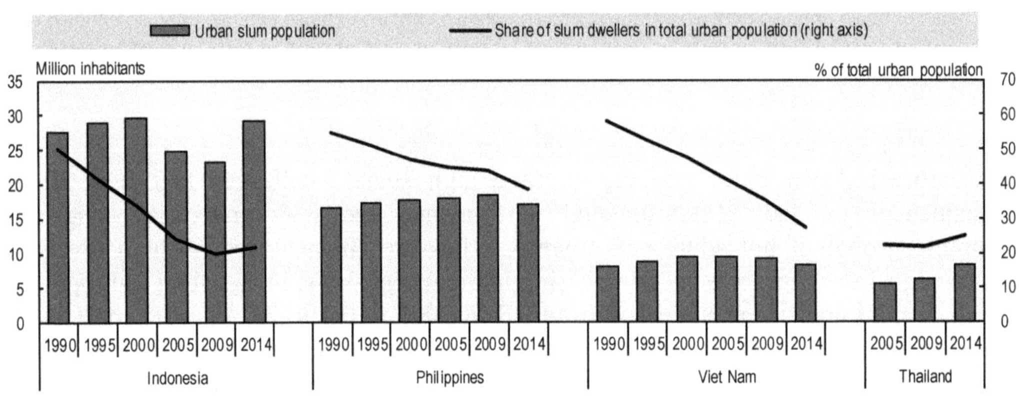

Sources: United Nations (2016b), "Slum population in urban areas (thousands)", Millennium Development Goals Indicators, http://mdgs.un.org/unsd/mdg/SeriesDetail.aspx?srid=711; UN DESA (2014), *World Urbanisation Prospects: The 2014 Revision*, https://esa.un.org/unpd/wup/Publications/Files/WUP2014-Report.pdf.

Slum dwellers tend to live under the poverty line and have low incomes, low levels of education, and low access to basic urban services and infrastructure. This undermines their economic opportunities and also provides them with little option but to adopt living behaviours which are harmful to the environment. Due to the lack of access to solid waste collection services, for instance, slum dwellers tend to burn waste, bury it in pits or dump it in the near environment, especially in canals, rivers or the sea. The lack of access to centralised water and energy networks also encourages the poorest populations to opt for alternatives which are less efficient and sustainable (e.g. communal or illegal water taps, old stoves, etc.) and which tend to be more expensive. Because of their location near water streams, or on hillsides and slopes, urban slum dwellers are also more exposed to floods and landslides, and are more vulnerable to such disasters as a result of insalubrious housing conditions and the lack of access to safety net mechanisms. Inadequate housing conditions and low levels of tenure security are central issues for slum dwellers, with consequences on their well-being, their environmental impact and economic security (UN HABITAT and UN ESCAP, 2015).

Many of the urban populations of Southeast Asia, especially those living in slums, are also "off the radar" and not registered in official databases. Their settlements often do not even appear on official maps. In the Bangkok Metropolitan Region, for instance, 10.6 million people were registered in 2014 according to official statistics, but it is estimated that the real number of inhabitants is around 14.6 million (OECD, 2015a). Likewise, many urban dwellers work in the informal economy: the number of persons in informal employment outside the agriculture sector in Indonesia (2009), the Philippines (2008), Thailand (2010) and Viet Nam (2009), was respectively estimated at around 3.2 million, 15.2 million, 9.6 million and 17.2 million (ILO, 2012). This situation creates difficulties for national and local governments in assessing urbanisation trends and their economic and environmental repercussions. For informal settlers and workers, this implies difficulties in accessing services, infrastructure, housing, land, economic opportunities (e.g. access to credit), pensions and other forms of social services (UN HABITAT and UN ESCAP, 2015). For buildings, industries and businesses, informality may result in higher environmental impact due to a lack of enforcement of environmental regulations.

Informality, nonetheless, is not always a burden on urban populations, but in some cases has developed as a practical means to compensate for the failure of governments to provide public services and infrastructure in fast-growing Southeast Asian cities. In many cities of the region, indeed, informal transport networks, informal waste picking and recycling communities, and informal water provision systems have emerged in the absence of formal structures. Such informal services have not necessarily developed in slums and informal settlements but wherever the public services and infrastructure are missing despite a need from the population.

Low educational performance and skills may drive urban economies into middle-income traps

Finally, low educational attainment and performance may undermine long-term economic growth and the transformation of urban economies in Southeast Asia. Scores from the OECD's Programme for International Student Assessment (PISA) demonstrate that on average the ASEAN region scores significantly lower than OECD countries in mathematics, reading and science (Figure 1.31). As the growth model of Southeast Asian economies is progressively shifting from a reliance on FDI and cheap labour to growth led by domestic markets and industry, with higher wages and decreasing cost competitiveness relative to least developed countries, Southeast Asian economies need effective strategies to transit from middle-income to high-income economies, and to avoid "middle-income traps" such as those experienced in Brazil and South Africa. In order to continue to grow in the long term, cities in this regard need to shift to higher value-added and technology-advanced goods and services, and investment in human capital to emphasise knowledge, skills, creativity and innovation (including in the environmental goods and services sector) will be paramount (UN HABITAT and UN ESCAP, 2015). In the shorter term, investment in human capital is also critical to improve the maintenance and development of urban infrastructure, and to raise awareness on the benefits of greening growth.

Figure 1.31. **Average PISA scores in OECD and ASEAN countries, 2012**

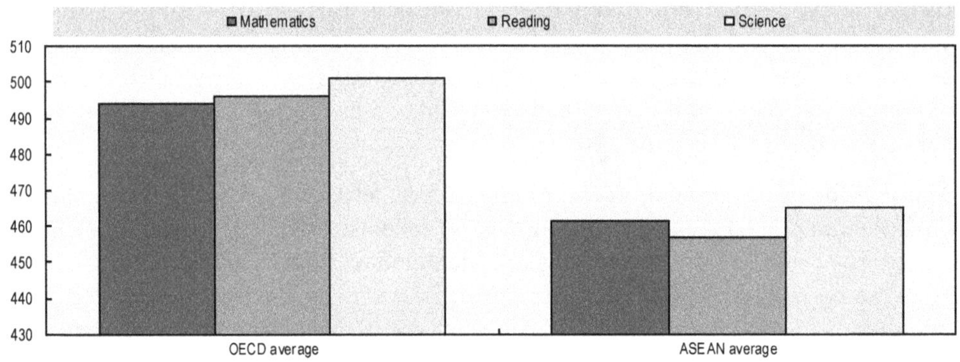

Source: OECD (2016b), *Economic Outlook for Southeast Asia, China and India 2016: Enhancing Regional Ties*, http://dx.doi.org/10.1787/saeo-2016-en.

Conclusion: The urgent need to green Southeast Asian cities' growth

Fast urbanisation and economic growth in Southeast Asian cities has triggered immense development challenges, in particular infrastructure gaps and unsustainable infrastructure lock-ins, local environmental degradation, acute climate change risks and social issues, which altogether threatens their long-term economic performance and well-being. The ongoing development process nonetheless still offers "windows of opportunities" to shift towards environmentally sustainable growth models. Such momentum must be seized immediately by all levels of governments as well as the private sector to avoid the consequences of business-as-usual development pathways.

The concept of urban green growth in this regard can be a powerful vector of sustainable development in Southeast Asian cities. Urban green growth is a multi-sectoral approach that aims to promote long-term economic and environmental sustainability, and which can thereby improve quality of life in cities (OECD, 2013a). Urban green growth emphasises the existence of co-benefits between economic and environmental performance. In the particular context of Southeast Asian cities, such co-benefits are potentially high in the sectors of land use, transport, energy, water and solid waste.

The development context in Southeast Asia also shows the need to consider the concept of green growth from an angle different than that in more developed countries. In the previous case studies of OECD cities, a strong focus was placed to demonstrate that urban green growth can be an instrument to generate new green jobs and boost the economy (OECD, 2013a). In contrast, the trends of urbanisation, economic growth and the associated challenges of Southeast Asian cities demonstrates that urban green growth priorities may lay in investing in urban infrastructure and in mitigating negative environmental impacts. There is more need to decouple environmental impacts and economic performance to ensure robust long-term economic growth and tackle development challenges rather than to revitalise economic growth (Figure 1.32). Social issues tend to also be more acute in Southeast Asian cities and testify to the importance of making green growth inclusive in this region.

Figure 1.32. **Urban green growth scenarios in OECD cities vs. Southeast Asian cities**

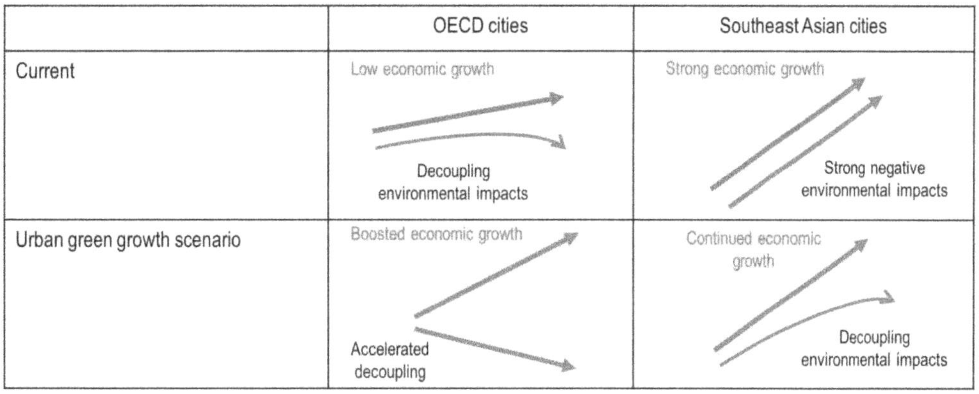

Source: Authors.

Notes

1. Southeast Asia here refers to Brunei Darussalam, Cambodia, Indonesia, Lao People's Democratic Republic, Malaysia, Myanmar, the Philippines, Singapore, Thailand and Viet Nam.

2. The list of high-income countries can be found at: https://esa.un.org/unpd/wup/CD-ROM/WUP2014_DOCUMENTATION/WUP2014_DEFINITION_OF_MAJOR_AREAS_AND_REGIONS.pdf.

3. The Philippines is among the top ten countries in the world to experience fastest rural population increase between 2014 and 2050, in absolute numbers. Conversely, Thailand, Indonesia and Viet Nam are amongst the top ten countries over the same period with the highest rural population decline in absolute numbers (UN DESA, 2014).

4. These figures only take into account cities; they do not take into account metropolitan regions.

5. Greenfield investment is defined as business investment for establishing new facilities or operations in a host country (fDi Markets, 2015).

6. This does not include Lao PDR, the only landlocked country of the region.

7. In trans-shipment ports, many vessels call in not for distribution in the country where the port is located but instead to unload the cargo onto smaller vessels, which will eventually call at other smaller ports in the region for distribution. Trans-shipment ports are highly attractive to shipping lines from an economic point of view, as they can load more cargo on a same boat, and thereby reduce transport costs. Most ports in the ASEAN-5 countries, with the exception of Malaysia, do not have the depth and capacity to handle large vessels.

8. Cargo accounts for all types of goods delivered in ports, including goods shipped in containers and other goods such as liquids (e.g. oil) and large-sized materials.

9. The environmental goods and services sector used in this sentence follows the classification of the European Union, which defines environmental goods and services as two main activities: environmental protection (e.g. wastewater management, waste management, protection of biodiversity and landscapes) and environmental management (e.g. water management, energy resource management).

10. The figures presented in this sentence do not include urban areas in the Pontian District, which is partly included in the official territory of Iskandar Malaysia.

11. Non-revenue water (NRW) refers to the difference between the volume of water put into a water distribution system and the volume that is billed to customers. The NRW can occur through physical losses from leaking and broken pipes, which are caused by poor operations and maintenance, the lack of active leakage control, and poor quality of underground assets. The NRW can also come from commercial losses caused by the under-registration of customer meters, data handling errors, illegal connections and theft. Another cause of the NRW is unbilled authorised consumption, which includes water used by utilities for operational purposes, water used for firefighting and water provided for free to certain consumer groups (van den Berg, 2014).

12. There is, however, a treatment plant for surface water of the Buhisan dam, and for groundwater of Jacluban, the main groundwater resource of Cebu.

13. Here, the Bangkok Metropolitan Electricity Authority service area.

14. Land subsidence is the lowering of the land-surface elevation from changes that take place underground.

References

ADB (2013), *Asian Water Development Outlook 2013, Measuring Water Security in Asia and the Pacific*, Asian Development Bank, Mandaluyong City, Philippines, https://www.adb.org/sites/default/files/publication/30190/asian-water-development-outlook-2013.pdf.

ADB (2011), "Republic of Indonesia: Preparing the Integrated Citarum Water Resources Management Investment Program periodic financing request 2", Technical Assistance Report, https://www.adb.org/sites/default/files/project-document/74867/37049-062-ino-tar.pdf.

Badan Pusat Statistik,(2016) / Central Bureau of Statistics, Gini Ratio Menurut Kabupaten/Kota Tahun 2008 – 2014 / Gini Ratio By Regency / City Year 2008 - 2014, Available at https://nganjukkab.bps.go.id/linkTabelStatis/view/id/45 (Accessed 07 November, 2016).

BMA (2014), *Statistical Profile of Bangkok Metropolitan Administration 2013*, Strategy and Evaluation Department, Bangkok Metropolitan Administration, Bangkok, www.bangkok.go.th/main/backoffice/upload_editor/file/stat2013%28ENG%29.pdf.

C40Cities (2014), "C40 GHG emissions 2014", webpage, www.c40.org/research/open_data/1.

City of Kitakyushu and City of Hai Phong (2015), *Green Growth Promotion Plan of the City of Hai Phong*, Hai Phong, Viet Nam, www.asiangreencamp.net/pdf/green_en.pdf.

City of Paris (2013), *Rapport Annuel sur le Prix et la Qualité du Service Public de Gestion des Déchets à Paris*, Paris.

Dissanayake, D. (2012), "Inter-regional and inter-temporal analysis of travel behaviour for Asian metropolitan cities: Case studies of Bangkok, Kuala Lumpur, Manila, and Nagoya", *Transport Policy*, Vol. 19/1, pp. 36-46, http://dx.doi.org/10.1016/j.tranpol.2011.07.002.

fDi Markets (2015), "fDi Markets: The in-depth crossborder investment monitor from the Financial Times", www.fdimarkets.com.

Fouré, J., A. Bénassy-Quéré and L. Fontagné (2012), "The great shift: Macroeconomic projections for the world economy at the 2050 horizon", CEPII Working Papers, No. 2012-3, CEPII, Paris, February, www.cepii.fr/PDF_PUB/wp/2012/wp2012-03.pdf.

Gouldson, A. et al. (2012), *The Economics of Low Carbon Cities: Johor Bahru and Pasir Gudang, Malaysia*, University of Leeds.

Guha-Sapir, D., R. Below and P. Hoyois (2016), *EM-DAT: The International Disaster* Database, Centre for Research on Epidemiology of Disasters-CRED, Université Catholique de Louvain, Brussels, www.emdat.be.

Hanson, S. et al. (2011), "A global ranking of port cities with high exposure to climate extremes", *Climatic Change*, Vol. 104/1, pp. 89-111, http://dx.doi.org/10.1007/s10584-010-9977-4.

IEA (2015), *Southeast Asia Energy Outlook 2015*, OECD/IEA, Paris, https://www.iea.org/publications/freepublications/publication/weo2015_southeastasia.pdf.

ILO (2012), "Statistical update on employment in the informal economy", International Labour Organization, Geneva, http://laborsta.ilo.org/applv8/data/INFORMAL_ECONOMY/2012-06-Statistical%20update%20-%20v2.pdf.

IPCC (2012) "Summary for policymakers" in: *Managing the Risks of Extreme Events and Disasters to Advance Climate Change Adaptation*, A Special Report of Working Groups I and II of the Intergovernmental Panel on Climate Change, International Panel on Climate Change, Cambridge University Press, Cambridge, United Kingdom and New York, pp. 1-19.

JICA and MCDCB (2015), *The Roadmap Study for Sustainable Urban Development in Metro Cebu.*

Khazanah Nasional (2014), "Mangrove matters. True value: Johor's Ramsar sites and solutions for conservation".

Maritime Insights (2014), "Container throughput and economic development: Container throughput in ports in the Philippines, Singapore, Thailand and Viet Nam", *Maritime Insights*, Vol. 2/3, autumn, https://www.polyu.edu.hk/lms/ICMS/research_maritimeInsight/2014-Autumn-en/1.pdf.

Matsumoto, T. and L. Daudey (2014), "Urban green growth in dynamic Asia: A conceptual framework", *OECD Regional Development Working Papers*, No. 2014/12, OECD Publishing, Paris, http://dx.doi.org/10.1787/5js7svlw8m0x-en.

Metropolitan Waterworks Authority (n.d.), "Water tariffs effective December 1999", webpage, www.mwa.co.th/ewtadmin/ewt/mwa_internet_eng/ewt_w3c/ewt_news.php?nid=309 (accessed 3 July 2015).

Metropolitan Waterworks Authority (2015), "Saving water together: Annual report 2015", Metropolitan Waterworks Authority, Bangkok, www.mwa.co.th/download/pln0201/annual2015/Annual_Report_2015_Eng.pdf.

NDRRMC (2014), "Effects of Typhoon Yolanda", National Disaster Risk Reduction Management Centre, Manila, Philippines.

OECD (2016a), *Green Growth in Hai Phong, Viet Nam*, OECD Publishing, Paris, forthcoming, http://dx.doi.org/10.1787/9789264260207-en.

OECD (2016b), *Economic Outlook for Southeast Asia, China and India: Enhancing Regional Ties*, OECD Publishing, Paris, http://dx.doi.org/10.1787/saeo-2016-en.

OECD (2016c), *Green Growth in Iskandar Malaysia, Malaysia*, OECD Publishing, Paris, forthcoming.

OECD (2016d), *Green Growth in Bandung, Indonesia*, OECD Publishing, Paris, http://dx.doi.org/10.1787/9789264264113-en.

OECD (2016e), *Green Growth in Cebu, Philippines*, OECD Publishing, Paris, forthcoming.

OECD (2015a), *Green Growth in Bangkok, Thailand*, OECD Publishing, Paris, http://dx.doi.org/10.1787/9789264237087-en.

OECD (2015b), *The Metropolitan Century: Understanding Urbanisation and its Consequences*, OECD Publishing, Paris, http://dx.doi.org/10.1787/9789264228733-en.

OECD (2014), *Green Growth Indicators 2014*, OECD Publishing, Paris, http://dx.doi.org/10.1787/9789264202030-en.

OECD (2013a), *Green Growth in Cities*, OECD Publishing, Paris, http://dx.doi.org/10.1787/9789264195325-en.

OECD (2013b), Green Growth in Stockholm, Sweden, http://dx.doi.org/10.1787/9789264195158-en.

OECD (2011), *Towards Green Growth*, OECD Publishing, Paris, http://dx.doi.org/10.1787/9789264111318-en.

OECD (2010) *Cities and Climate Change*, OECD Publishing, Paris, http://dx.doi.org/10.1787/9789264091375-en.

OECD/IEA (2015), *Southeast Asia Energy Outlook 2015*, OECD/IEA, Paris, https://www.iea.org/publications/freepublications/publication/weo2015_southeastasia.pdf.

OpenStreetMap (n.d.), www.openstreetmap.org/#map=5/51.500/-0.100 (accessed 15 May 2015).

Seoul Government Statistics (2015), http://stat.seoul.go.kr/octagonweb/jsp/WWS7/WWSDS7100.jsp.

Statistics Indonesia (2016), "Gini ratio by province 1996, 1999, 2002, 2005, 2007-2015", www.bps.go.id/linkTableDinamis/view/id/1116 (accessed 21 June 2016).

Statistics Jawa Barat (2016), "Gini ratio Menurut Kabupaten/Kota Tahun 2008-2014/Gini ratio by regency/city 2008-2014", http://jabar.bps.go.id (accessed 21 June 2016).

Statistics East Java (2016), "Gini ratio by regency/city 2008-2014", http://jatim.bps.go.id/linkTabelStatis/view/id/326 (accessed 21 June 2016).

Tuan, V.A. (2011), "Dynamic interactions between private passenger car and motorcycle ownership in Asia: A cross-country analysis", *Journal of the Eastern Asia Society of Transportation Studies*, Vol. 9, pp. 541-556, http://dx.doi.org/10.11175/easts.9.541.

UN DESA (2014), *World Urbanisation Prospects: The 2014 Revision*, United Nations Department of Economic and Social Affairs, Population Division, New York, https://esa.un.org/unpd/wup/Publications/Files/WUP2014-Report.pdf.

UN HABITAT and UN ESCAP (2015), *The State of Asia-Pacific Cities 2015: Urban Transformations – Shifting from Quantity to Quantity*, United Nations Human Settlement Programme and United Nations Economic and Social Commission for Asia and the Pacific, www.unescap.org/sites/default/files/The%20State%20of%20Asian%20and%20Pacific%20Cities%202015.pdf.

UNEP (2009), "Technology for waste management/infrastructure – Cebu (Philippines)".

United Nations (2016a), "Millennium Development Goals Indicators", http://mdgs.un.org/unsd/mdg/Data.aspx.

United Nations (2016b), "Slum population in urban areas (thousands)", Millennium Development Goals Indicators, http://mdgs.un.org/unsd/mdg/SeriesDetail.aspx?srid=711.

van den Berg, C. (2014), "The drivers of non-revenue water: How effective are non-revenue water reduction programs?", *Policy Research Working Papers*, No. WPS 6997, World Bank Group, Washington, DC, http://documents.worldbank.org/curated/en/949281468161359020/The-drivers-of-non-revenue-water-how-effective-are-non-revenue-water-reduction-programs.

Viet Nam Ministry of Natural Resources and Environment (2014), *Biennial Updated Report of Viet Nam to the United Nations Framework Convention on Climate Change*, http://unfccc.int/resource/docs/natc/vnmbur1.pdf (accessed 15 February 2016).

Viet Nam Seaports Association (2000), "Summary of throughput", www.vpa.org.vn/english/information/info_static2000.htm (accessed 22 September 2015).

World Bank (2016a), "Container port traffic (TEU: 20 foot equivalent units)", World Development Indicators, http://data.worldbank.org/indicator/IS.SHP.GOOD.TU/countries (accessed 20 July 2015).

World Bank (2016b), World Development Indicators, http://databank.worldbank.org/data/reports.aspx?source=world-development-indicators.

World Health Organization (2016 and 2014), *Ambient (Outdoor) Air Pollution in Cities Database*, www.who.int/phe/health_topics/outdoorair/databases/cities/en (accessed 30 June 2016).

Chapter 2.

Seizing untapped opportunities: Green growth policies in Southeast Asian cities

This chapter reviews current policies and practices in the Southeast Asian cities. It identifies opportunities and benefits existing in the green growth strategic areas and offers innovative policy recommendations for urgent implementation. The first section aims to answer the question "where are the potential areas?". It presents the numerous areas of opportunity at the disposal of cities in the following six policy areas: land use and transport, energy, housing and buildings, water resource management, solid waste management, and green industries and services. The second section provides an analysis of the six policy areas in the case study cities. Gaps are identified and recommendations and useful examples from other OECD/non-OECD cities are highlighted. The third section highlights key policy strategies to maximise the complementarities and synergies across policy areas. Other cross-sector policy strategies particularly relevant in the context of emerging economies (demand-side policies, policies for long-term growth, ICT innovation for growth, etc.) are also discussed. The final section summarises the key message and indicates the way forward.

Key findings

- In Southeast Asian cities, strong opportunities for urban green growth exist in six sectors: land use and transport, housing and buildings, energy, solid waste, water resource management, and green industries and services. Overall, land use and energy demonstrate the most important policy areas which can anchor other sectoral opportunities, although such opportunities have not been well explored.
- Several key strategies for effective urban green growth can be identified. Sustainable urban transport policies need to be put much higher on the green growth agenda, and be better co-ordinated with land-use planning (e.g. through transit-oriented development). Building standards and energy regulations need to be elaborated so as to include green growth considerations. It is also crucial for city governments to enhance local workers' skills to respond to green building demand. While exploring local potential to address the rapid increase in energy demand is crucial, the specific characteristics of Asian cities will call for a case-by-case analysis of the renewable potential of each city and country. More studies are urgently needed regarding what are feasible renewable energy options in different cities to harness their full potential. Promoting urban wastewater treatment is pivotal to fostering urban green growth and resilience. Policies to reduce the quantity of urban waste and to increase the capacity of waste treatment should go hand-in-hand. The "3Rs" (reduce, reuse and recycle) principle must be embedded into municipal solid waste strategies. In order to green industries, setting standards and ensuring expert inspections as well as stringent penalties for non-compliance would be key. An equally important measure to nudge industries into being more environmentally friendly and efficient is green labelling.
- Beyond sectoral policies for green growth, strong needs for policy complementarities have been identified in the case studies and show high potential to support green growth objectives. Such synergies can maximise policy outcomes and reduce trade-offs, in particular. For instance, waste-to-energy technology can support waste treatment efforts while easing the pressure on energy supply systems. Disaster risk management, likewise, requires close policy co-ordination between all of the aforementioned opportunity areas. The case study cities also shed light on additional policy objectives – in particular inclusiveness – that are essential and therefore complementary elements for urban green growth in Southeast Asia.
- Demand-side policies and the use of pricing mechanisms offer stronger potential to support green growth measures. Shifting tax burdens to encourage environmental performance or penalise negative environmental externalities would have high impact in Southeast Asian cities. Taxes, fees and charges, backed by adequate information on the consequences of action, can efficiently encourage consumers to behave in a more sustainable manner. For instance, progressive tariff structures and charges on groundwater extraction can help to optimise consumption.
- Innovation, quality infrastructure investment and human resource development are catalysts for the long-term growth of Southeast Asian cities and can support green growth objectives. It is important that long-term planning decisions for infrastructure in the coming years is not sacrificed for short-term expediencies given the huge demand. ICT application also holds tremendous potential in grassroots participation, government accountability, urban resilience and infrastructure such as bicycle sharing and low-carbon vehicles.

Untapped green growth opportunities in Southeast Asian cities

This first section aims to demonstrate the green growth potential which Southeast Asian cities have, as well as workable policy instruments, for the following six policy areas: 1) land use and transport; 2) housing and buildings; 3) energy; 4) water resource management; 5) solid waste management; and 6) green industries and services. These policy areas were conceptually proposed after extensive review of literature in the conceptual framework (Matsumoto and Daudey, 2014). The five case studies and the OECD Knowledge Sharing Workshops fine-tuned the areas for inclusion in the study and revealed where the untapped green growth opportunities lie in these areas.

Land use and transport

Land use represents an area of immediate opportunities for green growth, as land-use transformation is currently taking place at an unprecedented speed in Southeast Asian cities How effectively urban land is utilised may determine residents' access to local services and employment opportunities, the energy demands and energy efficiency of the transport sector, and a city's capacity to adapt to climate change through, for example, prevention of urban expansion to vulnerable areas and protection of productive farmland and natural biodiversity. It also directly affects public finances through the demands placed on maintaining existing infrastructure or the construction of new infrastructure, such as roads, electricity, water treatment plants or drainage systems. However, immediate actions are called for; as such, windows of opportunities are closing fast. Land-use decisions that will be made over the next 15 years (the time frame over which it is anticipated that more than two-thirds of the infrastructure for public services will be built in Southeast Asian cities) will lock in the levels of mobility within these urban areas, their energy use patterns and their greenhouse gas (GHG) emissions trajectory for decades, if not centuries, to come.

Strong opportunities are also seen in the transport sector because Southeast Asian cities are facing an unprecedented trend of motorisation. Improving public transport systems and investing in non-motorised transport options (i.e. walking and biking) have tremendous potential to cut down the levels of carbon emissions as well as air pollution, which would otherwise be prohibitive due to the increasing private motor transport. This does not mean that the residents in Southeast Asian cities will be restricted to have private cars; it would rather aim to provide them with alternatives so that they can optimise their mobility decisions. Furthermore, integrating land-use and transport policies with proper implementation can create synergies by guiding urban development along public transport corridors. The development of public transport can also create new industries and services.

Housing and buildings

The demand for housing investment in light of the rapid urbanisation and income growth in Asia generates high potential for urban green growth. Housing policies will open up opportunities for Southeast Asian cities to increase the quality of in-house environment and welfare of residents. It can also provide socially equitable and affordable housing options. High demand for building investment, characterising the booming economy, presents key opportunities to promote resource and energy efficiency, given the increasing energy and material consumption and GHG emissions in buildings. Building policies can also address vulnerability to risks such as floods, landslides and earthquakes, together with land-use policies. Retrofitting existing buildings stock for improved energy efficiency can create jobs, new services and innovation.

Energy

Energy presents untapped strong opportunities for urban green growth. While addressing the increasing energy demand is a pressing national issue for many countries and the policy frameworks vary across countries reflecting resource endowments and political interest (OECD/IEA, 2015), most national governments intend to diversify their energy supply and increase the share of renewable sources. Cities are well-positioned to address energy policies, as they greatly shape the energy landscape accounting for 60% of demand and 70% of energy related carbon emissions (IEA, 2016). As the rise in income spurs huge increases in energy consumption, opportunities for green growth exist for cities to encourage energy efficiency and promote decentralised clean energy options.

Renewable energy has untapped opportunities for cities to be integrated into the built environment; a recent study demonstrates that rooftop solar photovoltaic panels could meet 49% of the energy demand in Southeast Asian cities (Figure 2.1). Generating clean energy in cities could cut down on GHG emissions from traditional fossil fuels and energy loss through transmission. Renewable energy sources can also allow for micro grids, which could easily feed into or be disconnected from the main grid to respond to demand or emergencies. Cities investing in renewable energy and energy efficiency can also create jobs and economic opportunities.

Water resource management

Water resource management is another critical lever for urban green growth in Southeast Asian cities, due to the significant rise in demand. The rising water consumption implies that, as urbanisation continues, there will be fierce competition among the different categories of water users, such as agriculture, energy, industries and domestic consumers (OECD, 2016b). In parallel, persistent floods with increasing severity call for better management of water risks, in addition to enhanced need for protecting water resources from pollution. Moreover, as demonstrated in Chapter 1, investment in water infrastructure has not kept up with the pace of rapid urbanisation. Due to these urgencies, green growth policies in the water sector offer opportunities for Southeast Asian cities to address quantitative (including floods) and qualitative issues, encouraging water-related employment, innovation and investment in water infrastructure.

Figure 2.1. **Potential sources for energy generation in cities**

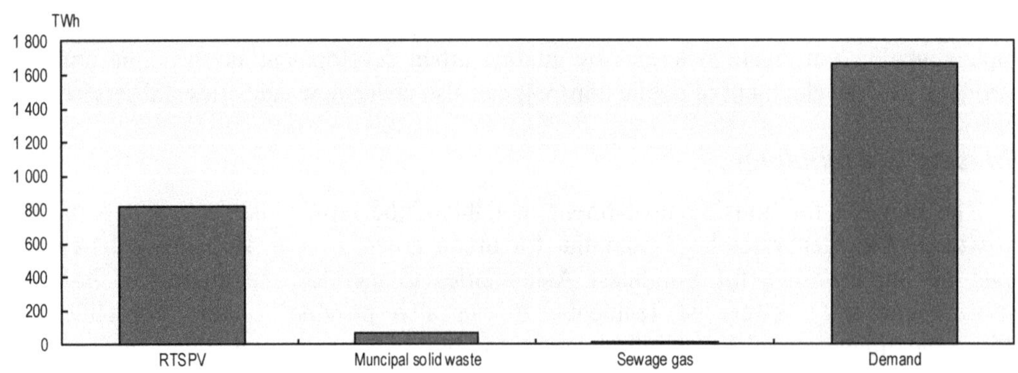

Note: RTSPV: rooftop solar photovoltaic panels.

Source: IEA (2016), *Energy Technology Perspectives 2016*, http://dx.doi.org/10.1787/energy_tech-2016-en.

Solid waste management

The increase in municipal waste has been a feature of the prospering economies of Southeast Asian cities, due to increasing material consumption. While cities are confronted by how to effectively collect and handle the increasing quantities of waste generated, and minimise its environmental impacts, this also offers untapped opportunities for Southeast Asian cities, mainly because they are still utilising landfills as a dominant method to dispose of municipal wastes. The increasing solid waste is also a huge burden for municipal budgets. Green growth enables cities to approach waste as a potential "resource" to unleash the associated chain of opportunities, including community-based job creation (waste pickers), promoting waste recycling and recovering energy from wastes. Waste-to-energy technologies offer multiple objectives, helping cities to simultaneously generate energy and reduce final waste residue that would otherwise be landfilled.

Green industries and services

A key green growth opportunity in Southeast Asian cities also lies in efforts to make local industries and services greener. The rapid urban economic growth in the region has been led by the manufacturing industry, although it is still emitting high levels of greenhouse gases and other pollutants. Dealing with this calls for a green growth model that reflects the realities of rapid urbanisation and industrialisation.

Greening industries also creates numerous opportunities for the service sector. Specialised services such as advisory, training and capacity building, research and development, as well as monitoring and evaluation, will be developed to render services to enable industries generate more positive environmental impact, when industries are deemed to become greener. The demand for the service sector, be it specialised or general services, creates jobs along the spectrum of the labour market, although certain skill development would be necessary for low-skilled workers to benefit from these new emerging job markets.

Summary: Land use as an anchor to leverage other green growth policies

Table 2.1 summarises the discussion above and presents potential contribution of the six policy areas to green growth in fast-growing Asian cities. The potential contribution by policy area is presented against major objectives of urban green growth. Though the table is not exhaustive, it provides what is going to be achieved by urban green growth policies, with the local context of Southeast Asian cities taken into consideration.

Overall, land use and energy stand out as the policy areas which can work as an anchor to leverage other policy sectors. Sustainable land use offers consideration for the environment, transit-oriented development, security to residence, and provides flexibility to respond to future societal changes. Land use is therefore an area of increasing focus and importance that Southeast Asian cities can benefit from. In terms of energy, cities have many activities which can enhance energy efficiencies such as transport, buildings, wastes and industries, in addition to contributing to cleaner energy production. In this report, such energy efficiency gains and policies are discussed in their respective policy areas.

The opportunities in the six policy areas identified in this section cannot be accomplished naturally but require deliberate action. The next two sections will thus look at policy strategies and instruments to unleash this potential.

Policy assessments and recommendations by sector

The following two sections provide an assessment of green growth policies in Southeast Asia. This is made by two steps: first by looking at policies by sector, then by looking at cross-sectoral policy approaches which can effectively promote green growth in cities. By putting them together, the two sections respond to the question "what policies need to be improved to accelerate green growth?". Examples from OECD and non-OECD cities are also provided to serve as "food for thought" to help define workable guidelines for consideration by policy makers in the design of green interventions for their cities.

Table 2.1. **Potential contribution of areas of opportunity to green growth in fast-growing Asian cities**

	Land use and transport	Housing and buildings	Energy	Water resource management	Solid waste management	Green industries and services
Green jobs and innovation	Development of public transport can create new industries and services	Retrofitting existing buildings can create jobs, new services and innovation	Investment in renewable energy can create jobs, new services and innovation	Investment in sanitation and new technologies (e.g. smart metering) can create jobs, new services and innovation	Promoting separation of waste can create jobs for the urban poor	Promoting recycling of industrial waste and energy-efficient industrial processes can create jobs, new services and innovation
Climate change adaptation and mitigation	Less automobile dependency can reduce greenhouse gas (GHG) emissions; risk-sensitive land use and preservation of natural ecosystems can reduce vulnerability to risks	Green buildings can reduce GHG emissions as well as the urban heat island effects; building codes can address vulnerability to risks	Investment in renewable energy can reduce GHG emissions	Managing water resources could reduce the incidence of inland floods, drought and improve water quality and quantity	Solid waste management can reduce GHG emissions resulting from waste and avoid pollution and diseases from improper solid waste management	Green manufacturing can reduce GHG emissions and ensure efficient use of resource
Healthier local environment and urban attractiveness	Compact cities can reduce pollution from automobiles and preserve productive farmland and natural biodiversity	Proper housing can increase the quality of in-house environment and welfare of residents	Cleaner energy production can reduce pollution and environmental stress	Proper wastewater treatment and water distribution can reduce the degradation of lakes and rivers	Solid waste management can reduce landfill and related pollution created by solid waste	Green manufacturing can reduce the amount of local air pollutants released

Source: Elaborated based on Matsumoto, T. and L. Daudey (2014), "Urban green growth in dynamic Asia: A conceptual framework", http://dx.doi.org/10.1787/5js7svlw8m0x-en.

Placing urban transport much higher on the agenda and integrating it with land use

The case studies underline an urgent need for a long-term land-use vision and an effective mechanism to implement the vision in Southeast Asian cities. Sustainable land use is crucial as converting greenfields (agricultural land and forests) into urban land is an irreversible process and can create serious land-use challenges, threatening agricultural and forested areas which have carbon sequestration capability and are essential for biodiversity. Not only is protecting the environmental assets on which well-being relies a challenge confronting cities but so is finding an optimal solution to foster long-term economic growth potential by providing flexible land-use options. This is common not only to Southeast Asian cities but to OECD countries as well, especially in accommodating housing and other urban development needs. The analysis of the case studies indicates that land-use decisions tend to prioritise short-term demands and therefore promote the ineffective use of land, e.g. housing development dispersed from existing built-up areas without access to public transport). Restrictions on land use are difficult tools for policy makers to introduce. For example, Iskandar Malaysia is the only city among the five case studies which has introduced an urban growth boundary at the metropolitan scale, intended to promote higher densities in urban centres and optimise mixed land uses. Hai Phong's Cat Ba Archipelago, which is not only a World Biosphere Reserve recognised by UNESCO but also a tourist attraction, is threatened by rapid urban development and water pollution which endangers its biodiversity (Cat Ba langur, 2016). This leads to an urgent need for Southeast Asian cities to develop professional experience and skills in land-use planning, especially at the metropolitan level, to achieve sustainable land use.

The results of the case studies also highlight that sustainable urban transport policies need to be placed much higher on the green growth agenda and co-ordinated with land-use planning (e.g. TOD). A pattern of long commutes and dependency on private motorised transport such as automobiles and motorcycles seriously affect the performance of the case study cities. In Hai Phong, Viet Nam, motorcycles accounted for 93% of the city's vehicle fleet in 2009 (World Bank, 2011). This appears to be exacerbated by the inefficient public transport systems, which together with the dependency on private vehicles lead to high traffic congestion, air pollution, loss of productive hours and health issues. Maximising the potential of informal minibuses such as *Jeepneys* (Philipines) and *Angkots* (Indonesia) is a promising policy in the case study cities. Though they contribute immensely to affordable urban mobility and to some extent are part of the rich cultural heritage of the city, their contribution to rising GHG emissions and other pollutants cannot be overlooked. This arises due to poor maintenance in addition to the use of aging vehicles. Making the minibuses a more viable element of the public transit system will require careful scrutiny if emission reduction and development goals are to be met.

A key factor to address this issue is to ensure mobility without over relying on private vehicles, (in particular on motorcycles) by accelerating investment in mass public transport. Low investment and attention to mass public transport has contributed to the dependence and proliferation of private motor transport, responsible for the rising GHG emissions and for all other economic and social costs. As described previously, Southeast Asian cities are currently offered a timely opportunity to invest in quality urban transport systems and other urban infrastructures for public service, thanks to strong economic growth, relatively low land prices and availability of land. It would be particularly unfortunate for them to miss this opportunity, because they will soon face the same challenges experienced in matured urban agglomerations, including high land value and more complicated land ownership systems, which lead to much higher costs for urban infrastructure investment. Once the automobile-oriented city form takes shape, a lock-in effect makes it difficult to shift to transit-oriented patterns, as the experience of many North American cities attests. Similarly, investing in infrastructure for non-motorised transport such as walking and cycling would equally contribute to reducing demand for private vehicles and create healthy and lively communities as well as social equity and contribute to climate change mitigation.

New emerging technology and societal dynamics (shared economy) are also helping to shift reliance on private petroleum vehicles to shared electric vehicles. Cities such as Paris, Shanghai and New York were early adopters of shared electric vehicles and benefited from carbon footprint reductions and cost savings (Amsterdam Roundtable Foundation and McKinsey & Company, 2014). This is extremely useful for local air pollution reduction as every kilometre driven without any pollution directly contributes to emission reduction targets. Though this might mean an increase in carbon emission from electric power production, which in Southeast Asian cities is highly dependent on fossil fuel, it nonetheless creates an opportunity for investment in power generation from cleaner sources such as thermal or hydro. Future-proofing Southeast Asian cities and reducing dependence on fossil fuel will require consideration for such technological advancements, which contribute to environmental conservation and economic prosperity.

The importance of integrating land-use and transport planning at the city level cannot be overstated. City governments largely manage land use. Their room for manoeuvre is often greater (than energy policies, for example) and they have more capacity and policy instruments to affect urban form and ensure integration of land-use plans with transport plans. Land-use regulations (e.g. zoning tools), transport demand management (e.g. traffic circulation, congestion charges, parking fees are examples of tools often in the hands of local governments that can help achieve green growth objectives, if different tools are effectively integrated and function organically.

National frameworks are yet critical to maintain strong influence on local affairs, especially when it comes to policy instruments and financing, highlighting the need for a co-ordinated policy approach (Chapter 3). For example, the high cost of implementing new transport infrastructure projects, such as mass transit, requires the financial and technical expertise of national governments, which therefore influence urban development. Likewise, fossil fuel subsidies, typically in the hands of national governments, can undermine green transport projects at the local level by providing incentives to use private motorised vehicles. Combining investment in urban transport with other economic instruments and legislative measures such as fossil fuel subsidy removal and carbon pricing can drastically help shift in favour of public transport.

Developing housing and buildings to meet green standards

The case study cities demonstrated the need for more comprehensive building standards so as to include green growth considerations. It was found that energy efficiency in buildings was being encouraged in the case study countries e.g phasing-out least energy efficient lighting source. Some cities were also pioneering innovative approaches, such as Bandung, which had announced that a green building certificate will be a requirement, not simply a recommendation, for obtaining a city building permit. Some challenges still remain. For example, the building standards in some countries are not sufficient to address their CO2 emission reduction targets. Other countries have only energy efficiency targets without codified building regulations, which make it difficult for builders to comply with the regulations. In addition, most Southeast Asian countries lack a comprehensive green building code (APEC, 2013). It will be important to develop a more comprehensive regulatory framework which considers water efficiency, indoor air quality and use of environmentally friendly materials. The Philippines' green building code aims to address these issues. Cebu City also introduced a green and disaster-resilient building programme (Ordinance No 2014-02) although it is voluntary. Since proper implementation of building codes is another critical issue, it will be important for national and subnational governments to discuss the types and levels of building codes which are implementable at the local level and sufficiently contribute to green growth.

Despite the absence of a green code, green building ratings and certificates are quickly gaining roots, influenced by a rising demand from businesses, investors and owners. Most of the case study countries had a rating system administered by mostly private bodies such as the LOTUS managed by the Vietnam Green Building Council and the GREENSHIP run by Green Building Council Indonesia. The Thai Green Building Institute, the main agency delivering green building standards, also promotes the Thailand Rating Energy and Environment System, a certification programme covering standards in energy consumption, material and resources, and indoor environmental quality, which provides advice and standards to building managers. The rating systems represent significant efforts towards ensuring greening even though there are concerns that some do not address the local built environmental context and are complex (Attia, 2014).

Green building ratings and certificates have been ascribed to only large-scale buildings (e.g. greater than 3 000 m^2) and new constructions because they have the greatest potential to achieve high efficiency. However, it will also be interesting for policies to include smaller buildings and promote renovation and retrofitting of existing old buildings to improve resource efficiency. While the main policy focus should be in new buildings, energy efficiency retrofits should also be considered in urban centres of Southeast Asian cities. Many OECD cities have been attracted to energy efficiency retrofits in existing buildings for their potential to generate jobs, contribute to energy savings and security, reduce pollution and contribute to global warming mitigation (OECD, 2013a):

- Given appropriate policies with respect to energy prices, the energy savings gained through retrofits can refinance the investment. With energy service companies, building owners can sometimes improve buildings' energy efficiency without upfront investment or special loans. In Berlin, energy service companies are meant to absorb upfront investments and offer average annual savings in energy costs of 26%, which should allow for payback periods of 8-12 years (New York City Global Partners Inc., 2011). If a price on carbon were to be introduced, retrofits could be an important way of lessening the impact of higher energy prices on poorer households. Property Assessed Clean Energy (PACE) financing is another business model which has been experimented in the United States. This is a mechanism by which property owners finance renewable energy and energy efficiency measures via an additional tax assessment on their property. The property owner repays over a period of 15-20 years through an increase in their property tax bills. When a property changes ownership, the remaining debt is transferred with the property to the new owner. This is applicable to renewable energy technology such as solar PV and solar thermal, efficient boilers and energy-efficient improvements (IEA-RETD, 2012).
- Retrofit investments can create jobs for a range of skill levels. These include low- to medium-skilled jobs that are accessible to a large range of workers, including unemployed manufacturing and construction workers (Schrock, 2009; Schrock and Sundquist, 2009).

Enhancing skills for green buildings

It is also crucial for city governments to strengthen local clusters by enhancing skills to respond to green building demand. With demand for green buildings increasing, case study cities can enhance skills of workers related to building design and construction to deliver on efficient green buildings. Skills requirements change with technology, and as technology has rapidly evolved over the years, so has the greening of the building sector been hampered by a shortage of skills (ILO, 2011). The essential skills across the value chain in the green buildings sector are crucial to ensure the effectiveness of all the policy instruments. Certainly, there are many business opportunities for green buildings which could be unleashed through training programmes and educational campaigns. Though roles in green building can be occupied by ordinary workers, many would require an upgrade of skills, especially for low-skilled workers such as electricians in installing solar panels and plumbers in installing new energy-efficient technologies such as solar water heaters. The availability of skilled workers makes clients confident of the standard of work being undertaken and serves as an incentive to drive more demand for green building. Furthermore, promoting green buildings on a metropolitan scale requires a greater understanding of local conditions, behavioural insights and socio-economic conditions to effectively design policies to respond to the needs of residents and at the same time achieve ecological impact. For this reason, professional occupational groups such as architects, engineers, urban planners and contractors require soft skills on environmental awareness, leadership, innovation and green growth to contribute to ensuring the uptake of green building initiatives (ibid). In essence, identifying skill gaps and labour shortages and adequately responding to them would be crucial to generate growth for greening buildings. Social partners such as worker organisations, along with government employees, play an important role in identifying the skills gap that their staff have and the partnering institutions to address it.

Addressing housing conditions and living environment

Insufficient quantity or quality of housing supply can be a major obstacle to urban green growth. In Southeast Asian cities developing countries, housing conditions such as construction materials, access to safe drinking water and hygienic toilet facilities are the most critical determinants of human health in urban areas. It also directly affects the vulnerability of urban dwellers: slum housing is often constructed of flimsy scrounged materials, such as plastic sheets, cardboard or scrap metal, or the cheapest construction materials. These structures are easily destroyed by storms, or floods since these are frequent in the locations (river banks, etc.) where many informal settlements are located (UN HABITAT, 2010). Moreover, slum houses are usually energy inefficient and their activities greatly impact the environment. City-wide green growth efforts need to strongly support slum dwellers to overcome barriers to their environmental sustainability.

Securing land tenure is critically important when it comes to generating better-quality housing and living environments for the urban poor (UN HABITAT, 2010). As in the slum upgrading programme implemented in Ahmedabad, India, issues of land tenure can be a major obstacle to urban green growth in Asian cities, limiting the urban poor's access to basic needs and services and their ability to escape the cycle of poverty. The urban poor tend to be priced out of formal land markets and to be deprived of secure tenure and land titles; vacant urban land is in the hands of private landowners and governments, so they are not free to settle there. This situation increases their distance from areas with income-earning opportunities (UN HABITAT, 2010). Tackling land tenure issues for the poor and making land markets more efficient in fast-growing Asian cities is not straightforward, however. While Singapore's public housing is unlikely to be a model for urbanising cities with limited public resources, private sector housing and housing finance for the poor often fail to benefit them because of their lack of collateral. As a response to land market failures, innovative schemes have emerged in many Asian cities, notably self-help and savings groups among the poor aimed at improving the local housing and infrastructure conditions (UN HABITAT, 2010). National and local governments could provide more support by improving domestic capital markets, legal and regulatory frameworks, and by encouraging housing microfinance (UN HABITAT, 2010).

Financing is pivotal to green buildings and the seemingly lack of it could stifle the achievement of overall green growth objectives. Many opportunities remain at the disposal of cities to directly or indirectly stimulate green cities. Property taxes for a case in point could discourage or encourage greening. For example, most Canadian municipalities impose the same charge on all properties of a particular type regardless of location (OECD, 2013c). Private finance also helps to fill the funding gaps. However, this requires three preconditions: 1) a market for green urban investment projects; 2) good returns on investment; and 3) limited risk (ibid). Public-private partnerships (PPPs) also appear an effective way for long-term contractual agreements between private operators and metropolitan governments to provide green housing. Detailed discussion of financing is presented in Chapter 3.

Promoting cleaner energy and efficiency to meet rising demand

Demand for energy in the case study cities has been escalating due to a burgeoning population and rapidly expanding economy driven by manufacturing industries. The rising demand is set to continue for the foreseeable future, leading to per capita energy consumption rising from 0.96 tonnes in oil equivalent (toe) in 2013 to 1.4 toe by 2040. By 2040, Southeast Asia's energy demand will grow by 80% (OECD/IEA, 2015). Meeting the rising energy demand is a challenge, as most affordable energy sources in the region are dependent on fossil fuel (74% in 2013) such as coal and petroleum, especially energy for transport and electricity. These sources raise concerns about energy security as well as environmental sustainability, as they contribute to high GHG emissions which invariably affect the eco-system and quality of life. In Peninsular Malaysia 96% of energy is from non-renewable sources. Reducing energy intensity, in addition to increasing the share of renewables in the energy mix, is of vital importance to Southeast Asian cities in reducing their carbon footprints and climate change mitigation efforts. Local governments therefore have the power to influence the energy choices of residents to achieve sustainable development and environmental objectives.

Disparities in access to energy are still prevalent among urban dwellers of some countries even though Malaysia, Thailand and Viet Nam have or are close to reaching universal access (OECD/IEA, 2015). Two major challenges remain which will need redress. First, policies still need to address the lack of access in slums and informal settlements in cities. Reasons such as irregular land tenure, ill-defined responsibilities for payment, poor access and low consumption explain the deficiencies in energy provision to the urban poor; this strongly influences their ability to participate in income-generating activities, which in turn affects their access to energy (UN HABITAT, 2010). Energy access is therefore at the heart of the poverty cycle that affects many urban dwellers, which must be addressed to achieve continued economic growth. Second, as the rise in income spurs huge increases in energy consumption, cities need to provide a more stable energy supply and to determine the appropriate price levels in conjunction with national governments.

While exploring local potential to address the rapid increase in energy demand is crucial, the specific characteristics of Asian cities will call for a case-by-case analysis of the renewable potential of each city and country. Comparatively, electricity production from renewable energy sources in ASEAN countries represented 18% of the region's total power production in 2013, lower than the share of electricity (21.15%) from renewables in OECD countries (OECD/IEA, 2015). For the built environment, rooftop solar photovoltaic electric generation offers immediate solutions and city policies could encourage assessment and mass deployment of it. An approach adopted by Barcelona could be a good option (Box 2.1). However, more studies will be urgently needed regarding what are feasible renewable energy options in different cities to harness their full potential.

Box 2.1. **The Barcelona Solar Ordinance**

The aim of this ordinance is to regulate, through local legislation, the implementation of systems for collecting and using active solar energy for the production of hot water for buildings. All new and renovated, private and public, commercial and residential buildings are required to supply at least 60% of the hot water demand through solar thermal collectors using the 2 350 annual hours of sunshine received. Other approved renewable energy heating technologies can be substituted by the building developer if desired. This ordinance first took effect in August 2000. It initially targeted buildings with a hot water heating demand of more than around 30 MJ/day, such as residential buildings with more than 16 apartments. Owners of buildings too small to comply were offered a subsidy to voluntarily install a solar system, but since the minimum requirement was removed in 2006, all buildings now have to comply regardless of size or use. It applies to all residential and commercial buildings, to industry where hot water is needed for the process or for staff facilities, and to buildings where there are kitchens or collective laundries such as in hospitals, sports centres and schools. In addition, all heating of swimming pools has to come from solar sources.

The Barcelona Energy Agency, a consortium of organisations with energy and environment interests, was established to evaluate the planned installations provided when a building developer seeks a planning permit or licence. Once approval has been granted, building inspectors ensure that construction meets the detailed design criteria and fines can be imposed for non-compliance. Buildings with co-generation systems installed or with roofs that are shaded from the sun can seek exemptions. The area of collectors per 1 000 population has increased twentyfold since the ordinance was introduced. As at 2008, solar thermal energy associated with the solar ordinance had drastically improved. Solar collectors to heat water had risen from 2 500m^2 in 1999to 65 506 m^2.

A crucial reason for the success of the policy was the support obtained from the citizens. A programme to communicate information on the use, costs and maintenance of solar water heating systems was conducted by the Barcelona Energy Agency in parallel with the ordinance first being introduced. The city published an explanatory guide to the ordinance in several languages; held regular meetings with stakeholders such as building contractors' associations, engineers, architects and environmental organisations; promoted the ordinance to neighbouring cities; implemented demonstration projects; and organised a "Solar Day". This programme was carried out alongside neighbourhood associations and body corporates of buildings to ensure that members of the public and tenants of the buildings also fully understood the benefits of solar water heating and would keep the systems operating efficiently. Monitoring existing systems was also undertaken.

The success of the Barcelona ordinance led to the Spanish government developing a national policy that, depending on the level of hot water consumption, the climate zone of the building location and the availability of back-up heating fuels, requires 30-70% of the energy demand for heating water in new buildings and those being renovated to come from solar systems. Many other municipalities throughout Spain are now considering or have developed a similar ordinance. Burgos, Seville, Madrid, Pamplona and other cities have followed Barcelona's lead and adopted regulations more stringent than those of the federal government.

Source: IEA (2009), *Cities, Towns and Renewable Energy: Yes In My Front Yard*, http://dx.doi.org/10.1787/9789264076884-en, p 80. Ajuntament de Barcelona(2010) Barcelona Energy Improvement Plan (PMEB), http://estatic.bcn.cat/MediAmbient/Continguts/Vectors_Ambientals/Agencia_de_lenergia/Documents/Fitxers/PMEB_integrat.pdf.

Managing water resources to ensure sustained access

The case studies demonstrated that sustainable water resource management is crucial to the future of Southeast Asian cities. The increasing water demand in the five case study cities has been met from surface water (rivers) and underground sources. The lack of abundant water resources in some cities is leading to situations of water stress and scarcity. Besides, many of the cities also face challenges with water supplies to cover actual and estimated growing domestic and non-domestic demand; along with concerns about the quality of drinking water. They also suffer from huge losses in the water distribution networks, intermittent supply and misuse of water sources. In addition, the over-exploitation of groundwater resources has resulted in negative environmental externalities such as groundwater depletion, salination, pollution and land subsidence in some case study cities. Such pressure is accentuated by the poor coverage and quality of urban pipe water. For instance, in Metro Cebu only 12.5% of drinking water is supplied through pipe connections yet groundwater accounts for 98% of water supply in the Metro Cebu Water District service area (OECD, forthcoming). Water sanitation infrastructure (wastewater treatment facilities and drainage) is also sub-optimal and has not kept up with the pace of urbanisation. Consequently, the frequency as well as intensity of floods has increased and the quality of water bodies has often fallen below established quality standards. Enhancing water security would be essential to guarantee the resilience and competitiveness of Southeast Asian cities. The key challenge is to align incentives and choose the relevant policy instruments to move from crisis response to adequate management and anticipation of water risks (OECD, 2016d).

Addressing water leakages and non-revenue water (NRW) in municipal water supply is essential to advancing sustainable water management and enhancing access to water. In Southeast Asia about 13 million m^3 of treated water, valued at USD 1.5 billion, is lost every year (ADB, 2010). NRW refers to the volume of treated water which cannot be accounted for after adjusting for (un)billed authorised consumption in the distribution system. Hai Phong's NRW stood at 13.7% of supply as of 2013. Thanks to long-term efforts to reduce non-revenue water, the current figure is much better than the national estimated average of 35% (Canales-Trujillo et al., 2015) and the national target of 15%, as stipulated in 2009 (under Decision No 1929/QD-TTg). However, this remains high in comparison with some cities such as Amsterdam (4%), Singapore (5%) and Kitakyushu (6.7%), whose average rate of NRW is below 10% (OECD, 2016a). Water loss has negative impacts and is a financial drain to local authorities. In some cases, investments will be needed to address ageing infrastructure in the water distribution system. The Sustainable Development Goal 6 (SDG) realises the importance of adequate water supply and implores signatories to improve water access, enhance efficiency, reduce pollution and enhance management. The temptation for most cities has been to expand water networks without putting in place mechanisms to remedy water losses. Yet, best practices indicate that engagements in non-revenue water reduction programmes yield performance and productivity results. Such programmes have brought significant gains to customers and utility companies such as efficient resource utilisation, enhanced consumer satisfaction, less capital-intensive additions to capacity and ability to service the urban poor (ADB, 2010). The improvement of water supply in Phnom Penh, Cambodia, which had nearly 83% in NRW, highlights the advantages and opportunities in addressing this issue. While it is highly encouraged that utility companies develop in-house capabilities to deal with non-revenue water, many others have explored performance-based contracting to the private sector which has also been a cost-effective and viable instrument to reduce water losses (3GF, 2013). From 2000 to 2006 Bangkok reduced NRW from around 40%

to 30% using performance-based service contracts for leakage reduction (OECD, forthcoming b).

Underground water depletion poses a high risk to cities and needs urgent attention. Underground water depletion has reached alarming levels in some of the case study cities. As a result, the water table has dropped, owing to the rate of underground water consumption which exceeds the natural aquifers recharge rate – a situation referred to as groundwater overdraft. Consequently, multiple impacts can be observed such as salination (intrusion of saltwater) in coastal cities and land subsidence (the sinking of land surface) in inland cities. Bangkok for one has experienced a high amount of land subsidence measured at 1 250 mm between 1900-2013 due to fast pumping of underground water (Taniguchi et al., 2008; Deltares – Taskforce Subsidence, 2013). Currently, various interventions in the BMR have helped to reduce the rate of land subsidence. It is worth noting that the interconnectedness of the impacts mentioned above breeds a potential disaster risk for the city related to public health, floods, earthquakes, destruction of buildings and interruption of utility services for which damages can be extensive (OECD, 2015). These threats are made more menacing due to the proximity of the case study cities to the sea and the increasing impact of climate change, which is accelerating sea-level rise. In Texas and California, groundwater overdraft is estimated to cause over USD 100 million worth of damage annually. Underground water is an increasing international problem as shown in Box 2.2, which presents cases of land subsidence in urban areas of OECD cities. Inaction by local authorities of Southeast Asian cities on underground water depletion is no longer a valid option (OECD, 2013a). Urgent attention is therefore needed to overcome this hindrance to green growth. Efficient monitoring through technological innovation such as satellite imagery and management of water resources through economic and regulatory instruments is needed. Good water governance would require supporting and strengthening mechanisms for co-ordination across policies, places and people as spelled out in *Water Governance in Cities* (OECD, 2016d). Similarly, excessive use of underground water for agricultural irrigation , though important, needs to be properly reviewed for the best optimum solution. Alternatives such as rainwater harvesting and storage have proven useful for some countries and could form part of policy strategies to enhance water management to advance green growth.

Pricing water right promotes judicious use and raises awareness on the scarcity value of water. The increasing water risk calls for effective pricing mechanisms as a means to rationalise consumption and manage demand. Water tariffs in some case study cities have been relatively low. For instance, the Metropolitan Waterworks Authority (Thailand) had a tariff structure flatter than East Manila and East Jarkata (Figure 2.2). Water service delivery should be properly priced to reflect the actual cost of production and raise awareness on its scarcity. Such pricing should permit consideration of social objectives in catering for the urban poor while allowing for adequate investment in the water sector. In OECD countries, a trend toward decreasing water consumption per capita has been observed over time attributable to water conservation measures, water loss reduction and increased pricing (OECD, 2016d). An OECD project on household behaviour and environmental policy found that households charged for water reduced consumption by 20% compared to those who are not charged. In addition, households subject to unit pricing had a higher probability to install water-efficient and energy-efficient equipment at home (OECD, 2011b). Furthermore, an observation across cities that have efficient pricing and low NRW shows a high service coverage and consistent water supply. Water pricing adjustments, though unpopular, would also need to be dissociated from political influence to ensure their effectiveness in accomplishing environmental objectives.

Box 2.2. Groundwater withdrawal induced land subsidence in OECD countries

UNESCO (1984) inventoried international cases of land subsidence related to the intensive use of groundwater. It found 42 cases, mainly located in urban agglomerations, perhaps due to better measurement. More recent efforts have included dozens of new cases. Notable examples in OECD countries include:

- Italy: Milan (subsidence of 0.2 m from 1952 to 1972); Venice (more than 0.2 m since the 1930s); and the Po Delta (more than 3 m during the 1950s)
- Mexico: Mexico City (since the 1920s up to 0.4 m per year in the Centre, up to 10 m and 300 mm/year during 2004-06); Toluca Valley (90 mm/year during 2003-08)
- United States: Denver, Houston, Las Vegas, San Francisco, Tucson, up to 2-9 m of subsidence in several cities in California and the San Joaquin Valley; Coachella Valley, California (70 mm/year during 2003-09); the Bolsón del Hueco basin around El Paso in Texas (0.3 m of subsidence since the 1950s)
- Japan: Tokyo (starting in 1910; subsidence up to 4 m; land surface fell to 1 m below sea level); Osaka (up to 2.5 m); the Sagamigawa alluvial plain (up to 0.32 m during 1975-95); and another 62 cases reported in 1998.

Sources: Margat, J. and J. van der Gun (2013), *Groundwater around the World: A Geographic Synopsis*; Famiglietti, J.S. and M. Rodell(2011), "Water in the balance", http://dx.doi.org/10.1126/science.1236460; UNESCO (1984), *Guidebook to Studies of Land Subsidence Due to Ground-water Withdrawal*, http://unesdoc.unesco.org/images/0006/000651/065167eo.pdf in OECD (2015c), *Drying Wells, Rising Stakes: Towards Sustainable Agricultural Groundwater Use*, http://dx.doi.org/10.1787/9789264238701-en.

Figure 2.2. **Water tariff structure of selected Southeast Asian cities**

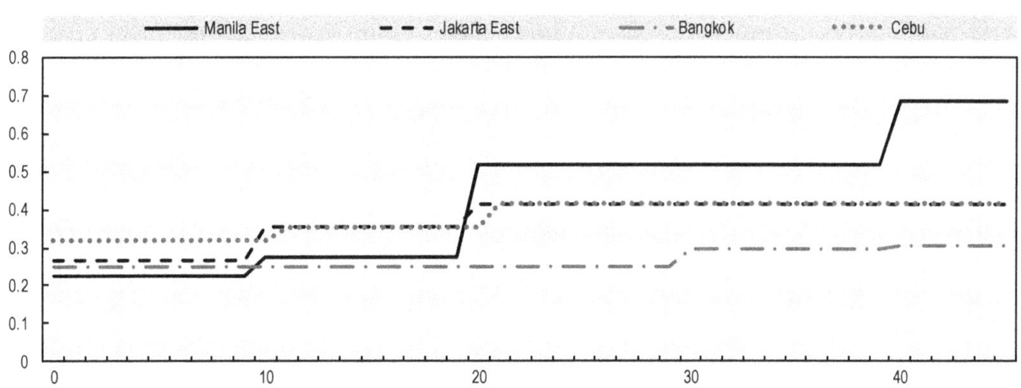

Sources: Manila Water (2015), Letter from Manila Water Company, http://www.manilawater.com/ir/Disclosures/ltr.pse.sec.biwci.tariff.adjustment.14december2015.pdf; PT Aetra Air Jakarta (Aetra) (2012), "Info Tariff Aetra", http://aat.co.id/en/rates-information ; Metropolitan Waterworks Authority (n.d.), www.mwa.co.th/ewtadmin/ewt/mwa_internet_eng/ewt_w3c/ewt_news.php?nid=309.

Improving access to water for poor urban households need to be considered. In some cities such as Cebu, field studies suggest that many people cannot afford to pay for water connection fees (ADB, 2014), forcing them to opt for alternative water supply systems which may be less efficient, less standardised and/or more expensive. Connection fees could be eradicated for poor households only based on social or economic assessment. The case of Viet Nam, in particular the cities of Hai Phong, Binh Buong and Ho Chi Minh City, has shown that the abolishment of connection fees can bring positive benefits

(McIntosh, 2014). An alternative could be to subsidise connection fees, as in Phnom Penh, for low-income households.

Promoting urban wastewater treatment

Promoting urban wastewater treatment is pivotal to building sustainability and urban resilience Among the case study cities, Bangkok was the only city where about half of wastewater is treated. In all other cities, most of wastewater is released in untreated form and pollutes rivers, groundwater and coastlines, the main natural bodies of water used for drinking, bathing, fishing and swimming Furthermore, the absence of sewage treatment facilities in some cites has led to high dependence on septic tanks which are often in poor condition. Though national regulations of the case study cities stipulate that industrial wastewater be treated before discharge, it is not effectively done as some treatment facilities have broken down or are absent. A similar dilemma hinders the treatment of domestic wastewater. Generally, wastewater treatment has been unsatisfactory, although improvements in country policy and institutional frameworks as well as practices have been observed.

To increase treatment capacity, two critical problems should be addressed. Firstly, appropriate financing policies and mechanisms should be developed for users to pay for the cost of wastewater treatment, as most of the case studies do not charge for this. The cities need to accelerate the ongoing discussion of introducing wastewater tariffs. The tariff should factor in distributional effects on the poor, and be based on per unit costs on water usage amounts (so that the marginal rate per unit goes up as consumption increases), to discourage over-consumption through marginal pricing structures. Local authorities could seek co-operation with water utility providers so that fees could be collected jointly with drinking water. Pricing wastewater would allow governments to finance the operation of the wastewater treatment plants and enable investment in new constructions. Secondly, more public-private partnerships should be encouraged in wastewater treatment projects. This is a key strategy for the local governments to pursue, and coupling water and wastewater tariffs could be an incentive for private developers/investors to get involved in these projects. In addition, since wastewater treatment operations need a lot of energy (50% of the total operation costs of the plants come from energy), policy complementarities with the energy sector can be explored so that new wastewater treatment projects could use renewable energy (solar, biomass, etc.) for their operations. In Gwangju, Korea, solar panels totalling a capacity of 6.82 MW were installed on an idle space on top of a sewage treatment plant. The installation was estimated to supply about 8 300 MWh of power annually, which is equivalent to a CO_2 emission reduction of 5 000 t (GTCK, 2013). Lastly, oversight function of the designated agency in terms of monitoring and enforcement of sanctions should be strengthened both for domestic and industrial waste.

Local governments need to pursue synergies and be aware of the complexities between water resource management and other policy areas such as land and flood management. This is fundamental to achieve water security and enable the evaluation of the trade-offs of water risk policy interventions (OECD, 2013c). For example, the risk of underground water depletion leading to land subsidence links land and water management. The management of risk of water excess (floods) or water scarcity could have an impact on agriculture or energy. Current local policies often act in "silos" and fail to recognise these connections so as to sustainably address them. Hence, it would be important for such trade-offs to be carefully analysed and the appropriate level of risk established. Green infrastructure offers the opportunity to enhance water security through effective water resource management, thereby contributing to biodiversity conservation, flood prevention, enhancing water quality and availability.

Transforming solid waste management by promoting the "3Rs"

Managing municipal solid waste

The findings from the case studies indicate a challenge of municipalities struggling to introduce effective policies to sustainably manage the high quantities of urban waste generated. This is most pressing considering that the majority of the waste collected in the case study cities are compacted at land fill sites (Chapter 1). The chronic issues – especially declining landfill capacity, leakages, emissions, insanitary open dumping, diseases and pest – as well as the foregone potential revenue are given little consideration. In some cities, scarce urban land competing for various uses for residential and commercial activities made it difficult to allocate land for waste management. Especially in Cebu City, finding space for waste landfilling has been daunting due to geographic constraints. Furthermore, access to municipal solid waste collection services is poor in some parts of the cities and has resulted in insanitary disposal practices. This is typically observed in urban slums. The urban poor, even though they generate less waste than the urban poor in higher-income countries, are also particularly affected, owing to their proximity to waste dumping sites.

While policy makers have been making much effort in improving the current situation by investing in solid waste management systems, a fundamental problem for Southeast Asian cities is a lack of policies to reduce the increasing volume of urban waste. Policies to increase the solid waste treatment capacity must go hand-in-hand with policies to reduce the volume. It is important to note that across the OECD municipal waste generated per capita has been reducing by a rate of over 1% since 2007, and many OECD cities are generating less waste per capita than cities in Southeast Asia (Chapter 1). This is the result of increasing recognition of environmental problems and political pressures from citizens, which forced governments to reassess their waste management policies. An important policy question for Southeast Asian cities is how soon they can reach a turning point from the mass consumption (and mass waste generation) economy to a greener economy with sustainable use of resources.

The "3Rs" (reduce, reuse and recycle) principle must be embedded into municipal solid waste management strategies. As previously discussed, the concept of green growth offers a strong rationale to promote the "3Rs". Waste is a "valuable resource" and transforming waste management practices can be a driver of economic growth. Both national and subnational governments need to rethink their approach to waste management to unleash the growth potential, by accelerating comprehensive measures to promote "3Rs". In parallel, sustainable materials management will be a key principle in the greening of fast-growing Asian cities through solid waste management. Sustainable materials management is defined by the OECD (2012) as "an approach to promote sustainable materials use, integrating actions targeted at reducing negative environmental impacts and preserving natural capital throughout the life-cycle of materials, taking into account economic efficiency and social equity". Sustainable materials management falls in line with the "3Rs", and although it encompasses the whole life cycle of materials, it is fully relevant here, as waste management policies are a major part of the sustainable materials management process (OECD, 2012). Tokyo's metropolitan government's Waste Management Plan is an example of successful sustainable materials management policy applied to solid waste management. The systems of law relating to the 3Rs and waste management are comprehensive and aim to build a sound material-cycle society.

Among the "3Rs" principle, waste reduction and reuse strategies are strongly related to the behaviour of households and firms. Policy options include promoting reusable items and avoiding single use items such as disposable plastic bags. Firms also have a role to play in green practices such as going paperless and encouraging the reuse of office supplies. While this generates cost savings for all parties and reduces the final residue that could have been sent to landfill sites, such policies are largely underdeveloped in Southeast Asian cities. Composting is an exception that many cities are putting in practice to make the best out of organic waste. The composted waste serves as fertilizer for household gardens and peri-urban farms. Yet the quality of the composting is affected due to poor waste segregation.

Recycling holds tremendous opportunity, yet many cities need to make more efforts to achieve this, as pointed out above. For example, the City of Bandung (Indonesia) hopes to reach a recycle target from 7% in 2013 to 30% by 2018. Bangkok in 2014 was recycling about 16% of municipal daily waste generated whilst Hai Phong (Viet Nam) recycled about 2.1%. This can be compared to other cities such as Singapore, where 61% of waste is recycled, and San Francisco that recycles 80% of waste (SF Environment, 2016; NEA, 2016). Southeast Asian cities would have to introduce critical measures to achieve sustainable management of solid waste.

Proper waste management also offers the avenue to address the issues of informal waste pickers, who are under serious health and safety risk. The metro areas studied had instances of informal waste workers who identify and pick out materials for recycling at open dump sites under unsanitary conditions. Proper waste management thereby allows public or private interests to engage the services of local workers under salubrious conditions. This also creates a higher efficiency for energy generation from the properly sorted out waste.

Promoting waste separation at source is the most important policy target to effectively implement the "3Rs". Cebu City has a policy of "No segregation, No collection", which compels waste sorting at source with penalties for non-compliance. This is a good starting point for emulation by other cities in order to begin a proper waste management and recycling practice. The benefit for sorting at source should enable a drastic reduction in the final quantity of residue needed to be permanently landfilled. The "No segregation, No collection" policy, though recently enacted, is influencing residents' behaviour to achieve impact in the waste sector to advance sustainable use of scant environmental resources. Optimism of this nascent policy lends to a favourable prognosis that Cebu would better be able to achieve sustainable resource and solid waste management provided other aspects of waste treatment and recovery systems are improved, including the development of small-scale waste business initiatives. Similarly, San Francisco's success in achieving high levels of waste recycling, nearing zero waste, is attributable to the policies, incentives and fines, educational campaigns and outreaches, as well as the convenience of its three bin system.

Price mechanisms can be an effective instrument to influence the volume of waste generated (see below for details). Fees charged for waste collection were found to be lowly priced in some cities and saddled the city government with an avoidable cost that could have been invested in more beneficial policy areas. Various economic instruments remain at the disposal of metropolitan governments to employ in waste service pricing based on the polluter-pays principle. "Pay as you throw", which is a variable system, and "flat rates" are by far the common methods used. Whatever model is adopted should enable full cost recovery as well as savings for investment to enhance service delivery. An appropriate fee model should induce a behavioural change for producers (domestic/commercial) to voluntarily reduce and recycle waste.

Managing hazardous, medical and industrial wastes

Promoting effective hazardous and medical waste collection has mostly been overlooked in the waste management stream, although it is essential for ecological conservation, public health and safety. Hazardous waste and, in some instances, medical waste, have been managed along with conventional waste without sufficient mechanisms for their safe treatment and disposal. The presence of toxic substances such as mercury, chromium and lead in old electronic equipment such as TVs, computers, radios and phones necessitate their proper disposal. In the case study cities, they are mostly landfilled and with time they release toxic metals and organic pollutants into the environment. E-waste collection should be an integral part of waste management systems due to their long-term hazardous impact on the environment and human life. Clearly, either the case study cites lack the needed regulation to adequately deal with this emerging trend of waste disposal or lack the capacity for enforcement. Public awareness campaigns and appropriate local legislation could be a starting point to address this environmental risk, supported by the needed infrastructure, such as fixed collection sites.

Managing industrial and hazardous waste is another important policy category which is underdeveloped in Southeast Asian cities. In optimising industrial waste, a collective approach permitting industries in close proximity to exchange by-products (materials, energy, water, etc.), referred to as industrial symbiosis, has gained popularity and it would be essential for Southeast Asian cities to explore this mechanism (Yuen and Kong, 2009). Industrial symbiosis creates a circular economy, or "closed-loop manufacturing process", where "waste" from one industry serves as an input for another. In Kalundborg, Denmark where this has been tried, it has led to exchange of about 3 million tonnes of material per year and 25% water savings, thereby yielding win-win environmental benefits and economic prosperity for local governments and businesses (ibid).

Greening industries and services for effective resource management

Industries are the backbone of the economy of the case study cities. They invariably have a tremendous contribution to make to achieving green growth objectives. However, they also pose challenges. For the case study cities, industries (both in terms of energy consumption and industrial processes), are the major sources of CO_2 emissions. For instance, in Hai Phong and Iskandar Malaysia the total CO_2 emissions from industries were 79.2% and 44.1% respectively. Industries, irrespective of size, can reduce their pollution, increase material resource efficiency and enhance their responsibility towards the environment without compromising their competitiveness. As noted by the OECD sustainable manufacturing toolkit (OECD, 2011c) "managing operations in an environmentally and socially responsible manner – "sustainable manufacturing" – is no longer just nice-to-have, but a business imperative".

The bifurcated role of industries in green growth can be viewed either as consumers or producers. Focusing on industries as consumers takes stock of the inputs used by manufacturing industries such as water, energy, raw materials and labour. Governments can use regulations (e.g. appliance standards) and financial tools (e.g. tax incentives to invest in energy-efficient technology) to encourage industries to be more resource efficient, bringing benefits to the city as well as the business itself with profit-making and improved competitiveness (OECD, 2011c). Lessons learned from cities such as Kitakyushu, Japan, can be helpful. Kitakyushu overcame severe pollution while retaining an economy based chiefly on manufacturing. Achieving energy efficiency in the industrial sector will be a necessary step in the greening process.

Focusing on industries as producers highlights the output, which are the by-products and consumables manufactured. The release of the by-products (emissions, solid waste and wastewater) creates challenges if not carried out in an environmentally friendly way in conformity with set out standards. In Hai Phong, analyses of river bodies reveal high contamination due to discharge of industrial and domestic waste (OECD, forthcoming). Appropriate technologies could be used to treat the waste products to acceptable standards before discharge into the environment. The role of local and national governments is to set standards and ensure expert inspections as well as stringent penalties for non-compliance with the standards.

The case studies find that green labelling for industries and consumer products can be an effective instrument. Green labelling schemes have been introduced in the case study countries, with some conforming to ISO 14020 series standards on environmental labelling. Green labelling communicates a product's environmental benefits while asserting its eco-sensitiveness. It assists users to make easier purchasing decisions based on environmental attributes.

Positive, environmentally conscious decisions produce benefits to governments and users manifesting in the form of cost savings, quality products, energy and material efficiency. In Thailand, green labelling schemes, aside from helping consumers identify and buy eco-friendly services and products, also encourage competition between manufacturers to produce greener products and services. Green procurement is also a powerful tool to incentivise green production in industries. In addition public awareness campaigns need to be intensified to provide information and tools to consumers and households to make greener purchasing choices for sustainable consumption. Though the eco-label schemes exist, consumer knowledge/awareness of such schemes is low, leading to a high preference for goods and services with little or no environmental consideration in their production process. An innovative approach that has gained popularity in OECD countries is the extended producer responsibility system. The OECD defines extended producer responsibility as an environmental policy approach in which a producer's responsibility for a product is extended to the post-consumer stage of a product's life cycle. The practice makes manufacturers responsible for the collection and recycling of consumer packaging waste (OECD, 2004). Finally, supporting and assisting industries with research and development ensures that consumer products are environmentally friendly.

Cross-sector policy approaches

Based on the policy assessment by sector in the previous section, this section will propose key strategies which can inform across the sectors and unleash the green growth opportunities. It highlights managing trade-offs across policy areas to maximise policy complementarities.

Box 2.3. Examples of eco-industries in OECD countries

Industrial symbiosis implies traditionally separate industries in geographic proximity, collaborating to harness synergistic possibilities for competitive advantage by exchange of energy, materials and by-products (Chertow, 2000). Industrial symbiosis deems the by-product/waste of one industry as a resource/input for another, allowing for innovation, cost reductions, increased revenues and, above all, additional economic prospects in an environmentally conscientious manner. Kalundborg Eco-Industrial Park in Denmark is one of the leading working industrial symbioses (IISD, 2013).

Similarly, cities can foster the growth of the green technology sector by creating green regional clusters that build on existing industries, services, research and innovation. Kitakyushu, Japan, has built an impressive recycling cluster, the Eco-Town, which recycles hundreds of tonnes of industrial waste every day while producing energy for residential and commercial neighbourhoods. Another area with great potential for energy efficiency is manufacturing industries. Greening manufacturing industries, as the example of Kitakyushu demonstrated, can make a significant contribution to energy savings and reduce the environmental impacts of this sector. Sustainable materials management will also be important for the greening of manufacturing industries in Asia. Although manufacturing industries are not the only actors that would be involved in the sustainable materials management process, they are absolutely central, notably in terms of natural resources policies (i.e. addressing the flow cycles that link natural and industrial systems).

In Kitakyushu, emissions from the iron, steel and other manufacturing sectors are largely responsible for high CO_2 emissions per capita, but the energy efficiency of its iron and steel manufacturing also makes this sector an asset for the city's green growth agenda. Kitakyushu's iron and steel industry offers a range of products with advanced energy performance, such as flat rolls, magnetic steel sheets, thin sheets or surface-treated steel sheets. These products represent about 75% of all products shipped (City of Kitakyushu, 2012). Growing exports of these products ensure the city's economic growth. They can also contribute to reducing CO_2 emissions globally, to the extent that such products maintain their leading positions in energy efficiency and the production processes reduce CO_2 intensity.

Besides iron and steel, successful energy-efficient and resource-saving products from a number of traditional local industries contribute strongly to Kitakyushu's growth. The local ceramic, chemical and electric manufacturing industries successfully sell resource-saving products to national and international markets. While most of these industries are resource-intensive, they can contribute to emission reductions through resource-efficient product manufacturing and reduction of their production process emissions. The city labels all types of technology, products and services that lead to the reduction of environmental impacts as "Eco-Premium" to help raise product awareness and stimulate product growth. To date, 124 companies have been labelled as "Eco-Premium".

Source: OECD (2013d), *Green Growth in Kitakyushu, Japan*, http://dx.doi.org/10.1787/9789264195134-en.

Prioritise policies which generate complementarity and synergies across sectors

Cities are critical drivers of national growth and are, as such, better positioned to realise synergies and green growth aspirations. Urban policy makers are more likely to identify and combine complementary climate policies within and across sectors given the interconnectedness of urban policy sectors such as transport, land-use planning and economic development (OECD, 2010a). Increasing the complementarity and coherence of policy packages across sectors and levels of government can help mitigate the trade-offs among environmental, growth and equity priorities. For example, congestion, pollution and public service constraints affect not only environmental quality, but also the efficiency of local economic activities and a city's ability to attract firms and skilled workers. Complementary policy packages address the costs of reducing environmental impact in a co-ordinated way and can have less regressive impacts. Complementarities among sectors are not only limited to green growth policy areas. Policy areas key to national and local development bordering on social and welfare issues such as inclusiveness have complementary links with green growth. These must be explored to generate shared prosperity and equitable growth. Similarly, bridging green growth with urban resilience and risk reduction is an important area that addresses the vulnerability of cities, thereby helping to protect assets and populations from harm's way. Through effective policy complementarities, green growth maximises economic and environmental outcomes and drastically reduces the impact of externalities on poor and vulnerable groups. This builds a solid foundation for continuous long-term sustained growth. Capitalising on this offers a sure hope for Southeast Asia to drive progress towards the attainment of the SDGs.

Policy complementarity and synergies within the green growth sectors

Maximising green growth outcomes requires policy complementarities at all scales of government. Policies that only focus on one element of the system, or one sector, are unlikely to be effective in enhancing the overall performance of green growth (OECD, 2011a). Various policy practices could achieve multiple objectives through comprehensive integration with other interconnected green growth areas of opportunity at the same time, thereby maximising outcomes. For example, green growth requires not only efficient and reliable water and electricity networks, but also risk-sensitive land use and building design. Green growth also requires an alignment of policies towards climate change mitigation.

Policy complementarities abound, as shown in Table 2.2. It presents the inter-relationships among policy areas and highlights the cross-sectoral policy outcomes that alignment of different sectors could yield for sustainable development. Identifying policy linkages and promoting complementarity leverages the trade-offs between economic and environmental goals among policy areas and sets off the drivers of long-term growth. For example, most cities aim to reduce waste landfilled, at the same time, most aim to increase electricity generation to meet rising demand. Exploring waste-to energy not only meets this dual objective, it also spawns employment and an associated chain of social and economic opportunities. Again, far-sighted policy decision making can be facilitated through identification of policy complementarities, for instance, land use and transport along with housing offer a means to ensure equal distribution of social opportunities in a city. As such, Southeast Asian cities can capitalise on transit-oriented developments to ensure equal spatial distribution of opportunities and shape the urban form into a desired results.

Furthermore, building policies can explore synergies between climate change adaptation and climate change mitigation. For the case study cities and already developed cities, retrofitting appears to be a prudent alternative. One initiative, taken by local communities and the local government in New York City, involved the use of white (or cool) rooftops. Similarly, green roofs have gained prominence and have been recognised as essential for healthy cities. These rooftops participate in climate change adaptation by helping to reduce the urban heat island effect; they are also part of a mitigation strategy as they make it possible to lower greenhouse gas emissions and air pollution by decreasing power demand. Green rooftops can also be used for climate change adaptation, as they can cool the building through shading and insulation and reduce vulnerability to storm waters. Green roofs have been experimented with in growing food and have been found to help in waste diversion by using composted organic material from the waste generated in the building. The city of Chicago is a good example when it comes to city-led efforts to promote green roofs to achieve complementary objectives. It has been placing green roofs on its municipal buildings since 2000. Realising its success, the city's sustainable development policy requires new buildings to have a green roof.[1] Mostly due to this policy, a recent study revealed that there was a total of nearly 5.6 million square feet of green roof coverage (City of Chicago, 2016).

Table 2.2. **Policy complementarities in urban green growth sectors in Southeast Asian cities**

	Land use and transport	Housing and buildings	Water	Solid waste	Green industries and services
Energy	Active mobility (cycling and walking) reduces dependence on fossil fuel to power transport	Green code: Promotes energy and resource efficiency in buildings	Water, energy and food security: Water and energy are reliant on each other for their respective commercial production, which together are essential for producing agricultural goods.	Waste-to-energy technology can reduce the amount of waste to be landfilled and at the same time generate energy	System and energy optimisation enables manufacturing industries to reduce energy intensity and reduce emissions
Land use and transport		Transit-oriented development: Leads to the creation of sustainable communities and reduces the need for private motor transport while enhancing access to social opportunities.	Green infrastructure: Provides ecological conservation while helping to address water risk and challenges Water bodies could also provide a means of sustainable transport	Material and energy recovery: Enables efficient resource utilisation over its lifecycle and generates energy to meet rising demand	Eco-parks/industries: Makes industries more sensitive to the environment thereby contributing to pollution reduction
Housing and buildings			Wastewater treatment: Reduces water pollution and contributes to water security Flood resilient architecture can reduce water risk	3Rs (reduce, reuse and recycle): Enables drastic reduction in waste generation at source	Green labelling and certification: Informs consumer choices and promotes economic and environmental efficiency
Water				Sustainable waste management: Prevents contamination of water resources from hazardous materials	Effluent charges and recycling wastewater: Reduces pollution from industries and makes industries more competitive in the market
Solid waste					Industrial symbiosis: Enables industries to reutilise by-products avoiding waste and promoting resource efficiency

Source: Author.

The case study analysis revealed that most of the cities have policies which appear to be complementary; however, upon a deeper analysis the linkages are weak and need to be strengthened. For example, all the case study cities are promoting energy efficiency appliances (Table 2.3), and though not developed fully in terms of the infrastructure and policies, active mobility is present in the case studies. In contrast, there are certain areas such as wastewater treatment and eco-industrial parks which need to be promoted to enhance water security. Experiences of policy complementarity abound and can be maximised through knowledge-sharing workshops (see Chapter 3) that enable city leaders to exchange best approaches. Similarly, governance arrangements to allow such cross-sector policy making as discussed in Chapter 3 can be extremely useful in identifying which programmes of different sectors inter-relate or could be integrated to achieve similar and more impactful results.

Table 2.3. **Examples of cross-sectoral policies practised in the case study cities**

	Bangkok	Iskandar Malaysia	Cebu	Bandung	Hai Phong
Active mobility	**	**	**	**	**
Renewable energy	**	**	*	**	**
Waste-to-energy/composting	**	–	*	*	–
Transit-oriented development	**	*	*	*	–
Eco-industrial parks	–	**	*	*	**
Wastewater treatment	***	**	**	**	**

Notes: Level of practice: – absent; *partial; ** moderate; ***fully practised.

Source: Author.

Inclusiveness as a crucial element for urban green growth

The adaptation of green growth as the policy framework to guide the development of Southeast Asian countries coincides with social disparities already prevalent in the case study cities. Brushing this situation under the carpet as if it does not exist would only compound its severity and generate unintended consequences for vulnerable and poor groups in the implementation of green growth strategies. It is imperative to ensure that green growth fosters economic growth in a more inclusive manner. Inclusive growth is defined by the OECD (2015c) as a new approach to economic growth that aims to improve living standards and share the benefits of increased prosperity more evenly across social groups. This perfectly blends in with the principles of green growth which dovetail into drivers of social and welfare improvements for sustainable development and poverty alleviation. As already identified by the joint force of the African Development Bank, OECD, United Nations and World Bank (2013) " inclusive green growth will not happen on its own, deliberate policy and investment decisions need to be taken at all levels, local to global, to ensure that economic growth is in fact green and inclusive".

Asian cities cannot be made greener at the expense of the less well off. Exploring complementarities of the green growth agenda with social issues is key to successful outcomes. This is important as it not only contributes to the SDGs, but translates into tangible results with positive outcomes on economic self-sufficiency, health, governance, education and social cohesion. Moreover, it also draws attention to specific needs of segments of the population such as the elderly, physically challenged, youth, unemployed, women and the poor. Most policies on social issues are currently developed and implemented in isolation. Furthermore, implementation of some measures in green growth might have a negative effect on some households and businesses, especially in Southeast Asia where safety nets and welfare systems are not well developed. Bridging the policy gaps permits an enhanced implementation which is able to overcome these setbacks. Poor social equity in Asian cities is reinforced by the low social status, low levels of education, low access to public entitlements, low protection, little provision of basic infrastructures, and little or no political voice or formal representation of informal settlers and slum dwellers, who lack a formal identity (Bartlett et al., 2012). Their vulnerability to local environmental degradation and natural hazards also participates in the "urban divide" between rich and poor areas. These conditions create a structural poverty that is exacerbated by the pace of urban growth and does not allow for inclusive economic growth. It will be necessary to evaluate the scale of the informal sector and the obstacles it represents for policy implementation in each Southeast Asian city to avoid policy failures and to clarify policy opportunities and challenges.

Informal housing and slums were identified as an area in need of intervention that the green growth approach should address. Informal settlements often emerge as expedient solutions to the failure of formal systems to adequately meet the housing needs of the urban poor. Greening the urban informal sector for inclusiveness requires slum upgrading and provision of basic services. Advanced slum upgrading in Jakarta is a potentially efficient policy example. Not only would it reduce GHG emissions through relocation of slum dwellers to safer areas with energy-efficient homes and through improved access to public transport (electricity and road transport are the city's two leading emitters of GHG), it would also reduce the vulnerability of the community formerly located in flood-prone areas (Sugar et al., 2013). Bangkok City has implemented several community-driven housing development initiatives, such as the Ban Mankong project, launched in 2003 by the Community Organisations Development Institute. It successfully provided clean and secure housing to approximately 1 000 households, with social support systems to empower citizens (OECD, 2015g). Similarly, to enhance complementarity in slum upgrading, it would be essential that cities willing to engage in this adopt inclusive approaches with slum dwellers to provide sustainable arrangements. By so doing, green interventions are responsive to the needs of slum dwellers as opposed to implementing a top-down project that is not reflective of local needs and only makes slum dwellers passive recipients of assistance.

Involving communities in solid waste management can also be a good example of complementarity. UNIDO (2011) stresses that greening the informal waste management sector involves not only bringing it under the purview of the formal system, but also modernising its operational techniques. This unleashes the opportunities along the value chain of waste management. Bandung City's new recycling programme also aims to co-operate with the city's active waste pickers. In seeking complementarity in informal waste management. This enables waste pickers to be reliable service providers who abide by high standards in diligently executing their duties. In India, Waste Ventures provides door-to-door waste collection services and directly employs some of the poorest and most unskilled workers, whose livelihoods are put at risk by large-scale waste management operations that do not recycle sufficient waste or provide effective services. To date, the company has recruited 53 "pickers", who traditionally collect rubbish from roadsides and dump yards to earn their living. Providing employment and training, Waste Ventures equips them with skills and protective clothing so they can collect waste directly from the local households in the communities in which they work. The training gives them the skills to segregate waste on the spot into recyclable, organic and inert portions. Generally, 80% of the waste is processed for recycling, and by selling the by-products, additional revenue is generated from which Waste Ventures is able to pay the pickers a salary about twice that they would normally earn (OECD, 2015g).

Disaster risk management as a crucial element for urban green growth

Green growth strategies contribute to building stronger urban resilience against environmental and climatic risk which often leads to disaster. This plays an important role in systematically addressing uncertainties, mitigating the adverse effects of shocks, and empowering urban areas to adapt and immediately recover from disasters. The quality of the sustainable growth of Southeast Asian cities would be dependent on their ability to minimise disaster risk. Presently, urban development and climate change trends exacerbate natural disaster risks in Southeast Asian cities. The assessment of the case studies indicates that Southeast Asian cities lack strong planning for disaster risk reduction. Risks of disasters in these cities are higher than in many other parts of the world, mainly owing to tropical storms, earthquakes, floods and settlements in low-lying areas as presented in Chapter 1. For instance, the Bangkok Metropolitan Region is at high risk of inland flooding owing to land subsidence resulting from over-pumping of ground water. Ports are also vulnerable to such risks. As Asian cities host some of the world's largest ports, their vulnerability is a source of concern, as disruption of their activities can have disastrous consequences for local and global economies. Furthermore, owing to limited access to affordable land and housing, slums and informal settlements tend to be located in fragile environmental areas, such as banks of rivers or lakes, steep slopes or low-elevation coastal zones. These areas are extremely vulnerable to natural disasters such as floods, tropical storms, rises in sea level, earthquakes or tsunamis, which could increase with climate change and could deprive slum dwellers and informal settlers of their assets and drive them into extreme poverty traps. Considering that the majority of disasters now occur on a small scale and are managed at the local level, with the economic and social cost seldom recognised, communities which are the first responders need to be better prepared (GRC, 2011). Complementarities between green growth strategies and disaster risk management offer a, long-term cost saving approach to address the interaction between urban development and vulnerability.

A good example of such complementarity between urban resilience and green growth can be observed in the green infrastructure policy. Green infrastructures are defined as "a strategically planned network of natural and semi-natural areas with other environmental features designed and managed to deliver a wide range of ecosystem services" (OECD, 2015d; EU, 2015). In contrast, grey infrastructure refers to the stock of manmade physical developments which are put up to serve a particular function of the society (e.g. roads) which are not primarily for an environmental service. Combining grey infrastructure with more flexible and green infrastructure contributes to urban resilience, especially on undeveloped land where this is more feasible. Grey infrastructure has several limitations, such as not being easily being adaptive to the dynamics of the society in terms of socio-economic or environmental demands (Gartner and DiFrancesco, 2015). On the other hand, green infrastructure provides environmental services; it is more flexible and cost-effective. Equally important, green infrastructure plays a crucial role in mitigating climate change risk by protecting urban areas from floods, conserving the ecosystem and enhancing quality of life. On the whole, government policy in Southeast Asia needs to support investments in green infrastructure. Grey infrastructure to some extent can also be made "green", that is retrofitted to reduce environmental impact, thereby contributing to environmental objectives. Notably, city and national governments have revenue tied to infrastructure delivery for different sectors such as water, energy, housing and transport, whose design can be made green. Moreover, revenue sources of cities such as property taxes can be used as a means to stimulate greening (Merk et al., 2012). Private sector engagement for green infrastructure investment should also be promoted considering the fiscal challenges of governments. On the other hand, the economic life of grey infrastructure (e.g. coal-fired power stations) could prematurely be curtailed to promote environmental objectives (OECD, 2015a). A case in point of curtailing the life of a grey infrastructure for a green infrastructure is the Cheonggyecheon stream restoration project in Seoul, Korea. In 2002, as a part of a revitalisation project of the downtown area, the city decided to demolish an elevated highway and structure covering the stream in order to restore the stream and shift the city's urban policy paradigm to be more sustainable (Lah, 2012). Aside the many ecological functions, flood management was integrated into the project design with an embankment capable of withstanding a 200-year severe flood. In the case study cities, examples of green infrastructure were few, although it emerged that discussions are underway to increase the investment to the sector, such as the "green loop" project in Cebu.

Box 2.4. **Green infrastructure**

Green infrastructure uses the natural environment in a way that maximises its functions. Through regulatory or planning policy as well as mechanisms, it seeks to ensure the protection of the natural environment. This is achieved through landscaping or engineering. Green infrastructure is nuanced by regional approaches. For example, while in European countries (European Commission,2013) green infrastructure is broadly a strategically planned network of high-quality natural and semi-natural areas with environmental features designed and managed to deliver a wide range of eco-system services and protect biodiversity, the United States Environmental Protection Agency (US EPA, 2016), identifies it as a cost-effective, resilient approach to managing wet weather impacts that provides many community benefits. The US EPA identifies green infrastructure more as a storm water management approach requiring parks, gardens, bio-swales, permeable pavements and green roofs. The EU approach, on the other hand, identifies it as an integral part of an interconnected network capable of delivering different environmental features, for example an urban park in a city qualifies for green infrastructure if it acts as a cool air corridor, absorbs excess water run-off, and offers an attractive outdoor area for recreation and wildlife (European Commission, 2013). Similarly, rural farm land qualifies for green infrastructure if it is specifically managed so that it supports local biodiversity or encourages a more multifunctional land use which combines food production with other benefits, such as recreation or water purification (ibid).

Green infrastructure is increasingly recognised as part of the answer to water challenges in OECD countries, especially when cities compete with other users (e.g. agriculture and thermal energy) to access the water they need, and when water management is considered in relation to land use and other policies. A point made by UNEP (2014) is worth repeating: green infrastructures work best in combination with existing grey ones, when appropriately sited and designed. The point is not to substitute grey with green, but to combine grey and green, retrofitting green infrastructures to grey ones.

Sources: European Commission (2013), *Building a Green Infrastructure for Europe*, http://dx.doi.org/10.2779/54125; US EPA (2016), "What is green infrastructure?", webpage, https://www.epa.gov/green-infrastructure/what-green-infrastructure; Ranjah, S. (2016), "Green infrastructure: Planning for sustainable and resilient urban environment", https://sustainabledevelopment.un.org/content/documents/95599_Ranjha_Green%20infrastructure_planning%20for%20sustainable%20and%20resilient%20urban%20environment.pdf; OECD (2015f), *Water and Cities: Ensuring Sustainable Futures*, http://dx.doi.org/10.1787/9789264230149-en.

Among different infrastructure, port infrastructure is one of the most critical ones to be prepared and protected from disasters. For example, one remarkable measure listed in the 2012-25 Environmental Conservation Programme of the City of Hai Phong is a project with a budget estimated at VND 4 billion (Vietnamese dong) to strengthen communication systems to warn vessels in case of typhoons. However, no comprehensive emergency response strategy is in place for the port. Since most of the Southeast Asian countries have major ports, it would be essential that response capacity and plans are developed to ensure the economic resilience of the port. In this regard, port companies should develop business continuity plans to minimise the impact of disaster on their activities.

In order to manage urban disaster risks, hard infrastructure can perform best when it is complemented by "soft" measures. Among different measures, the study revealed that while national governments have developed insurance schemes or contingency lines of credit, comparable local financial instruments are lacking across the five cities. Pre-arranged insurance policies, contingency financial plans and agreements of reciprocal assistance in emergencies are fundamental components of effective response planning. These "soft" measures play a key role as a financial bridge towards a more resilient future. However, the affordability of flood insurance policies can be a significant barrier, especially considering the frequency of such disasters, which increases the cost of premiums. For example, after the 2011 floods in Bangkok, many businesses and individuals struggled to find affordable insurance policies to cover flood damages and losses. Of the total losses in 2011, only about USD 10 billion were insured (as compared to losses of about USD 45 billion). In response, the Thai government set up the National Catastrophe Insurance Fund in 2012, which is used as a reinsurance reserve, and regularly raises awareness about it and other insurance products at seminars and events (OECD, 2013b). In Bandung, the central government's Rehabilitation and Reconstruction Fund finances public post-disaster expenditure as part of state government budgets (OECD, 2013c). Despite the increasing frequency of natural disasters, insured losses remain low in Indonesia and the majority of post-disaster costs are borne by the central government. For example, Indonesia's Disaster Management Authority reports that local disaster risk management agencies are reluctant to use their limited provincial budgets and instead rely on Indonesia's national disaster funds (Give2Asia, 2016). Insurance and contingency lines of credit are the backbone of effective response planning and should be developed, in particular at the local level. A common regional insurance fund for city governments to avoid "peak losses and risk concentration" could spread risk across Southeast Asia and therefore reduce the burden on any one city. Equally, national governments could take the lead domestically and introduce subnational insurance and contingency lines of credit.

Moreover, the response capacity of all stakeholders, including administrations, companies and local communities, especially in poor neighbourhoods, need to be improved. Preparedness and response capacities are determinant factors of resilience. Disaster response is not only the prerogative of the police and fire brigade, all stakeholders have a role to play. Empirical experience from previous disasters have shown that in almost all cases it was family members, friends and neighbours who lived nearby who saved the majority of lives, property and assets in the first few minutes and hours after a disaster. Response simulation exercises need to be organised to test and improve response capacities, as well as ensure staff communicate and receive training to equip them to discharge their duties in emergency response. Especially in high-risk areas of Southeast Asian cities, residents and responsible agencies need to be familiarised with such response and preparedness activities. Digital technologies can also help to make urban planning more resilient through flood simulation tools, co-ordination of emergency response infrastructure and the reaching out to local communities and the private sector more efficiently.

Finally, the complementarity also needs to be pursued for social aspects. Disasters disproportionately affect the urban poor by deepening poverty and inequalities and resulting in weaker long-term economic growth. While this can be explained by their poor access to urban services – such as electricity, transport, and water supply and treatment – it also stems from a lack of efficient policies to directly protect them from disaster risk. To increase the resilience of poor and vulnerable groups to disaster, it will be critical to enhance the preparedness and response capacity of local communities, especially that of the aforementioned groups.

Developing demand-side policies

The case studies have demonstrated that compared to OECD countries, demand-side policies are yet to gain root in Southeast Asian countries. Demand policies are meant to encourage green innovation and foster the market for new products and services. Often, responsibility for demand-side polices such as tax incentives, regulations or public procurement have been distanced from the ministries and agencies responsible for ensuring that demand from public need is met (IPP, 2015). Demand-side measures include pricing mechanisms, consumer information policies, innovation-oriented regulation and standards including procurement. Typically, benefits of demand-side policies have the potential to reduce excess energy or water consumption, reduce solid waste generation and traffic congestion, and strengthen markets for green innovation, thereby fostering markets for new products and ensuring that policies do not get locked into poor supply decisions (OECD, 2011a). At the same time it fosters markets for new products.

Pricing mechanisms could be explored more aggressively to influence the behaviour of people. Chinese cities with free district heating at point of use emit some 45% more GHG per household from domestic sources than similar cities where domestic heating is priced. Pricing can also work well to influence traffic demand (e.g. congestion charge) and waste volumes (e.g. fees for domestic waste). Faced with rising waste, an effective waste-charging system witnessed waste volume reduce by 60% after charges were reviewed and implemented in Chinese Tapei (Green Power, 2012). Management of water resources is a good example of a green growth policy area for which pricing can make a significant difference. Water pricing can be seen both as an incentive mechanism to increase resource and allocation efficiency and as a strategy to raise revenues. However, water pricing can be a delicate issue insofar as it is often at the heart of trade-offs between the financial sustainability of service providers on the one hand and environmental protection and economic efficiency on the other. It also raises affordability and distributional issues if not done right. Water pricing instruments which are being used in cities comprise of: water pollution levies, water use levies, water service levies (e.g. flood control, wastewater treatment), and damage compensation penalties (EU Water Initiative, 2012). Price-based instruments can also be useful for energy efficiency policies in buildings, because pricing energy right will stimulate investment in energy efficiency in buildings such as insulation and more energy-efficient heating. Where price-based instruments are employed, the market is likely to take care of many of the energy efficiency challenges in response to changing prices, but public intervention is likely to be needed to assist low-income groups and to enhance the energy efficiency of social housing, public buildings and public infrastructure. Pricing policies must be considered in a multi-level governance context, since a lack of co-ordination at national scale or, in some cases, across adjacent municipalities in a complex metropolitan area, may simply lead to the displacement of people or activities, penalising those adopting greener policies and fuelling growth elsewhere. For example, in considering fees on waste collection, adequate measures should be put in place at the same time to address illegal dumping. Another important issue affecting the capacity of cities to make efficient use of pricing tools, is the actors in charge of design and implementation. In the water sector, for instance, river basins authorities, provinces or national governments may be in charge of water pricing rather than cities.

Fossil fuel subsidies undermine cities' efforts to promote sustainable transport modes. Reducing or eliminating these subsidies is urgent and can have a positive impact on green growth in Southeast Asian cities, provided it is integrated with complementary social protection measures, such as cash transfers and measures to protect the poor from increases in energy, water and agricultural input prices (OECD, 2012).

Extreme demand-side polices come with challenges also. Government-led demand-side policies may be driven by political interest rather than consideration of emerging market needs. At the same time, some economic instruments may not suffice alone to influence consumption patterns and may rather encourage relatively lowly priced technologies (ibid). Nevertheless getting the demand-side policy right remains an important decision for city and national governments to make.

Awareness-raising campaigns and information dissemination are important but often undermine demand-side instruments that can promote urban green growth in Southeast Asia. The Roadmap strategy for the various countries of the case studies highlights such campaigns. However, they are not strong and could be intensified. The transition to a low-carbon, green economy could be misconstrued as a threat to the interest of some actors. As such, compelling messages outlining the benefits of green growth with credible analysis must be communicated to such vested interests. Awareness raising can bridge the knowledge gap of consumers, ensuring the buy-in of all stakeholders into the environmental transformation the city seeks. Various media platforms, well suited to the needs of the population (demographics), can be an effective means to mobilise popular support and place the green growth agenda on a path of least resistance. In particular, since formulating values begins at a tender age, introducing environmental stewardship into classroom curricula could shape the behaviour of the youth to be more environmentally conscious of their actions. Much attention has been paid to this for which some OECD countries have collaborated to develop comprehensive educational programmes. Similarly, making consumers aware of the environmental consequences of their purchases would be important to promote sustainable consumption. Consumer education programmes could highlight energy and resource efficiency, as well as the role of residents in militating against climate change. As has already been mentioned, green labelling could also be promoted to serve as a guide to consumers in their lifestyle and purchasing choices to opt for more environmentally friendly products.

Prioritising policies to ensure long-term growth

Investment decisions must consider long-term impact on society and aim to create growth. It is widely recognised that urban infrastructure, innovation and human capital are drivers for long-term economic growth (OECD, 2009). However, confronted by the challenge of managing extremely rapid urbanisation, fast-growing Southeast Asian cities tend to prioritise short-term economic benefits over long-term considerations, which often do not lead to sustainable environmental outcomes.

Long-term infrastructure investment

Investing in infrastructure for long-term growth is critical for sustained long-term competitiveness and productivity gains. Cities are responsible for a momentous share of investments in infrastructure, which if invested wisely can contribute to national efforts to combine growth with environmental performance. However, confronted by the challenge of managing extremely rapid urbanisation, fast-growing Southeast Asian cities tend to prioritise short-term economic benefits over long-term considerations, which often do not lead to sustainable environmental outcomes. As there will be huge demands for urban infrastructure in the next decades, it is crucial for urban policy makers to consider not only how to meet these demands, but also how to make infrastructure investment greener. The rail transport systems in Paris and London, which were established in 1900 and 1863 respectively, demonstrate how carefully planned long-term infrastructure investments can tremendously benefit cities.

The case study cities have a need for a long-term vision and policy framework for these urban investments to have impact. The absence of a long-term integrated infrastructure plan in most cities could undermine green growth efforts and lead to inefficient resource allocation. The development of a long-term plan provides confidence to investors and residents about the city's priorities and how they would be delivered. A policy framework for long-term green infrastructure investment might include: goal setting and aligning policies across and within levels of government; reforming policies to enable investment and strengthen market incentives for low-carbon, climate resilient infrastructure; establishing specific financial policies, regulations, tools and instruments that provide transitional support for new green technologies; harnessing resources for capacity building; and promoting green business and consumer behaviour (Corfee-Morlot et al., 2012). Moreover, it would be prudent for Southeast Asian cities to future proof the city by reserving public space for infrastructure. Currently, a crucial area identified is for investment to favour public transport over private vehicle use. Yet a major challenge realised by most case studies, especially with implementation of urban infrastructure investment projects, is the lack of reserved space. The scarcity of space for urban infrastructure projects such as bus rapid transit or rail lines increases the cost and even delays the projects, as processes for resettlement and compensation are made complex. This would, of course, emanate from the long-term plan which could guide such reservation efforts.

While Southeast Asian cities have urgent demand for new infrastructure investment, keeping the quality of the infrastructure high is essential for long-term growth and a strategy that they should pursue. The G7 summit held in Japan in May 2016 made this recognition stressing that "investment without the quality perspective could end up introducing infrastructure with higher lifecycle costs, less durability, inequitable distributive effects, highly negative environmental and social impacts, vulnerability against natural disasters and the impacts of climate change" (Government of Japan, 2016). Promoting quality infrastructure is therefore not a luxury but a necessary step for leapfrogging into a low-carbon economy. The summit endorsed the G7 Ise-Shima Principles for Promoting Quality Infrastructure Investment, which can be streamlined with the investment decisions of governments and stakeholders in Southeast Asia to bridge the infrastructure demand-supply gap (Box 2.5).

Box 2.5. Ise-Shima Principles for Promoting Quality Infrastructure Investment

The G7 Ise-Shima summit endorsed the G7 Ise-Shima Principles for Promoting Quality Infrastructure Investment as follows:

Principle 1: Ensuring effective governance, reliable operation and economic efficiency in view of life-cycle cost as well as safety and resilience against natural disaster, terrorism and cyber-attack risks: Quality infrastructure investment should ensure effective governance, economic efficiency, sustainability and reliable operation during the life span of a project as well as safety and resilience against natural disaster, terrorism and cyber-attack risks.

Principle 2: Ensuring job creation, capacity building and transfer of expertise and know-how for local communities: Quality infrastructure investment should seek to contribute to job creation for local work forces and to transfer of expertise and know-how to local communities.

Principle 3: Addressing social and environmental impacts: Quality infrastructure investment must consider the social and environmental impacts of infrastructure projects and duly address such impacts including by applying social and environmental safeguards that are in line with international best practices as reflected in the most relevant standards including those of existing [multilateral development banks].

Principle 4: Ensuring alignment with economic and development strategies including aspect of climate change and environment at the national and regional levels: Quality infrastructure investment should be aligned with economic and development strategies at the national and regional levels, through dialogues with stakeholders from the project preparation and prioritization phases. Relevant elements of economic and development strategies to be considered include the development of a global supply chain through enhanced connectivity; use of latest technology such as information and communication technology; promotion of private investment and attraction of new industries; medium and long-term plans based on a long-term and cross-sector demand forecast and other relevant information; and debt sustainability and fiscal outlook. Climate change resilience, energy security and sustainability, conservation of biodiversity, disaster risk reduction should be considered including through further promotion of ecosystem-based approaches and green infrastructure.

Principle 5: Enhancing effective resource mobilization including through PPP: Quality infrastructure investment should effectively mobilize resources including from the private sector through PPP and other forms of innovative financing, including through MDBs. To this end, joint efforts among stakeholders including host country governments to strengthen the enabling investment environment at national and sub-national government levels, as well as to enhance due process and transparency are essential.

Source: Government of Japan (2015), *G7 Ise-Shima Principles for Promoting Quality Infrastructure Investment*, www.mofa.go.jp/files/000160272.pdf.

Local and national governments can leverage official development assistance (ODA) to advance green growth. In Thailand, a blending of ODA and non-concessional other official flows (OOF) has leveraged private sector investment in renewable energy and energy efficiency to avoid lock-in to carbon-intensive development pathways (OECD, 2013c). Bilateral and multilateral initiatives are already increasingly involved in the financing of urban green growth projects in Asia. The Asian Development Bank's (ADB) 2010-20 Sustainable Transport Initiative plans to increase the share of the ADB's investments in urban transport in Asian cities from 2% to 30% of its total transport lending by 2020, which could encourage more sustainable infrastructure development patterns in cities (EMBARQ, 2013). Another example is the Cities-Environment-Transport in the ASEAN region. In this project, GIZ (the German International Co-operation Agency) works with Cambodia, Indonesia, Lao PDR,

Malaysia, the Philippines and Viet Nam to reduce emissions from transport and other sectors and to achieve co-benefits such as improved air quality and more competitive urban centres. They achieve this by promoting clean air measures, increasing the energy efficiency of land transport, and reducing exhaust emissions and local waste related to port activities. Such activities should be scaled up and replicated. One option is to explore possibilities of direct involvement with local governments and to increase joint actions between national and local governments.

Investment in human capital and innovation

Positive results have been observed with regards to the human resources of the case study cities. In general, there are favourable national policies promoting high educational attainments of the labour force in Indonesia, Malaysia, the Philippines, Singapore, Thailand and Viet Nam (Goujon and Samir, 2008). The high educational attainment of the labour force with the rising share of tertiary educated labour force is an asset to drive green growth. Nonetheless, many opportunity areas remain that can be improved. With regards to gender in the labour force, though female participation continues to rise, it remains relatively low compared to that of men. In Southeast Asia the labour participation rates for males and females are 82% and 59% respectively (ADB, 2013). Ensuring gender equity is key to sustainable economic and social growth, as closing the gender gap generates a 30% increase in per capita income in the economy (ibid). Furthermore, mismatch between employer skill demand and workforce qualification, especially among the youth, creates issues of under and over qualification, which debases productivity growth and hinders the structural transition to higher valued activities (ILO, 2015). Moreover, the increased migration from rural to urban areas creates a large pool of low-skilled workers who are unable to fully integrate into mainstream society. Failure to provide the needed skills for these groups has potential to create social and political discontent (OECD, 2009).

Investing in capacity building (at the community, local and national government levels) is also necessary for green growth in Southeast Asian cities. Southeast Asian cities should ensure that skills developments are linked to areas of opportunities or industrial development. Thinking about long-term growth also implies that policy frameworks must develop an outlook towards the future, not just understand the present needs. Strategies to adopt in this area include using labour market and economic information to help identify the evolution of the economy and using proactive strategies to meet skills demand instead of reacting to labour shortages. Furthermore, policies at the national level should allow for flexibility for programmes to be customised at the local level and use local partnerships to stimulate policy co-ordination (OECD, 2009).

Finally, the issue of short-term and long-term innovation should be addressed. Levels of investment in education and in R&D are still too low in dynamic Asia to attract and retain talent and to develop local capacities sufficiently, although efforts are being made. Chapter 3 explores this topic further.

Promoting the use of ICT in green growth policies

Information and communication technology (ICT) access, skills and use are pivotal for achieving efficiency in environmental and economic performance. In essence, ICT is a cornerstone to the green growth agenda, especially when analysed from the standpoint of application in transport and land use, energy, housing and utilities. It now permeates every aspect of the economy, transforming the traditional approach society used to interact and conduct its affairs. In all sectors such as energy, transport, education, media and health, the impact of ICT as a major driver of innovation and inclusive growth can be felt through the use of fixed and mobile computing devices. Most importantly, governments are capturing the opportunities available in ICT to inform policy- and decision making in many countries and cities through e-governance. ICT is also a potentially useful approach to urban resilience; it encompasses strategies such as investing in social and human capital and modern ICT infrastructure, enhancing the availability and quality of knowledge communication and social infrastructure, and innovation in emerging technologies (OECD, 2013b). ICT is useful in making historical and real-time data available for deeper analysis which encourages rapid response to urban challenges (see discussion in Chapter 3). In transport, this could be very relevant in the distribution of traffic and the provision of real-time transit information to commuters. This is essential in reducing carbon emissions and allowing commuters to save on time and cost. Furthermore, dynamic road pricing (tolls or congestion fees) can be better optimised through such systems (OECD, 2015d).

Southeast Asia remains a dynamic region for ICT use, mostly driven by smartphone and mobile broadband growth with a surging Internet adoption (Ericsson, 2015). Areas of opportunity for application of ICT in green growth remain high in the case study cities and Southeast Asia as a whole. For example in Bandung, the city capitalises on monitoring its social media activity to provide city administrators with insights into challenges of citizens. An online reporting system also offers the chance for citizens to report problems. The time taken for the assigned department to resolve the problem forms part of a performance metric (Kwang, 2015).

A promising green growth option for Southeast Asian cities is to apply ICT to enhance the shared economy. This can be seen in terms of services (car rentals – Zipcar; ride sharing – Uber, Lyft, blablacar; accommodations –Airbnb, shared parking spaces – Justpark) or station-based infrastructure (bicycle sharing – Velib, electric cars – Autolib'). Benefits to cities not only arise from taxation but also from better government regulation of the sectors. The sharing economy can reduce "redundant ownership" and resource consumption as well as lend support to the tourism sector. Applications in the shared economy have penetrated most of the cities in Southeast Asia though the initial reaction of most local governments was to ban them (Liem, 2015). A full understanding of the trade-offs and impacts on existing industries are required. While some sectors could benefit, it could result in high competition to existing traditional industries (e.g. hotels). In the field of road transport, it becomes a challenge when it does not lead to any marginal returns to environmental performance considering the already high traffic congestion and traffic emissions from the transport sector. It would be essential for transport policies relating to shared usage platforms to ensure they are integrated into existing systems rather than add to the already high stock of vehicles plying the road. Alternatively, new vehicle stock should only be permitted if they contribute to GHG emissions reduction by using hybrid or low-carbon cars. This in no way should also preclude investments in mass public transport.

Another important option is to invest in data and statistics for better green growth policy making and accountability to citizens. Open data portals are increasingly helping private agencies and individuals to contribute meaningfully to city innovation and development. Recently, many OECD member countries have lunched municipal open data portals and provided assistance to enable developers to tap into this to create useful apps for the cities. The city of Melbourne in Australia, for instance, provides application programming interface related to transport for third-party app developers to easily use the open data it provides in enhancing travel information (Institute for Sensible Transport, 2016). This creates new business opportunities for innovative start-ups to respond to demands in the urban market. Many cities over the world are likewise stimulating concentrations of start-up incubators in their vicinities realising its importance in job creation and responding to challenges of the society. How start-up ecosystems like the Silicon Valley have contributed to the economic development of Northern California are compelling stories on their own.

Opportunities are also available for cities in Southeast Asia to become a "living lab" where different ICT applications can be introduced and tested. They could attract private ICT investment by providing such space for experimentation of new technologies. The "Smarter Cities Challenge" is an initiative of IBM with contributions valued at more than USD 66 million in 2016. Since 2010, more than 130 cities around the world have benefited from the initiative, including Cebu and Jakarta. It deploys experts to work with city leaders in using innovative methods to draw up effective recommendations on how to make the city smarter for long-term growth (IBM, 2013). Such approaches transform cities into large-scale experimental test beds for data-driven innovation (OECD, 2015d) that enables cities to learn from one another in collaborating to solve societal challenges. Some common applications of ICT-based smart city tools are summarised in Table 2.4.

Currently, there are obstacles to the implementation of ICT and strategies must be put in place to ensure that the region benefits. Some challenges identified include: low government spending on ICT, lack of interdepartmental co-ordination for ICT policies, low broadband penetration, poor Internet access outside major cities and relatively high tariffs (Rao, 2008). Addressing these obstacles has a trickling down effect which promotes efficiency and allows for a greater integration of the urban systems.

Box 2.6. **Bandung Command Centre**

The Bandung Command Centre is the flagship project developed by the city of Bandung to achieve its vision to become a smart city. It was initiated in early 2015 in partnership with IBM and the Institut Teknologi Bandung, one of the top universities in Indonesia, and is similar to other existing command centres in Japan and Korea, aiming to improve public services. The centre consists of a digital control board allowing city staff to remotely monitor traffic and manage crisis situations in the city (in case of accidents, crime, etc.). Fifteen operators from the Bandung Telecommunication and Information Agency work permanently in the Command Centre, but it is also accessible to other city departments, such as firefighter brigades, police officers and transportation agencies. It collects information from the street level in order to make informed decisions to improve the delivery of public services, such as ambulances, fire fighters and police intervention. The information is shown on a digital screen in the Command Centre. Two types of methods are used to collect street-level data:

- It uses CCTV cameras in streets and GPS tracking installed in school buses, ambulances, public buses and garbage trucks. For instance, a traffic violation could be easily spotted by the cameras and the information would be immediately transmitted to the centre and appear on the screen.
- An interesting method used by the Command Centre to collect information from the street level is the use of social media. The Command Centre can be reached directly by the citizens from Twitter, for instance, and they can transmit via their smartphones or computers any concerns they have regarding safety and traffic (e.g. poor road conditions).

Box 2.6. Bandung Command Centre *(continued)*

Some of the information gathered by the Command Centre is also accessible to the public. For instance, the data collected through GPS devices in school buses can be viewed by the local population who can make an informed decision in case the bus is late due to traffic. The Command Centre is therefore being developed so as to become a privileged interface of communication between the local governments and local communities in the city.

The Bandung Command Centre also works as a data bank unit, by storing information on traffic violations, road infrastructure conditions, safety performance, disaster frequency and locations, etc. Another benefit is that it can allow visualising the types of problems most frequently encountered in every district of the city, and make a performance assessment for each of them. In the future, smaller operations centres will be opened in each district, in a strategy to decentralise smart city tool management. The centre is being developed in three stages. Currently, only the first stage is completed. It is expected to cover management of other sectors in the future.

Source: OECD (2016b), *Green Growth in Bandung, Indonesia*, http://dx.doi.org/10.1787/9789264264113-en.

Table 2.4. Main types of ICT application in cities

Sector	Main smart city initiatives in the world
General environment	– Air pollution monitoring (Louisville, Kentucky; Chicago, Illinois)
	– Greenhouse gas emissions sensors
	– Weather forecast sensors
Energy	– Smart electricity grid (People's Republic of China)
	– Street lighting regulation (Besancon, France)
	– Smart metering in households (Italy)
	– Home/building energy management system (Lyon, France; Yokohama, Japan)
	– Renewable energy generation: smart shacks with solar charging for mobile phones (Stellenbosh, South Africa)
	– Resilience of the electricity grid (Maryland, Pennsylvania)
Water	– Smart metering in households (Washington, DC)
	– Flood management through simulation software (Paris, France; London, United Kingdom; Rotterdam, Netherlands)
	– Control of water levels in canals and rivers (Bangkok, Thailand)
	– Study of impacts of sewer overflow due to storm water (Philadelphia, Pennsylvania)
	– Reduction of water leaks (Aquamatix; Leesburg, Virginia)
Transport	– Smart card/integrated fare collection service (Paris, France)
	– Bicycle sharing (Lyon, France)
	– Free-service car sharing (Paris, France)
	– Online platform for car sharing (France)
	– Smart parking system (San Francisco, California)
	– Electronic congestion toll (Singapore)
	– Smart taxi service (Uber)
	– Mapping informal public transport routes (Nairobi, Kenya)
	– Maintenance of bridge conditions (New York City)
	– Traffic management centre (including forecast and distribution)
	– Emergency services
	– Spatial flows

Table 2.4. **Main types of ICT application in cities** (*continued*)

Sector	Main smart city initiatives in the world
Solid waste	– Sensors in trash to reduce waste consumption (Barcelona, Spain) – Smart bins (Groningen, Netherlands) – Improvement in the solid waste collection system (Maputo, Mozambique) – Smart optical sorters – Automated waste collection system (Singapore) – Radio frequency identification swipe card (Korea) – Environmental reporting (London, United Kingdom)
Land use	– GIS mapping – Cadastre improvement (Mexico)
Governance	– Increase efficiency of social services (New York City) – Open Data (New York City; Chicago, Illinois)
Others	– Earthquake detection (Japan) – Early warning systems (Rio de Janeiro, Brazil; Austin, Texas) – Resilience through safe banking (Nairobi, Kenya) – Prediction of medical needs in case of disaster (United States) – Better identification of citizens in need of support in case of disaster (New York City) – Crowdsourcing post-disaster recovery (New York City) – E-learning – Electronic delivery to citizens – Video crime monitoring

Source: OECD (2016b), *Green Growth in Bandung, Indonesia*, http://dx.doi.org/10.1787/9789264264113-en.

Conclusion

This chapter demonstrated that numerous opportunities exist for Southeast Asian cities to ensure a sustained growth not only for the short but the long term as well. An important message to stress is the need to ensure policy complementarities and synergies across the various areas of opportunity to maximise the green growth objectives and outcomes for the benefit of different stakeholders, including residents, city and national governments. Cities are well positioned to realise these complementarities and synergies. Table 2.5 summarises the main policy assessments and recommendations to the six policy areas of green growth opportunities in Southeast Asian cities.

Table 2.5. **Main policy assessments and recommendations**

Policy areas	Strengths observed in Southeast Asia	Issues encountered in Southeast Asia	Recommendations
Land use and transport	– The needed urban institutions and legal frameworks are present in Southeast Asian cities	– Weak implementation of spatial plans and uncontrolled urban sprawl – Low investments in public transport and high levels of private motor vehicle use	– Promote integrated land use and transport (transit-oriented development) – Invest in quality and low-carbon infrastructure for long-term growth - Improve existing public transport for integration into improved transport system – Promote mixed land-use development
Housing and buildings	– Increase in eco-friendly buildings and the rise in organisations supporting green certification and resource efficiency	– Housing backlog and low investment in social housing	– Localities should set green standards and promote green building codes – Encourage building energy audit and labelling – Promote retrofitting of old buildings to be resource efficient – Provide support to improve housing conditions and energy efficiency, especially for low-income households – Develop the skills base to deliver on green buildings
Energy	– Regional and national efforts to decarbonise and increase renewable energy – Falling prices of renewable energy	– Rapid increase in energy consumption per capita – Not all households have access to energy – Fossil fuel subsidies - High reliance on fossil fuel for energy supply - Low levels of renewable energy	– Promote research on the feasibility of different renewable energy options – Promote energy-efficient equipment and appliances – Carbon pricing and removal of fuel subsidies
Water	– Increasing efforts to reduce non-revenue water	– Low tariffs – Low coverage of standardised water supply infrastructure – Low wastewater treatment rates – High underground water exploitation – Fragmentation of responsibilities	– Introduce fees for wastewater treatment and invest in treatment facilities – Proper fee charging reflecting the scarcity value of water with social considerations – Build internal capacity to reduce non-revenue water – Promote a comprehensive approach to water security (supply, sanitation, floods)
Solid waste management	– National laws and local ordinances on environmental sanitation	– Low user fees – Low rates of recycling – Need to enhance waste collection service	– Promote at source waste segregation by providing households with the needed disposal tools – Generate energy from waste with emission control facilities – Awareness campaigns
Green industries and services	– Strong recognition to green industries	– High greenhouse gas emissions – Breach of regulations – High pollution – Lack of control over small industries and small and medium-sized enterprises	– Green procurement to encourage local production – Development of skills and capacity required by the industry – Frequent expert supervision and enforcement of standards – Establish eco-industrial parks – Intensify public awareness and education campaigns for green labelling

Note

1. Since 2004, all building projects that receive financial assistance from the city, are part of a planned development or located on the Chicago waterway system or near Lake Michigan should have a green roof (Berkshire, 2015). More information is available at: https://www.cityofchicago.org/dam/city/depts/zlup/Sustainable_Development/Publications/GreenMatrix2011DHED.pdf (accessed 24 October 2014).

References

3GF (2013), "Financing urban water leakage solutions: Why do we not see more performance-based contracts in the water sector", http://3gf.dk/en/events/3gf-2013/partnerships/solving-urban-water-leakage-through-performance-based-contracts (accessed 24 August 2016).

ADB (2015), *Women in the Workforce: An Unmet Potential in Asia and Pacific*, Asian Development Bank, Mandaluyong City, Philippines, https://www.adb.org/sites/default/files/publication/158480/women-workforce-unmet-potential.pdf.

ADB (2010), *The Issues and Challenges of Reducing Non-revenue Water*, Asian Development Bank, Manila, Philippines, www.adb.org/sites/default/files/publication/27473/reducing-nonrevenue-water.pdf.

African Development Bank, OECD, United Nations and World Bank (2013), "A toolkit of policy options to support inclusive green growth", Submission to the G20 Development Working Group by the AfDB, the OECD, the UN and the World Bank, www.oecd.org/greengrowth/toolkit.pdf (accessed 4 November 2016).

Albino, V., L. Fraccascia and T. Savino (2015), "Industrial symbiosis for a sustainable city: Technical, economical and organizational issues", *Procedia Engineering*, Vol. 118, pp. 950-957, http://dx.doi.org/10.1016/j.proeng.2015.08.536.

Amsterdam Roundtable Foundation and McKinsey & Company (2014), "Evolution: Electric vehicles in Europe: Gearing up for a new phase?", Amsterdam Roundtable Foundation, Netherlands, www.mckinsey.com/~/media/McKinsey%20Offices/Netherlands/Latest%20thinking/PDFs/Electric-Vehicle-Report-EN_AS%20FINAL.ashx.

APEC (2013), "APEC building codes, regulations, and standards: Minimum, mandatory, and green", Asia-Pacific Economic Cooperation, Singapore, http://publications.apec.org/publication-detail.php?pub_id=1442.

Attia, S. (2014), "The usability of green building rating systems in hot arid climates", in: *ASHRAE Energy & Indoor Environment for Hot Climates*, http://hdl.handle.net/2268/164015.

Bartlett, S., D. Mitlin and D. Satterthwaite (2012), "Urban inequalities", Global Thematic Consultation.

Berkshire (2015), Chicago green roof initiative. http://www.gisclimat.fr/sites/default/files/MBerkshire.pdf.

Canales-Trujillo, N., V.X.H. Vu and S. Whitley (2015), "Mapping current incentives and investment in Viet Nam's water and sanitation sector: Informing private climate finance", Overseas Development Institute, London.

Cat Ba langur (2016), Community Based Conservation Project. http://www.catbalangur.org/Community.htm.

Chertow, M.R. (2000), "Industrial symbiosis: Literature and taxonomy", *Annual Review of Energy and the Environment*, Vol. 25, pp. 313-337, http://dx.doi.org/10.1146/annurev.energy.25.1.313.

City of Chicago (2016), Chicago Green roofs, https://www.cityofchicago.org/city/en/depts/dcd/supp_info/chicago_green_roofs.html.

City of Kitakyushu (2012), "Background paper on the City of Kitakyushu – OECD Green Cities Programme", internal document, City of Kitakyushu, Japan.

Corfee-Morlot, J. et al. (2012), "Towards a green investment policy framework: The case of low-carbon, climate-resilient infrastructure", *OECD Environment Working Papers*, No. 48, OECD Publishing, Paris http://dx.doi.org/10.1787/5k8zth7s6s6d-en.

Deltares – Taskforce Subsidence (2013), "Sinking cities: An integrated approach towards solutions", Deltares, Delft/Utrecht, Netherlands, https://www.deltares.nl/app/uploads/2015/09/Sinking-cities.pdf (accessed 25 September 2016).

Desrochers, P. (2001), "Cities and industrial symbiosis: Some historical perspectives and policy implications", *Journal of Industrial Ecology*, Vol. 5/4, pp. 29-44, http://dx.doi.org/10.1162/10881980160084024.

EMBARQ (2013), "Financing needs for sustainable transport systems for the 21st century", background paper presented at the 7th Regional Environmentally Sustainable Transport Forum in Asia, 23-25 April, Bali, Indonesia.

Ericsson (2015), "South East Asia and Oceania", Ericsson Mobility Report, Ericsson, Stockholm, https://www.ericsson.com/res/docs/2015/mobility-report/emr-nov-2015-regional-report-south-east-asia-and-oceania.pdf.

European Commission (2013), *Building a Green Infrastructure for Europe*, European Union, http://dx.doi.org/10.2779/54125.

EU Water Initiative (2012), *Pricing Water Resources to Finance their Sustainable Management*, Stockholm.

Famiglietti, J.S. ad M. Rodell (2013), "Water in the balance", *Science*, Vol. 340/6138, pp. 1 300-1 301, http://dx.doi.org/10.1126/science.1236460.

Gartner, T. and K. DiFrancesco (2015), "From gray to green: Investing in natural infrastructure to address water, food and energy challenges", World Resources Institute blog, www.wri.org/blog/2015/08/gray-green-investing-natural-infrastructure-address-water-food-and-energy-challenges (accessed 21 August 2016).

Give2Asia (2016), "Disaster preparedness and resiliency: Indonesia", webpage, www.give2asia.org/disaster-preparedness-and-resilience-indonesia (accessed 24 February 2016).

Global Cool Cities Alliance (n.d.), Global Cool Cities Alliance website, www.globalcoolcities.org.

Goujon, A. and K.C. Samir (2008), "The past and future of human capital in South-East Asia: From 1970 to 2030", *Asian Population Studies*, Vol. 4/1, pp. 31-56, http://dx.doi.org/10.1080/17441730801966428.

Government of Japan (2015), *G7 Ise-Shima Principles for Promoting Quality Infrastructure Investment*, www.mofa.go.jp/files/000160272.pdf (accessed 2 October 2016).

Green Power (2012), "Don't delay on waste charging! – Learning from the successful case of Taipei", webpage, www.greenpower.org.hk/html/eng/2012_2.shtml (accessed 25 August 2016).

GRC (2011), Disaster Risk Reduction in South East Asia; Analysing hazards, preventing disasters and reinforcing resilience http://www.preventionweb.net/files/globalplatform/entry_bg_paper~grc2011drrinsoutheastasia.pdf.

GTCK (2013), "Eco-energy town, energy self-reliant city and green city", Green Technology Center Korea, Seoul, www.gtck.re.kr/frt/center/en/tech/green_focus.do?pageMode=View&nttId=3697&nowNum=4 (accessed 1 August 2016).

IBM (2013), "How to reinvent a city: Mayors' lessons from the Smarter Cities Challenge", *IBM Smarter Cities White Paper*, IBM Corporation, Armonk, New York, https://smartercitieschallenge.org/assets/documents/IBM-SCC-How-to-Reinvent-a-City-January-2013.pdf (accessed 1 October 2016).

IEA (2016), *Energy Technology Perspectives 2016*, OECD Publishing, Paris, http://dx.doi.org/10.1787/energy_tech-2016-en.

IEA (2015), *Fossil Fuel Subsidy Database*, www.worldenergyoutlook.org/resources/energysubsidies/fossilfuelsubsidydatabase.

IEA (2009), *Cities, Towns and Renewable Energy: Yes In My Front Yard*, OECD Publishing, Paris, http://dx.doi.org/10.1787/9789264076884-en.

IISD (2013), "Kalundborg", webpage, International Institute for Sustainable Development, https://www.iisd.org/business/viewcasestudy.aspx?id=77, (accessed 30 September 2013).

ILO (2015), "Asia Pacific labour market update", ILO Regional Office for Asia and the Pacific, International Labour Organization, Geneva, www.ilo.org/wcmsp5/groups/public/---asia/---ro-bangkok/documents/publication/wcms_410962.pdf (accessed 30 September 2016).

ILO (2011), "Greening the global economy: The skills challenge", *Skills for Employment Policy Brief*, International Labour Organization, Geneva, www.ilo.org/wcmsp5/groups/public/---ed_emp/---ifp_skills/documents/publication/wcms_164630.pdf.

Institute for Sensible Transport (2016), "Emerging transport technologies: Assessing impacts and implications for the city of Melbourne", City of Melbourne, www.melbourne.vic.gov.au/sitecollectiondocuments/emerging-transport-technologies-report.pdf (accessed 2 October 2016).

IPP (2015), "Policy coherence for green innovation", The Innovation Policy Platform, https://innovationpolicyplatform.org/content/policy-coherence-green-innovation (accessed 17 August 2016).

K-water Institute and World Water Council (2015), "Water and green growth: Beyond the theory for sustainable future", Volume 1, K-water Institute and World Water Council, Daejeon, Korea and Marseille France, www.worldwatercouncil.org/fileadmin/world_water_council/documents/publications/forum_documents/Water_and_Green_Growth_vol_1.pdf (accessed 4 November 2016).

Kwang, T.W. (2015), "Bandung's smart city initiatives", www.enterpriseinnovation.net/article/bandungs-smart-city-initiatives-246675038 (accessed 1 October 2016).

Lah (2012), The Dilemma of Cheonggyecheon Restoration in Seoul. http://prospernet.ias.unu.edu/wp-content/uploads/2012/09/SPC-learning-case-2_final.pdf.

Liem, C. (2015), "The rise of the sharing economy in Indonesia", blog, Bruegel, 22 December, http://bruegel.org/2015/12/the-rise-of-the-sharing-economy-in-indonesia (accessed 1 October 2016).

Manila Water (2015), Letter from Manila Water Company, http://www.manilawater.com/ir/Disclosures/ltr.pse.sec.biwci.tariff.adjustment.14december2015.pdf.

Margat, J. and J. van der Gun (2013) *Groundwater around the World: A Geographic Synopsis*, CRCPress/Balkema, Taylor and Francis, London.

Matsumoto, T. and L. Daudey (2014), "Urban green growth in dynamic Asia: A conceptual framework", *OECD Regional Development Working Papers*, No. 2014/12, OECD Publishing, Paris, http://dx.doi.org/10.1787/5js7svlw8m0x-en.

Merk, O. et al. (2012), "Financing green urban infrastructure", *OECD Regional Development Working Papers*, Vol. 2012/10, OECD Publishing, Paris, http://dx.doi.org/10.1787/5k92p0c6j6r0-en.

Metropolitan Waterworks Authority (n.d.), Water Tariffs. http://www.mwa.co.th/ewtadmin/ewt/mwa_internet_eng/ewt_news.php?nid=309 (accessed 7 November 2016).

McIntosh, A.C. (2014), *Urban Water Supply and Sanitation in Southeast Asia: A Guide to Good Practice*, Asian Development Bank, Manila, Philippines, https://www.adb.org/sites/default/files/publication/42583/urban-water-supply-sanitation-southeast-asia.pdf.

NEA (2016), "Waste statistics and overall recycling", National Environment Agency, www.nea.gov.sg/energy-waste/waste-management/waste-statistics-and-overall-recycling (accessed 2 August 2016).

OECD (forthcoming a), *Green Growth in Hai Phong, Viet Nam*, OECD Publishing, Paris, forthcoming.

OECD (forthcoming b), *Green Growth in Cebu, Philippines*, OECD Publishing, Paris, forthcoming.OECD (2016a), *Economic Outlook for Southeast Asia, China and India 2016: Enhancing Regional Ties*, OECD Publishing, Paris, http://dx.doi.org/10.1787/saeo-2016-en.

OECD (2016b), *Green Growth in Bandung, Indonesia*, OECD Publishing, Paris, http://dx.doi.org/10.1787/9789264264113-en.

OECD (2016c), *Green Growth in Cebu, the Philippines*, OECD Publishing, Paris, forthcoming.

OECD (2016d), *Water Governance in Cities*, OECD Publishing, Paris, http://dx.doi.org/10.1787/9789264251090-en.

OECD (2015a), *All on Board: Making Inclusive Growth Happen*, OECD Publishing, Paris, http://dx.doi.org/10.1787/9789264218512-en.

OECD (2015b), *Data-Driven Innovation: Big Data for Growth and Well-Being*, OECD Publishing, Paris, http://dx.doi.org/10.1787/9789264229358-en.

OECD (2015c), *Drying Wells, Rising Stakes: Towards Sustainable Agricultural Groundwater Use*, OECD Publishing, Paris, http://dx.doi.org/10.1787/9789264238701-en.

OECD (2015d), *Policy Guidance for Investment in Clean Energy Infrastructure: Expanding Access to Clean Energy for Green Growth and Development*, OECD Publishing, Paris, http://dx.doi.org/10.1787/9789264212664-en.

OECD (2015e), *Towards Green Growth?: Tracking Progress*, OECD Publishing, Paris, http://dx.doi.org/10.1787/9789264234437-en.

OECD (2015f), *Water and Cities: Ensuring Sustainable Futures*, OECD Publishing, Paris, http://dx.doi.org/10.1787/9789264230149-en.

OECD (2015g), *Green Growth in Bangkok, Thailand*, OECD Publishing, Paris, http://dx.doi.org/10.1787/9789264237087-en.

OECD (2014a), "Cities and climate change: Policy perspectives: National governments enabling local action", OECD, Paris, https://www.oecd.org/env/cc/Cities-and-climate-change-2014-Policy-Perspectives-Final-web.pdf.

OECD (2014b), *Green Growth Indicators 2014*, OECD Publishing, Paris, http://dx.doi.org/10.1787/9789264202030-en.

OECD (2013a), "Costs and distributional impacts of inaction", in: *Water Security for Better Lives*, OECD Publishing, Paris, http://dx.doi.org/10.1787/9789264202405-10-en.

OECD (2013b), "Opening roundtable: Building the future of our cities, bridging national and local policies", Fifth OECD Roundtable of Mayors and Ministers, Sessions at a glance, OECD, www.oecd.org/urban/roundtable/Sessions-at-a-glance.pdf.

OECD (2013c), *Green Growth in Cities*, OECD Publishing, Paris, http://dx.doi.org/10.1787/9789264195325-en.

OECD (2013d), *Green Growth in Kitakyushu, Japan*, OECD Publishing, Paris, http://dx.doi.org/10.1787/9789264195134-en.

OECD (2013e), *Putting Green Growth at the Heart of Development*, OECD Publishing, Paris, http://dx.doi.org/10.1787/9789264181144-4-en.

OECD (2012), "Policy instruments for sustainable materials management", in: *Sustainable Materials Management: Making Better Use of Resources*, OECD Publishing, Paris, http://dx.doi.org/10.1787/9789264174269-7-en.

OECD (2011a), *Fostering Innovation for Green Growth*, OECD Publishing, Paris, http://dx.doi.org/10.1787/9789264119925-en.

OECD (2011b), *Greening Household Behaviour: The Role of Public Policy*, OECD Publishing, Paris, http://dx.doi.org/10.1787/9789264096875-en.

OECD, (2011c) OECD Sustainable Manufacturing Toolkit; Seven Steps To Environmental Excellence. https://www.oecd.org/sti/inno/48101937.pdf.

OECD (2010a), *Cities and Climate Change*, OECD Publishing, Paris, http://dx.doi.org/10.1787/9789264091375-en.

OECD (2010b), *Eco-Innovation in Industry: Enabling Green Growth*, OECD Publishing, Paris, http://dx.doi.org/10.1787/9789264077225-en.

OECD (2009), *How Regions Grow: Trends and Analysis*, OECD Publishing, Paris, http://dx.doi.org/10.1787/9789264039469-en.

OECD (2004), Economic Aspects of Extended Producer Responsibility, OECD Publishing, Paris, http://dx.doi.org/10.1787/9789264105270-en.

OECD/IEA (2015), *Southeast Asia Energy Outlook 2015*, OECD/IEA, Paris, https://www.iea.org/publications/freepublications/publication/weo2015_southeastasia.pdf.

PT Aetra Air Jakarta (Aetra) (2012), "Info tariff Aetra", http://aat.co.id/en/rates-information.

Ranjah, S. (2016), "Green infrastructure: Planning for sustainable and resilient urban environment", Brief for GSDR, 2016 update, https://sustainabledevelopment.un.org/content/documents/95599_Ranjha_Green%20infrastructure_planning%20for%20sustainable%20and%20resilient%20urban%20environment.pdf (accessed 22 August 2016).

Rao, M. (2008), "Regional report: South East Asia", *Global Information Society Watch*, pp. 72-75, http://www.giswatch.org/en/2008 (accessed 19 August 2016).

Schrock, G. (2009), "Career ladders and training gaps in CCAP workforce impact areas: Energy efficiency, landscape/horticulture, and recycling/reuse", report to the Chicago Climate Action Plan Workforce Advisory Committee, University of Illinois-Chicago, Center for Urban Economic Development.

Schrock, G. and E. Sundquist (2009), "Potential workforce impacts of the Chicago Climate Action Plan (CCAP): Quantitative and qualitative assessments", report to the Chicago Climate Action Plan Workforce Advisory Committee, UIC Center for Urban Economic Development, Chicago, Illinois.

SF Environment (2016), "San Francisco sets North American record for recycling & composting with 80 percent diversion rate", San Francisco Department of the Environment, http://sfenvironment.org/news/update/san-francisco-sets-north-american-record-for-recycling-composting-with-80-percent-diversion-rate (accessed 2 August 2016).

Sugar, L. et al. (2013), "Synergies between climate change adaptation and mitigation in development: Case studies of Amman, Jakarta, and Dar es Salaam", *International Journal of Climate Change Strategies and Management*, Vol. 5/1, pp. 95-111, http://dx.doi.org/10.1108/17568691311299381.

Taniguchi, M., W.C. Burnett and G.D. Ness (2008), "Integrated research on subsurface environments in Asian urban areas", *Science of the Total Environment*, Vol. 404/2, pp. 377-392, http://dx.doi.org/10.1016/j.scitotenv.2008.04.033.

UN HABITAT (2010), *The State of Asian Cities 2010/11*, United Nations Human Settlements Programme, Fukuoka, Japan, http://mirror.unhabitat.org/pmss/getElectronicVersion.aspx?nr=3078&alt=1.

UNEP (2014), *Green Infrastructure Guide for Water Management: Ecosystem-based Management Approaches for Water-related Infrastructure Projects*, United Nations Environment Programme, http://www.unepdhi.org/-/media/microsite_unepdhi/publications/documents/unep/web-unep-dhigroup-green-infrastructure-guide-en-20140814.pdf

UNESCO (1984), *Guidebook to Studies of Land Subsidence Due to Ground-water Withdrawal*, Poland, J.F. (ed.), United Nations Educational, Scientific and Cultural Organization, Paris, http://unesdoc.unesco.org/images/0006/000651/065167eo.pdf.

UNIDO (2011), "Green Idustry Initiative for Sustainable Industrial Development", United Nations Industrial Development Organization, Vienna, October, www.greenindustryplatform.org/wp-content/uploads/2013/05/Green-Industry-Initiative-for-Sustainable-Industrial-Development.pdf.

UNISDR (2004), "Disaster risk reduction tools and methods for climate change adaptation", Inter-Agency Task Force on Climate Change and Disaster Risk Reduction, www.unisdr.org/files/5654_DRRtoolsCCAUNFCC.pdf (accessed 21 August 2016).

United States Department of Energy (2012), "Green building codes", webpage, https://www.energycodes.gov/development/green/codes (accessed 23 August 2016).

US EPA (2016), "What is green infrastructure?", webpage, https://www.epa.gov/green-infrastructure/what-green-infrastructure (accessed 22 August 2016).

Yuen, B. and L. Kong (2009), "Climate change and urban planning in Southeast Asia", *Cities and Climate Change*, Vol. 2/3, SAPIENS, https://sapiens.revues.org/881.

Chapter 3.

Governance levers to enable urban green growth in Southeast Asia

This chapter examines governance bottlenecks and opportunities for urban green growth in Southeast Asia. The chapter analyses the following topics: vertical policy co-ordination for urban green growth; metropolitan governance for urban green growth; financing urban green growth; enhancing data collection and production capacities; and mobilising local communities and research capacities.

Key findings

- National governments in Southeast Asia are central decision makers and holders of authority in all green growth opportunity areas. Decentralisation trends in the region since the 1990s, however, have progressively transferred some responsibilities to local governments, which has increased the need for vertical policy co-ordination. Such co-ordination is mostly exercised through national plans and strategies emanating from the national government to be translated at the local level. In practice, however, such co-ordination is not always effective. This is due to lack of policy frameworks at both national and local levels and co-ordinating mechanisms in some sectors. For example, national policy frameworks in the water and solid waste sectors tend to be weak and unclear; in parallel, many cities have not adopted energy master plans and have failed to implement many existing national guidelines. National governments need to recognise the role cities can play in each green growth opportunity area. Regulatory mechanisms should also be coupled with further outreach and capacity-building programmes encouraging a collaborative approach to green growth policy making.
- Many metropolitan areas in Southeast Asia are characterised by a lack of formal and informal forms of horizontal collaboration between local governments, and therefore a lack of metropolitan planning for green growth, despite critical needs for co-ordination in many opportunity areas. Such co-ordination needs have been exacerbated by decentralisation processes and the relative withdrawal of national governments from local affairs. Metropolitan forms of governance should be built with the mission to foster green growth. The Iskandar Malaysia Regional Development Authority and the Metro Cebu Development Co-ordinating Board (MCDCB) provide two different types of inspiration, but their impact could be further enhanced. The OECD's functional urban areas (FUA) could be applied to Southeast Asian countries in order to seek the most appropriate scale of action. It is also critical that metropolitan forms of governance encourage the adoption or "mainstreaming" of metropolitan-wide development and green growth plans into the constituting local governments' annual planning and budgeting cycle and are supported by national governments.
- Financing urban green growth is one of the main critical green growth implementation levers. Increases in revenues are observed in many Southeast Asian cities, mainly owing to significant increases in the share of own-source revenues following decentralisation reforms. Nonetheless, such increases have not kept pace with the needs and new functions of local governments in Southeast Asia. Many urban governments still depend to a very large extent on fiscal transfers. In Indonesia, the General Allocation Fund and the Special Allocation Fund accounted for 51% and 5%, respectively, of regencies' and cities' revenues in 2015. In this regard, central governments could earmark special funds for green growth-related activities. Local governments, in parallel should improve the efficiency of tax collection and raise revenues from fees and charges. Fees and charges account for only 2% of the Bangkok Metropolitan Administration's total revenues, 6% in all of Metro Cebu's local government units combined and 0.5% in Hai Phong, against 14.9% for subnational governments on average in the OECD area. Opportunities lie in green growth sectors, such as wastewater treatment fees. Conditions for private investment should also be enhanced, in particular public-private partnerships (PPP). National governments should design capacity-building and technical assistance programmes to help subnational governments design PPPs. The cost recovery in green growth sectors must also be raised to attract private investors.

Key findings *(continued)*

- In parallel, the amounts and effectiveness of environment-related official development finance (ODF) must be increased. Among ODF committed for environmental purposes in ASEAN-5 countries, around 37.2% can be clearly identified as targeting cities in 2002-14, with no significant evolution over time. However, around 40% of such funds were committed to capital cities, while they account for only around 16% of the total urban population. Secondary cities such as Bandung or Cebu only received very small amounts in comparison. This is mainly due to lack of autonomy and capacity of local governments to contract loans from and interact with donors, and poor co-ordination with the national government. ODF projects also tend to be undertaken in silos and not embedded in broader local sustainability plans.
- Achieving green growth is ambitious and the different profile of cities implies different policy needs. A first step for cities in order to invest more efficiently and promote the green growth agenda at all levels of government is to build technical capacities to produce, collect and analyse data, and create results-based monitoring and evaluation systems, so as to identify their specific green growth challenges. Indeed, despite strong evidence for the need to green Southeast Asian cities' growth given in Chapter 1, significant effort remains to be made to produce such data, as even basic statistical information is often missing, and not produced at the metropolitan scale. The issue lies in the lack of resources but also in some cases the lack of technical skills in local governments. In addition, there is a significant lack of time-series data and projections to assess the evolution of cities' performance over time. This report proposes a framework for green growth indicators in Southeast Asian cities. Local governments should build capacities to produce such data for metropolitan areas and make greater use of digital technologies to monitor their performance.
- More emphasis should be placed on mobilising local stakeholders and external partners to foster urban green growth. In particular, the involvement of local communities can be an option to local governments facing under-capacity, in order to govern more efficiently, raise public awareness and tackle poverty. As the cases of Bangkok and Bandung have shown, there are great opportunities in the solid waste management sector. Building capacities to track progress towards green growth and to innovate (e.g. smart city) will also require more efficient involvement of local education and research capacities. Finally, outside the jurisdiction of cities, knowledge-sharing activities amongst cities, between cities and higher levels of government, and between cities and development partners can potentially bring high benefits, if developed as a long-term process.

Enhancing vertical policy co-ordination between local, regional and national governments

Gaps between national, regional and local policy frameworks should be filled

National governments in Southeast Asia are central decision makers and holders of authority. They exert various degrees of influence over the main opportunity areas for urban green growth (transport, land use, energy, solid waste and water management; see Chapter 2), through their financial power (see below for more details), and policy and legal authority. National medium-term and long-term plans, in particular, are powerful instruments employed to guide development in the respective countries. Each of the ASEAN-5 national governments has indeed elaborated general economic and social development plans, and in most cases sectoral plans in the opportunity areas listed above or in similar cross-cutting fields, such as climate change (Table 3.1). Indonesia and Viet Nam are the only ASEAN-5 countries having developed a specific green growth strategy at the national level, although Malaysia's Eleventh Malaysia Plan includes green growth as one of its development pillars. Indonesia's Green Growth Programme is less ambitious and binding than Viet Nam's Green Growth Strategy and National Action Plan (Box 3.1).

Besides, the national governments have kept direct management functions of some urban utilities: in the Bangkok Metropolitan Region, the Metropolitan Electricity, Waterworks, and Rapid Transit Authorities (MEA, MWA and MRTA) are state-owned corporate entities that exert the functions of local governments in their respective areas. Associated ministries exert a planning authority in the capital city. In Metro Manila, the national government is also often directly involved in major urban projects (e.g. Flood Management Master Plan for Metro Manila). In some sectors also, the national government retains significant authority on all cities: many local governments in Southeast Asia in particular are not very active in the energy sector, and their responsibilities are limited to small tasks such as managing street lights.

The 1990s, however, saw greater recognition of the role of cities as drivers of national development (UN HABITAT and UN DESA, 2015). ASEAN-5 countries have undertaken decentralisation processes since the late 1990s or early 2000s – in particular in Indonesia, the Philippines and Thailand – and local governments have progressively obtained responsibilities and some autonomy in the management of their own cities. In Indonesia, the decentralisation process, initiated by the Decentralisation Act 22/1999 and continued under Act 32/2004 and Act No.23/2014 on local governance, transferred both decision making and financial resources for the delivery of basic services, such as the provision of road and wastewater infrastructure, to local governments. As a result, the central government's share in infrastructure investment fell from around 80% to about 35% (Chaudhuri and Taylor, 2013). In the Philippines, the 1991 Local Government Code devolved to local government units[1] (LGUs) the responsibility for delivery of basic services that previously had been the responsibility of the national government, and also considerable discretion over local taxes. It granted LGUs regulatory powers and increased available financial resources (OECD, 2016c). In Thailand, the 1997 Decentralisation Action Plan transferred authority to local governments in six critical areas: 1) infrastructure; 2) quality of life; 3) order and security of communities and society; 4) planning, investment promotion, and commerce and tourism; 5) natural resources and environmental protection; and 6) arts and culture, traditions and local wisdom (Ratanawaraha, 2010).

Table 3.1. **Major national plans in green growth-related sectors in ASEAN-5 countries**

Sector	Indonesia	Malaysia	Philippines	Thailand	Viet Nam
General	– National Long Term and Medium-Term Development Plan (RPJPN 2005-2025, RPJMN 2015-2019)	– Eleventh Malaysia Plan 2016-2020	– Philippines Development Plan 2011-2016	– 11th National Economic and Social Development Plan	– 10th Five-year Plan (2016-20)
Green growth	– Delivering Green Growth in Indonesia (2015) – Green Growth Programme (2013)	–	–	–	– Viet Nam Green Growth Strategy and National Action Plan
Climate change (mitigation and adaptation)	– National Action Plan to Reduce Greenhouse Gas Emissions (2011) – National Action Plan for Climate Change Adaptation (2012)	– National Policy on Climate Change (2009) – Low Carbon Cities Framework and Assessment System (2011)	– National Climate Change Action Plan 2011-2018 – National Disaster Risk Reduction and Management Plan (2011-28)	– Thailand Climate Change Master Plan (2012-50) – National Disaster Prevention and Mitigation Plan (2010-14)	– National Climate Change Strategy (2011) and Action Plan (2012)
Land use	– National Spatial Plan (Rencana Tata Ruang Wilayah Nasional)	– Second National Physical Plan (2010-20)	– National Physical Framework Plan (2016-45)	– National Spatial Development Policy Plan (2007-57)	– Master Plan Orientation for Viet Nam's Urban System Development to 2025 with Vision to 2050
Transport	– Sustainable Urban Transport Programme (NAMASUTRI)	– National Land Public Transport Master Plan (2013)	–	– National Transport Master Plan (2011-20)	– National Railway Master Plan 2020
Energy	– National Energy Master Plan Toward 2050 (RUEN)	– National Energy Efficiency Master Plan (2014)	– Philippines energy sector plans and programmes (2013-30)	– 20-year Energy Efficiency Development Plan (2011-30) – 10-year Alternative Energy Development Plan (2012-21)	– National Master Plan for Power Development (2011-20)
Solid waste	– Solid Waste Management Act 18/2008	– Solid Waste and Public Cleansing Management Act (2007)	–	– National Roadmap of Solid Waste Management Plan (2015-19)	– National Strategy for Integrated Management of Solid Waste until 2025 and Vision Towards 2050
Water	– Presidential Decree 185/2014 on the Acceleration of Drinking Water and Sanitation Provision	–	– Clean Water Act (2004)	–	–
Others	– National Urban Development Strategy and Policy (KSPPN)	– Environmental Quality Act	–	–	– Viet Nam Seaport Master Plan 2020

Sources: OECD (2015b), *Green Growth in Bangkok, Thailand*, http://dx.doi.org/10.1787/9789264237087-en; OECD (2016d), *Green Growth in Hai Phong, Viet Nam*, forthcoming, http://dx.doi.org/10.1787/9789264260207-en; OECD (2016b), *Green Growth in Bandung, Indonesia*, http://dx.doi.org/10.1787/9789264264113-en; OECD (2016c), *Green Growth in Cebu, the Philippines*, forthcoming; OECD (2016e), *Green Growth in Iskandar Malaysia, Malaysia*, forthcoming.

In such decentralisation contexts, national development plans have become important mechanisms that structure development strategies across different government levels and should ensure vertical policy co-ordination. Indeed, the main economic and spatial development plans in some countries possess a legal character and must be translated into regional and local plans by subnational government authorities. In Iskandar Malaysia, for instance, the Comprehensive Development Plan integrates the strategies of the National

Physical Plan and the Johor State Development Plan. In Indonesia, the main components of the National Development Plans (RPJPN 2005-2025 and RPJMN 2015-2019) are translated at lower levels of government into the West Java Province development plans and into each development plan of the five municipalities of the Bandung Metropolitan Area. The same mechanisms are applied in the Philippines, Thailand and Viet Nam.

Box 3.1. **Viet Nam Green Growth Strategy and National Action Plan**

The Viet Nam Green Growth Strategy (VGGS) aims to achieve sustainable economic development by reducing carbon emissions, increasing ability to absorb greenhouse gases (GHG) and enriching natural capital. The strategy outlines short-, medium- and long-term objectives, prioritised for implementation, as well as a vision for 2050. It is anchored in three strategic tasks:

1. Low-carbon growth: the VGGS sets out systematic targets starting from the period 2011-20 through 2030 to 2050 in hopes of reducing the intensity of GHG emissions per unit of GDP (8-10% or double the target with international support) and encourages the use of clean and renewable energy.
2. Greening of production: a "clean industrialisation'' strategy will green existing business and create new ones, adopting environmentally friendly technology, preventing and remediating pollution and investing in natural capital.
3. Greening of lifestyle: the traditional lifestyle is to be combined with modernised yet comfortable, high-quality living standards that are rooted in nature, as experienced in the rural areas, and at the same time in tune within the context of global integration. The focus is on promoting green growth, expanding public transport, and effective waste collection and treatment.

Ten priority programmes and projects were outlined for implementation from 2011-15.

After the VGGS, the Prime Minister's Office launched the National Green Growth Action Plan(GGAP) for 2014-20. The action plan designates 12 actions: 1) formulating institutions to support the implementation of the VGGS; 2) localities formulate local GGAP and implement small-scale green pilot projects; 3) implementing efficient use of energy and reducing GHG emissions in some energy-consuming industrial sectors; 4) implementing efficient and effective use of energy and reducing GHG emissions in the transport sector; 5) changing cultivation techniques to reduce GHG emissions in agriculture, forestry and aquaculture; 6) developing clean and renewable sources of energy; 7) reviewing development strategies, master plans and plans and formulating a programme for restructuring the economy towards green growth; 8) efficient and sustainable use of natural resources and developing green economic sectors; 9) developing sustainable infrastructure; 10) promoting the "Enterprises for Sustainable Development" campaign and improving capacity, as well as developing technical and management services market for green growth; 11) developing green and sustainable urban areas (cities); and 12) promoting a green lifestyle.

Each action is supplemented by 65 activities, of which 23 are listed as priorities. One such activity is an inter-ministerial Co-ordinating Board for Green Growth Strategy, which was established under the National Committee on Climate Change to implement the strategy. Another priority is to formulate local green growth action plans in some provinces and cities.

Sources: Government of Viet Nam (2012), *Viet Nam National Green Growth Strategy for the Period 2011-2020, with a Vision to 2050*, https://www.giz.de/en/downloads/VietNam-GreenGrowth-Strategy.pdf; Government of Viet Nam (2014), *National Action Plan on Green Growth for Period 2014-2020*.

In practice, national development plans have, however, proved to be limited to ensure policy alignment and co-ordination across levels of government. A primary reason lies in the absence of policy frameworks and effective co-ordinating mechanisms in green growth opportunity areas, which have repercussions at the local level. This is particularly an issue in the water sector, which has no clear national policy framework in any of the ASEAN-5 countries (Table 3.1). In the Philippines, for instance, there is no comprehensive policy framework guiding water supply and sanitation, or flood management, at the national level. Responsibilities are shared between the National Economic and Development Authority, the Local Water Utilities Association, the National Water Resources Board, the Department of Environment and Natural Resources, the Department of Health, and the Department of Public Works and Highways, without any official co-ordinating body or strategy. Such a policy gap has repercussions at the local level: in Metro Cebu, the allocation of responsibilities between water districts and the LGUs is sometimes unclear and not efficient, and there is no appointed body for disaster risk reduction in the LGUs, creating a lot of management inconsistencies across jurisdictions. National policy frameworks also tend to be weak in the solid waste sector. In Indonesia, the lack of comprehensive national policies and legal framework for solid waste management makes it difficult for provincial and local governments to establish clear strategies and financial resources to tackle solid waste issues (OECD, 2016b).

Likewise, some local initiatives may be hindered by the lack of policy and legal support at the national level. The Smart City Strategy developed in the Bandung 2015 ICT Master Plan, for example, has no similar counterpart from the national and provincial governments. Smart Cities is one of the five pillars of the National Urban Development Strategy and Policy but is loosely defined as "the capability of a city to utilise human resources, social capital and information and communication technology to support more competitive and sustainable cities in the future". The lack of a specific and detailed strategy for a smart city is an issue to unlock large funds to support smart cities in the whole country, especially because infrastructure-based smart city initiatives (e.g. air pollution monitoring systems, sensors in rivers, operations centres) may be costly. In addition, many smart city projects depend on the quality of national infrastructure systems: for instance, without good broadband connection, Wi-Fi technology and reliable electricity networks, the impact of mobile applications and smart metres cannot be optimised. Similarly, many smart city initiatives are dependent on regulations from the national government: for instance, the introduction of smart electricity metres can only be introduced with a national reform introducing real-time dynamic pricing of energy consumption, instead of the current metering based on installed capacity of supply networks.

Conversely, lack of policy frameworks in green growth opportunity areas at the local level are also observed in Southeast Asia. Many national plans are not translated effectively into local plans, despite of the urgent needs and untapped opportunity. Most city-regional spatial development plans in Asian agglomerations are not formally adopted as legally binding documents and are mainly regarded as "indicative guidelines" (Laquian, 2011). Regional governments also tend to have a weak role in countries such as Indonesia, the Philippines and Thailand. In Indonesia, the national Green Growth Programme has not been translated at the regional and local levels (OECD, 2016b). While the lack of binding character of some national plans may be pointed out, a major reason for such a policy gap partly lies in the absence of recognition by national governments in Southeast Asia of the role cities can play to foster green growth, and prescribing them resources to do so. This particularly happens when the national guidelines are missing, such as in the water sector in the Philippines, but also sometimes in existing guidelines. In Indonesia, the RPJMN 2015-2019 aims to create and increase the development of green cities as a part of climate and disaster security, improve governance in natural resources, reduce greenhouse gas emissions, and increase community resilience to the impacts of climate changes. However, the role to be played by cities and the way different levels of government co-ordinate are not well explained in each sectoral plan in green growth opportunity areas. In Iskandar Malaysia, the translation of strategies from the national level to the local level meets challenges. While the 11th Malaysia Plan places significant emphasis on green growth, there is still a lack of clarity about how it will cascade down to regional and local plans. The plan does not explain how green growth strategies can be implemented at the local level; it is instead envisioned only as a national challenge and lacks any analysis or proposed role for the local dimension of adopting a green growth pathway. In this context, it is difficult for regional and local authorities to understand clearly how to integrate national green growth strategies into their plans and strategies.

Clear national policy frameworks and co-ordinating mechanisms in each green growth-related sector would help to clarify responsibilities, especially for local governments. In parallel, such sectoral and more comprehensive green growth action plans should be developed at the regional and local levels (OECD, 2016b). Korea provides a good example of integrated national and subnational action for smart cities. Following the green growth vision of the national government and the 2006 U-Korea Master Plan, the Ministry of Construction and Transportation and the Ministry of Information and Communication signed a Memorandum of Understanding on Smart City implementation in 2008 to collaborate and define the role of government agencies in this programme. The national government then supported industries through the establishment of the Smart City Law and the standardisation of relevant technologies, and co-ordinated with several targeted cities (e.g. Dongtan, Songdo) to implement the vision. Municipalities, in particular, were given a critical role of managing smart city assets and preparing local regulations. Collaboration with public land developers and private companies was also essential to the projects (Korea Telecom, 2015).

In Southeast Asia, the central government in Viet Nam recognises the roles that cities can play in encouraging green growth. Among the 12 measures laid out by the National Action Plan on Green Growth for the period 2014-20, Action 11 (to develop green and sustainable urban areas) specifically targets urban actions. In addition, Action 2 requests some provinces and cities to formulate a local green growth action plan, implement small-scale green pilot projects and to synthesise and disseminate best practices, with the Ministry of Planning and Investment as a co-ordinating agency. Based on these national initiatives, Hai Phong adopted the Green Growth Strategy Action Plan (2014) and the Green Growth Promotion Plan (2015), with the support of the city of Kitakyushu, Japan (OECD, 2016d). The federal government of Malaysia has also undertaken initiatives to promote the role of cities, in particular through the Low Carbon Cities Framework, which provides a framework to achieve sustainable development at the city level (UTM Low Carbon Asia Research Centre, 2013). Both initiatives in Viet Nam and Malaysia would, however, need enhanced vertical co-ordination, at the image of Korea's smart cities. Co-ordinating regulations and buildings capacities at the local level should complement planning efforts, in particular.

Outreach, collaboration and capacity building must complement plans and strategies

The existence of a national policy framework and co-ordination mechanism is not sufficient per se to ensure effective implementation. There seems to be an over-reliance on statutory frameworks and guidelines, instead of outreach and capacity building to local governments. This is particularly an issue in decentralisation contexts. There is no sufficient financial support and capacity-building programme to transfer further resources and skills from the national to the subnational levels. In Indonesia, local governments have been transferred extensive responsibilities but have not gained sufficient financial autonomy and resources or the necessary skills to undertake their assigned tasks, which leads to disparity across cities and regions (Tarigan et al., 2015). The same issue has been observed in Thailand (OECD, 2015b). One study has shown that the benefits of decentralisation on electricity, water infrastructure quality and local economic governance in Indonesia are not clearly observed (Patunru and Rahman, 2014).[2] In the Philippines, the mandate of cities and municipalities to prepare, implement and enforce comprehensive land-use plans resides in the Constitution and provisions of the 1991 Local Government Code. The LGUs are required to complete comprehensive land-use plans and update them every six years. In Metro Cebu, some LGUs have stated that the national guidelines are overly technical for local government application. In addition, there is no binding mechanism to force the LGUs to implement the guidelines. As a consequence, there is not one completed, updated comprehensive land-use plan in Metro Cebu, despite the legislative requirement and the guidelines created by Region VII.

As local authorities are relatively autonomous in the way they choose to implement national, state or regional development strategies in Malaysia and Thailand, for instance, collaborative approaches are more likely to succeed. Strong linkages among completed local and regional plans, and the nationally prepared plans should be ensured. This could either be done through an outright requirement for alignment in legislation, coupled with an outreach and capacity-building programme to make it happen, or through an instrument such as the "regional context statement" as present in British Columbia, Canada (Box 3.2). The case of Morocco is also inspiring: the National Agency for the Development of Renewable Energy and Energy Efficiency launched the Jiha Tinou pilot programme in Morocco (2012-14), with the long-term goal of reducing energy dependence and increasing the use of renewable energy at the subnational level to contribute to the national energy targets for 2020 (ADEREE, 2012). The national government launched the "advanced regionalization" process in parallel with "decentralization reinforcement". Such initiatives have provided a legal framework for transferring resources authority to subnational levels of government, thus allowing regions/territories to have ownership of their renewable energy and energy efficiency development initiatives with the support of the national government (Green Growth Best Practice, n.d.). The French Regional Climate-Air-Energy Plan (Schéma Régional du Climat, de l'Air et de l'Energie), created under the Grenelle II Law (passed in 2012) for the purpose of guiding climate and energy policy in the 26 French regions through to 2050, also offers a good example of integrated and flexible co-ordination across levels of government (Green Growth Best Practice, n.d.). Training local government staff and improving e-government tools are also potential instruments for greater vertical co-ordination for urban green growth. Such need for outreach and collaboration not only applies to plans and policies but also to urban project management. The city of Bandung, for instance, which is currently developing a range of urban projects including PPP projects where the involvement of the national government will be critical, should maintain constant contact with relevant national agencies and ministries to ensure that national regulations will not be an obstacle to their initiatives.

Box 3.2. British Columbia's regional context statement

In British Columbia, Canada, prior to 1983, all local plans had to be consistent and aligned with regional plans. In 1996, new legislation softened the regional role and strengthened that of municipal governments in relation to the regional growth management plan. The legislation instituted what is called a "regional context statement", which essentially is a linking document housed in the municipal official community plan, that demonstrates how the official community plan is aligned with, and supports, the regional growth strategy, or how it will be made more consistent over time. The regional context statement is adopted as part of the official community plan by the municipality and must be submitted to the regional district Board of Directors for acceptance. It is an agreement. There is a dispute resolution process prescribed if the two parties are unable to agree. The regional context statement must be submitted to the regional district within two years of a new regional growth strategy being adopted, and must be renewed every five years. However, there is no recourse described in the legislation if the regional context statement is not submitted.

Metro Vancouver, as the largest regional district in the province of British Columbia, focuses on collaboration, early and frequent communication, moral suasion, and ensuring a good value proposition in its regional planning function and relationship with member municipalities. As of January 2016, four and half years after the adoption of the most recent regional growth strategy, 18 out of 20 regional context statements have been successfully completed and accepted.

Metro Vancouver's Board of Directors is made up of elected officials from all member municipalities – it is a federation, and as such, Metro Vancouver staff are the stewards of the regional vision created by that federation.

Source: City of Vancouver (2016), "Regional Context Statement", http://vancouver.ca/home-property-development/regional-context-statement.aspx.

The need for metropolitan green growth policies

Urban green growth challenges extend far beyond the jurisdiction of core cities, but in many cases policies remain spatially secluded

Urbanisation and economic development trends in Southeast Asia typically occur in the wider metropolitan areas, not only in the core cities. As shown in Figure 1.2, urbanisation has extended the built-up areas further into local government units adjacent to the core city of metropolitan areas. This means that urbanisation is often occurring beyond the reach of a city's governance, service provision and planning mandate, including land-use planning (UN HABITAT and UN DESA, 2015). In addition, in many metropolitan areas, faster population growth rates are observed in municipalities and urban areas surrounding the core city: in the Bangkok Metropolitan Region, Samut Prakan grew at an average annual rate of 10.9% between 1990 and 2015, against only 1.8% in Bangkok City (see Table 1.1). In Metro Cebu, the municipalities of Consolacion, Cordoba and Liloan have grown at a respective average annual rate of 5.1%, 3.2% and 4.1% between 2000 and 2015, while Cebu City has grown at an average annual rate of 1.7% (JICA and MCDCB, 2015).

The continuity of the urban space across local jurisdictions has generated urban development issues that extend beyond the administrative borders of core cities into the wider metropolitan areas. In Iskandar Malaysia, for instance, commuting flows link

Johor Bahru to surrounding urban centres such as Nusajaya, Senai-Skudai, Pasir Gudang and Tanjung Pelepas. Such commuting flows are increasing fast as the metropolitan area grows: the number of daily commuters between Nusajaya and Johor Bahru increased from 26 000 to 300 000 between 2007 and 2015, and is set to reach 447 000 in 2020. Large daily commuting flows also exist and are increasing between Iskandar Malaysia and Singapore, creating common transport management issues across national borders. These fast-increasing commuting flows have resulted in heavy congestion and risks in terms of air pollution, GHG emissions and loss of productivity. Generally speaking, transport management, land-use, solid waste management and water resources management (including flood risks) are typical urban issues affected by urbanisation and economic growth and which extend beyond the historic boundaries of core cities in Southeast Asia.

Meanwhile, co-ordination between local governments in Southeast Asian metropolitan areas has been a major challenge, aggravating the above-mentioned issues. Many metropolitan areas are characterised by a lack of formal and informal forms of horizontal collaboration between local governments, and therefore a lack of metropolitan planning for green growth. Bangkok City, for instance, has adopted an advanced set of plans to foster green growth, such as the BMA Action Plan on Global Warming Mitigation (2007-12), the Bangkok Master Plan on Climate Change (2013-23), and other sectoral plans, but such plans have rarely been created in adjacent provinces. Municipal mergers to legally capture the urban catchment area beyond the city limits is a time-consuming procedure and most often politically contested by the territorial unit whose land is being infringed upon. Lack of data on rapidly expanding developments in peri-urban areas makes any kind of intervention even more difficult (UN HABITAT and UN DESA, 2015).

Decentralisation reforms have also reinforced the need for horizontal co-operation, due to the relative withdrawal of the national government from local affairs. In Indonesia, decentralisation reforms have empowered cities but the lack of incentives for horizontal collaboration has had perverse consequences, notably disencouraging local governments to make efforts to talk and govern with their neighbours.[3] In addition, many local government officials lack awareness on the co-ordination needs created by decentralisation reforms and their potential benefits. The parochialism attitude of many local governments has caused a number of problems in services which require cross-border co-operation, including solid waste management and water supply, in many regions in the country (Firman, 2009). The perverse consequences of decentralisation and the lack of incentives for horizontal co-operation are also encountered in the Philippines and Thailand. More specifically, the following examples of co-ordination challenges across local governments in the metropolitan area have been observed from the case studies:

- In Bandung Metropolitan Area (BMA), traffic volumes have expanded by 10-15% annually (City of Bandung, 2014), and contribute to deteriorating average travel times during the week which have increased from 30 to 65 minutes, and more than an hour on weekends. There is no BMA-wide strategy to improve transport systems, including mass transit, to reduce increasing congestion and its externalities in terms of air pollution, GHG emissions and potential losses in productivity. The lack of land-use and transport co-ordination has also led to an origin-destination mismatch reinforcing inefficient mobility patterns (Tarigan et al., 2015). The city of Bandung also lacks appropriate space to dump collected solid waste in sanitary landfills and adapt to the increasing amounts of waste generated and which already exceeds current collection and treatment capacities. At present, the BMA's five municipal areas rely on the same landfill site, which is under great stress and has been repeatedly scheduled to close, most recently in 2015 (IGES and City of Kawasaki, 2015). Negotiations to use vacant lands in the surrounding areas of the BMA have been unsuccessful (Tarigan et al., 2015) and further co-operation is needed. Some current green projects such as the introduction of bio-digesters in Bandung City will also receive waste from the surrounding municipalities and require efficient co-operation on the conveyance system. It also needs to be accepted by all local governments in the region and integrated in their strategies. The landfill project led by the West Java provincial government and a national guideline to promote incineration, for example, do not follow the same strategic orientation as the bio-digester project. Other horizontal challenges affecting the BMA include solid waste management, water supply and flood risk management (OECD, 2016b).

- In the Bangkok Metropolitan Region, a major metropolitan co-ordination issue relates to flood risk management. The failure to contain and minimise the damage from the 2011 floods partly owed to the lack of good metropolitan governance. Most of the runoff came from the northern mountains of the Chao Phraya Basin and the lack of efficient polder and drainage infrastructure in the vicinities of Bangkok City was responsible for damages even in Bangkok City itself. Indeed, although Bangkok City had built massive dikes and drainage tunnels over the past decades, the lack of similar infrastructure in surrounding provinces made it more vulnerable. Other factors of vulnerability of the BMR were urban sprawl and the loss of natural habitats, which is partly due to a lack of co-ordination of land use in the region, and the lack of protection for industries (OECD, 2015b). By protecting one location, policies may simply shift the risk to adjacent locations (an example of "mal-adaptation"), instead of addressing the issue in a lasting, comprehensive manner.
- In Metro Cebu, the bus rapid transit (BRT) is only being designed and implemented in Cebu City. Even though Cebu City is the largest local government unit of the metropolitan area, it would benefit much more from a bus network that reaches out to adjacent LGUs, as many residents commute from these areas to Cebu City, or vice versa. In addition, the current expansion of the metropolitan area towards its outskirts creates increasing demand for public transport in these areas. The BRT system is relatively flexible compared to a metro system, but not building it right from the start and letting adjacent LGUs expand their built-up areas without including BRT will nonetheless create an infrastructure lock-in that will be difficult to circumvent in the future. Similarly, road widths are not being maintained across LGU boundaries, which precludes good, co-ordinated transport (and land-use) planning (OECD, 2016c).

Metropolitan forms of governance can be powerful setups to foster urban green growth and harmonise policies in metropolitan areas

While the need for metropolitan governance is obvious in many Southeast Asian cities, they should first find the appropriate scale for metropolitan actions and build governance systems accordingly. The OECD's functional urban areas (FUA) could be applied to Southeast Asian countries to define metropolitan areas in the country, taking into account population density and commuting between urban areas (OECD, 2012). This would help to identify the most appropriate spatial scale for policy making and implementation. The national government, with the support of provinces and province-level cities, could develop the concept of an FUA and a metropolitan planning framework to build synergies for green growth.

Based on FUAs, metropolitan forms of governance or projects should be built with the mission to foster green growth. By systematising forms of collaboration, joint visions and urban projects, they have the power to tackle the co-ordination challenges mentioned previously and generate high impacts on the economic, environmental and social performance of cities. The benefits of metropolitan thinking have been widely observed in OECD cities (Box 3.3). In France, subnational governments have formulated the Territorial Coherence Scheme (Schéma de cohérence territorial), to ensure a balance between urban renewal and the rural periphery, to preserve the diversity of urban functions and social mix, and to achieve competitive and sustainable development. Such benefits are increasingly acknowledged in Southeast Asia. Different forms of metropolitan governance systems are indeed observable in the five case study cities. In Hai Phong, 53% of the population within the city's jurisdiction is rural. In the case of Bangkok City, however, which comprises more than 8 million inhabitants, the relevance of the administrative limits is still questionable, despite the status of province, since the Bangkok Metropolitan Region – which is not headed by any form of metropolitan government – comprises more than 14 million inhabitants and faces some co-ordination challenges. Currently, there is no form of metropolitan governance in the Bandung Metropolitan Area, but the establishment of a BMA co-ordinating body is currently under discussion and pending approval by presidential decree in 2016. Such a metropolitan body would be the first of its kind outside Jakarta in Indonesia.[4] The objective of this body would be to co-ordinate policies through BMA-wide master plans, but also to facilitate private investment in the region. It would be chaired by the Governor of West Java Province and the Mayor of the City of Bandung would sit as a Vice-Chair (OECD, 2016b).

Box 3.3. The benefits of metropolitan thinking

Well-functioning cities require a combination of a multitude of factors. Some are similar to those that make societies and countries function well, but a large number of factors are specific or at least have a particular relevance for cities. For example, the benefits of adequate governance structures may be particularly high in cities. This is because the very density of opportunities for contact and exchange that makes cities so dynamic and productive also implies that the actions of households and firms, as well as the interactions among different strands of public policy, typically have larger positive or negative spillover effects in cities than in less dense places. In this context, it is especially important that governance structures take the functional realities of metropolitan areas into account. Often, administrative boundaries are based on centuries-old borders that do not correspond – if they ever did – to patterns of human settlement and economic activity. Getting administrative structures right typically allows for better outcomes in most dimensions that make cities function well. These prominently include economic performance. Indeed, the fragmentation of a metropolitan area into a large number of municipalities tends to result in lower levels of productivity: for a given population size, a metropolitan area with twice the number of municipalities is associated with lower productivity of around 6%. This effect is mitigated by almost half by the existence of a governance body at the metropolitan level. Transport planning and land-use planning are also dependent on governance structures, as well as the co-ordination of both processes. In particular, land-use regulations need to find the right balance between protecting existing neighbourhoods and green spaces and allowing new construction. Also, the quality of public transport provision usually increases when services are integrated.

Source: OECD (2015e), *The Metropolitan Century: Understanding Urbanisation and its Consequences*, http://dx.doi.org/10.1787/9789264228733-en.

Two distinct metropolitan forms of governance are found in Iskandar Malaysia (Box 3.4) and in Metro Cebu (Box 3.5). The Iskandar Regional Development Authority (IRDA) was established by the federal government of Malaysia as a statutory body in 2007 and has been appointed as the development authority for the Iskandar Malaysia Economic Region (IMER), within the state of Johor. The IRDA represents a joint and co-ordinated approach between federal, state and local governments. Co-ordination with the five local governments in the IMER is one of the tasks of the IRDA, especially in the implementation of the comprehensive development plans, but the approach is less participatory than the Metro Cebu Development Co-ordinating Board (MCDCB). The MCDCB is a co-ordinating body for metro-wide planning and development that was created in 2011. It is a consortium of the 13 LGUs composing Metro Cebu, regional line agencies of the national government, private sector representatives and civil society organisations. Contrary to the IRDA, Metro Cebu has no official mandate to design metropolitan plans, but is more of an open form of governance involving a wide spectrum of stakeholders. The MCDCB is set to evolve into the Metro Cebu Development Authority (MCDA), pending approval by the National Congress. The main purposes of the creation of the MCDA are: 1) to recognise a more institutional approach to metropolitan and integrated development planning; 2) to foster co-operative relations between and among metropolitan and surrounding cities and towns; 3) to ensure active participation by the private, business and civil society sector; and 4) to implement a national government-approved Metropolitan Cebu Roadmap and other subsequent and related metro-wide roadmaps and plans (OECD, 2016c).

Local governments in Southeast Asia could take some inspiration from the initiatives of the IRDA and the MCDCB. While the process of creating metropolitan co-ordinating bodies may be time-consuming at the beginning, it should yield higher returns in the long run, especially in relation to better management of natural resources and the transport sector because each municipality will be engaged in the amelioration of the metropolitan area as a whole, and will not focus on its own affairs to the detriment of another. A single metropolitan development plan would not only facilitate more effective service provision, but have the dual effect of providing greater economic certitude for investors and improved environmental amenity as well as enhanced quality of life. The planning institutes of Barcelona (Spain) and Guadalajara (Mexico) could also prove an inspiration here (OECD, 2015b). Such institutes work on critical urban systems/functions that lead to green growth and greater resilience, including energy, land use and transport, housing and buildings, water supply and sanitation, solid waste management and green manufacturing. In the context of green growth, it is critical that such bodies undertake the following tasks:

- After agreeing on the priorities, they could formulate co-ordinated strategies, policies and programmes. In particular, they should encourage the adoption or "mainstreaming" of metropolitan-wide development and green growth plans into the constituting local governments' annual planning and budgeting cycle, and provide technical assistance to ensure that such metropolitan plans are translated to lower levels of government. Advisory boards in each green growth opportunity area could be created to gather experts and government officials and support the creation of such plans.
- They should follow up and assess progress towards green growth targets through indicators applied regionally, and set up monitoring protocols and reporting mechanisms to encourage all of the local governments to implement the decisions taken by the metropolitan body/institute (see discussion on indicators in the next section).

- Outreach and advocacy roles. They should share information on green growth issues and initiatives with the public and media, to update residents and local and national policy makers on the progress of specific green growth policies and actions.
- Metropolitan funds can also be set up to support the activities of metropolitan bodies/institutes, including planning, technical assistance and information sharing.

Box 3.4. Iskandar Malaysia Regional Development Authority

The Iskandar Regional Development Authority (IRDA) was established as a statutory body under the IRDA Act of 2007 (Act 664) and has been appointed as the development authority for the Iskandar Malaysia Economic Region (IMER). It was created at the same time as the Northern Corridor Implementation Authority and the East Coast Economic Regional Development Council. These economic regions were part of the Ninth Malaysia Plan to tackle development imbalances throughout the country (MLIT, 2015).

The IRDA represents a joint and co-ordinated approach between federal, state and local governments, and is co-chaired by the Prime Minister of Malaysia and the Chief Minister of Johor. The IRDA's mandate includes implementing the vision and objectives of Iskandar Malaysia in its efforts to become a metropolis of international standing. The IRDA's main functions are to establish national policy directions and strategies that have a direct impact on the development with Iskandar Malaysia; to co-ordinate the performance of development activities carried out by government departments and agencies in Iskandar Malaysia; to plan, promote and facilitate; to stimulate and undertake development in Iskandar Malaysia; and to act as the principal co-ordinating agent on behalf of government agencies in relation to receiving, processing and expediting the required approvals (Government of Malaysia, 2007). The creation of the IRDA was not meant as a transfer of power: Act 664 specifically claims that nothing in the act limits the state of Johor's jurisdictions, powers and functions over land and local government matters (Government of Malaysia, 2007).

An important contribution of the IRDA has been in assisting Khazanah Nasional (Malaysia's Sovereign Wealth Fund) in the development of the Comprehensive Development Plan for Iskandar Malaysia that translates national and state spatial developments plans (National Physical Plan and State Structure Plan). The IRDA's role is to facilitate negotiations and co-ordination processes between different government institutions in the region, in particular to integrate inputs from the five local authorities of Iskandar Malaysia (Majlis Bandaraya Johor Bahru, Majlis Perbandaran Pasir Gudang, Majlis Bandaraya Johor Bahru Tengah, Majlis Perbandaran Kulai and the District of Pontian). The Comprehensive Development Plan is a long-range developmental road map intended to guide decision makers, city planners, designers and builders over the next 20 years. The first plan was enacted in 2006 for the period 2006-25, and was revised in 2013 for the period 2014-25. Another important contribution of the IRDA has been the 24 blueprints, which elaborate specific details in policy sectors, and which support the comprehensive development plans.

Sources: OECD (2016e), *Green Growth in Iskandar Malaysia*, forthcoming; MLIT (2015), "An overview of spatial policy in ASEAN and European countries", webpage, www.mlit.go.jp/kokudokeikaku/international/spw/general/malaysia/index_e.html; Government of Malaysia (2007), Iskandar Malaysia Development Authority Act.

Box 3.5. Metro Cebu Development and Coordinating Board

The Metro Cebu Development and Coordinating Board (MCDCB) is a consortium of the 13 local government units (LGUs) comprised of Metro Cebu (seven cities – Cebu, Danao, Mandaue, Lapu-Lapu, Naga, Talisay and Carcar; and six municipalities – Compostella, Liloan, Consolacion, Cordova, Minglanilla and San Fernando), regional line agencies of the national government, private sector representatives and civil society organisations. The key objectives of the MCDCB are to:

- act as a co-ordinating body and platform for inter-jurisdictional challenges and responsibilities
- be a platform for inter-jurisdictional co-ordination between the public and private sectors and local and national governments
- be a launch pad for collective action and impact (recognising the importance of collaboration in developing policy and priority coherence, improving capacity, etc.)
- be a vehicle for regional, national and international co-operation.

The MCDCB model is unique in its explicit engagement with, and leadership from, the private sector and civil society. This model of having both the private sector and civil society at the Board level of a regional organisation can be seen as a means to institutionalise innovation, accountability and transparency. The private sector offers resources and is a main driver of economic growth and in bringing in technology and innovation. Having the private sector at the table as a co-chair sends a clear message in terms of integration and in providing an environment conducive to business and investment. Having the idea for co-ordination stem from the private sector also facilitates broad local government engagement in that project ownership is seeded more broadly, rather than with one or two local governments or officials. However, there is some question as to the role of the private sector in establishing public policy where elected officials must be responsible for implementation (e.g. zoning, parking restrictions, etc.).

The own financial resources and power of the MCDCB are, however, very limited, which prevents a strong impact of the promising dialogue and outreach initiative it represents. Currently, the operations of the MCDCB are supported through non-specific financial contributions from the member LGUs as well as through grants, donations, national government appropriation and other sources. In addition, the LGUs are still the units in charge of adopting the comprehensive land-use plans, and the MCDCB only pushes them to follow through. There is only a Memorandum of Understanding between the MCDCB and the LGUs, but not a regulatory relationship.

Source: OECD (2016c), *Green Growth in Cebu, the Philippines*, forthcoming.

A critical factor of success of metropolitan forms of governments in Southeast Asia is the involvement of the national government. In Metro Cebu and the future Bandung Metropolitan Area co-ordinating body, the participation of the central government is unclear. The presence of the national government is crucial not only to translate effectively national policy guidelines at the provincial and local levels, but also so that the new metropolitan body serves as a platform where local governments can communicate on the national policy gaps and regulations that are obstacles to urban green growth. In addition, this would create a channel whereby the national government could offer technical assistance to the provincial and local governments. In this regard, the national government can facilitate metropolitan planning, even if it does not direct it.

Successful multi-level co-operative frameworks in other countries can offer further inspiration. In Barcelona, three sectoral inter-municipal authorities were created in 1987, each of them covering a different geographical area: a planning authority, a transport authority and an environmental authority. Co-operation between municipalities in the metropolitan area through these metropolitan-wide entities has resulted in metropolitan strategic plans covering many municipalities (Box 3.6). Southeast Asian cities could try to replicate such an initiative (particularly in planning and environmental issues), as such sectoral inter-municipal authorities could progressively demonstrate the benefits of metropolitan-wide governance, and might even evolve into further forms of co-operation in the long term. In Barcelona, high political tensions surrounded the creation of a Metropolitan Corporation in the 1970s and 1980s, but the manifest benefits of inter-municipal co-operation after more than 20 years led to the creation of a metropolitan authority in 2011 that brought together the three inter-municipal authorities. As already noted, the national government's participation will also be critical in the case of Southeast Asian cities.

Box 3.6. Inter-municipal co-operation in Barcelona

In 1975, Spain's central government created a Metropolitan Corporation of Barcelona (Corporación Metropolitana de Barcelona), covering 27 municipalities. However, it was dissolved in 1987 when political tensions escalated between the city of Barcelona and the autonomous community of Catalonia, after Barcelona was chosen in 1986 to host the 1992 Olympics. Three sectoral inter-municipal authorities were instead created in 1987, each covering a different geography:

1. a planning authority, covering 31 municipalities (3.1 million people)
2. a transport authority, covering 18 municipalities (2.9 million people)
3. an environmental authority, covering 33 municipalities (3.2 million people), in charge of the water network and waste treatment.

Before and after the Olympics, a process of strategic planning took place, starting with a focus on the core city and gradually evolving towards the metropolitan scale. The city of Barcelona published its first strategic plan in 1990, a second one in 1994 and the third in 1999 with the three sectoral inter-municipal authorities. These strategic plans involved the regional government, all the municipalities, universities, the private sector, the port and civic organisations. The Association for the Strategic Plan of Barcelona, a non-profit organisation created in 2000 with 300 members of the political, business and social communities, launched the first Metropolitan Strategic Plan in 2003, which covered 36 municipalities. A new plan, Barcelona Visió 2020, was published in 2010 as a continuation of the 2003 plan. Finally, a metropolitan authority was set up in 2011 by Law 31/2010 of the Parliament of Catalonia. The Àrea Metropolitana de Barcelona (AMB) brings together the three sectoral inter-municipal authorities. Its Metropolitan Council is composed of the mayors of all 36 municipalities covered under the strategic plan, including the city of Barcelona. The AMB is in charge of planning, transport, water, waste treatment, social cohesion and economic development. In 2013, its budget was around EUR 600 million, composed mainly of subsidies and transfers (56%), fees and user charges (24%), and own taxes (17%). A specific authority in charge of public transport runs an integrated public transport network with a single unified fare system.

Source: OECD (2015a), *Governing the City*, http://dx.doi.org/10.1787/9789264226500-en.

Opportunities to raise finance for urban green growth

Despite increases in revenues, local governments in Southeast Asia still face significant financial constraints. This particularly affects opportunities to foster urban green growth, as enhancing infrastructure in key sectors such as transport, water and energy can be costly. Several options can be explored to raise opportunities to finance urban green growth, in particular: 1) making better use of and enhancing public finance at both national and local levels; 2) creating favourable conditions for private investment in green growth opportunity areas; and 3) enhancing the impact of official development assistance in cities.

Public finance must be designed to foster urban green growth

Local revenues have significantly increased in Southeast Asia

Significant increases in total and per capita local revenues have been observed in Southeast Asian cities. The nominal revenues of Bandung City increased dramatically from USD 620 million (at purchasing power parity prices) in 2010 to USD 1.6 billion in 2016. In Hai Phong, they increased from USD 2.5 billion in 2004 to USD 6.5 billion in 2014. In parallel, revenues per capita have increased from USD 258 to USD 620, and from USD 1 422 to USD 3 340 (Figure 3.1). The real budgets of these cities (controlling for inflation) have also increased significantly. Such trends are not observable in the case studies only: in the Philippines, from 2001 to 2013, provinces' revenues increased from USD 2.4 billion to USD 5 billion, cities' revenues from USD 4 billion to USD 9.4 billion, and municipalities' revenues from USD 3.3 billion to USD 7.9 billion (Philippines Department of Finance, n.d.).

Figure 3.1. **Total and per capita local revenues in Metro Cebu, Bandung City, Hai Phong and Bangkok City**

PPP

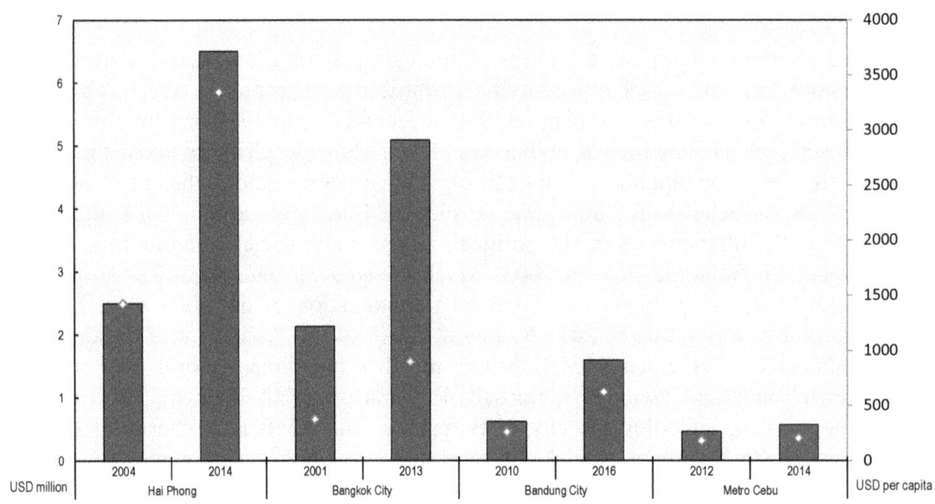

Note: Calculations for Metro Cebu are based on 2010 population for the fiscal year 2012, and on 2015 population for the fiscal year 2014.

Sources: OECD (2015b), *Green Growth in Bangkok, Thailand,* http://dx.doi.org/10.1787/9789264237087-en; OECD (2016d), *Green Growth in Hai Phong, Viet Nam,* forthcoming, http://dx.doi.org/10.1787/9789264260207-en; OECD (2016b), *Green Growth in Bandung, Indonesia,* http://dx.doi.org/10.1787/9789264264113-en; OECD (2016c), *Green Growth in Cebu, the Philippines,* forthcoming.

The significant rise in local revenues in Southeast Asian cities can be explained by various factors depending on the context of the city at focus. In Bandung City, such an increase is largely explained by a raise in own-source revenues, whose share in total revenues have increased from 16.7% in 2010 to 43.3% in 2016. This is a direct consequence of the Decentralisation Act 22/1999, updated later as Act No. 32/2004 and more recently Act No 28/2009 on Local Taxes and Charges and Act No.23/2014 on Local Governance, which included fiscal decentralisation and granted local governments rights to manage local finance. For instance, property taxes and land acquisition fees have been delegated to local governments. In Hai Phong, the increase in local revenues is largely explained by a surge in customs revenues thanks to the growth in port activities, which increased from 66.2% of total revenues in 2004 to 70.5% in 2014.

National governments should further support financial efforts for urban green growth

Despite increases in revenues, local governments in Southeast Asia still face significant financial constraints and difficulties to spend for green growth. Despite the 1991 Local Government Code, the LGU expenditures in the Philippines remain very low by international standards. Total LGU spending increased from an average of 1.6% of GDP during 1985-91 to about 3% in the late 2000s (compared to 16% of GDP in the OECD). The LGUs represent nearly 17% of total government expenditures and around 14% of public investment (compared to 59% in OECD countries), and have very limited ambitions for funding infrastructure development (OECD, 2015f), although they have substantial responsibilities in the environment sector (e.g. solid waste disposal, water supply systems, seawalls and dikes, drainage and sewerage, flood control) (Philippines Department of Finance, 2015). The national government shoulders about two-thirds of the investment programme of the Philippine Development Plan 2011-2016, including official development assistance grants, followed by private sector investment at an 18.5% share of the cost. The LGUs will only supply about 1.1% of the investments. In Indonesia, regencies and cities accounted for 30% of government expenditures (all levels of government included) but only accounted for 4% of government revenues in 2015. In contrast, the central government accounted for 57% of government expenditures and 89% of government revenues (OECD, 2016f). The lack of local budget is a common problem forcing local governments to look for alternative funding solutions (PPPs, grants, etc.).

Although local government revenues are increasingly dominated by own-source revenues, national governments still retain a very significant share of tax revenues at the country level and therefore retain the main bulk of funds: in Malaysia and the Philippines, only 3.3% and 5.2% of total tax revenues are attributed to local governments, and the central governments retain 95.2% and 82.2% of tax revenues, respectively. In Indonesia, 9.6% of total tax revenues were attributed to local governments in 2013, but was a significant increase from 2000 when only 3.2% of tax revenues were attributed to local governments, owing to decentralisation processes. In comparison, 12% of total tax revenues are attributed to local governments on average in OECD unitary countries, and 7.6% in federal countries. It is as high as 15.5% in Korea and 24.7% in Japan (Table 3.2).

In addition, transfers and grants from the national government still account for a large share of total local revenues. In Bandung City, transfers and grants from the national governments account for 44% of local revenues, respectively. In Indonesia, the General Allocation Fund and the Special Allocation Fund accounted for 51% and 5%, respectively, of regencies' and cities' revenues in 2015 (OECD, 2016b). In Metro Cebu, the Internal Revenue Allotment accounts for around 40% of the 13 local government units: in municipalities and component cities, which are more dependent on the Internal Revenue Allotment than independent cities such as Cebu City, Mandaue City and

Lapu-Lapu, the share oscillates between 60% and 90% of total local revenues (Figure 3.2). Generally speaking, the Internal Revenue Allotment accounted for 80.5% of provinces' revenues, 43.5% of cities' revenues and 80% of municipalities' revenues in the Philippines in 2014 (Philippines Department of Finance, n.d.). In Hai Phong, transfers from the central government "only" account for 6.8% of total local revenues, but this is mainly due to the large customs revenues perceived by the local government through port activities, implying other local governments with fewer revenues are more dependent on transfers from the central government.[5]

Table 3.2. **Attribution of tax revenues to sub-sectors of general government as a percentage of total tax revenue in selected countries and regions of the world**

	Central government			State or regional government			Local government			Social security funds		
	2000	2010	2013	2000	2010	2013	2000	2010	2013	2000	2010	2013
Federal countries												
Malaysia	94.7	94.3	95.2	..	..	..	3.4	4.0	3.3	1.9	1.7	1.5
OECD	56.5	53.8	54.5	15.3	16.3	16.5	6.9	7.9	7.6	21.1	21.8	21.3
Unitary countries												
Indonesia	96.8	92.8	90.4	..	..	..	3.2	7.2	9.6	..	..	..
Philippines	81.5	82.2	82.2	..	..	..	5.3	5.2	5.2	13.2	12.7	12.7
Japan	38.7	33.0	33.7	..	..	..	26.1	25.9	24.7	35.2	41.1	41.6
Korea	68.2	60.4	58.2	..	..	..	15.1	16.7	15.5	16.7	22.8	26.3
OECD	66.5	63.4	62.9	..	..	..	11.0	11.9	12.0	22.3	24.4	24.8

Source: OECD (2015d), *Revenue Statistics in Asian Countries 2015: Trends in Indonesia, Malaysia and the Philippines*, http://dx.doi.org/10.1787/9789264234277-en.

Figure 3.2. **Share of internal revenue allotment in total revenues of local government units in Metro Cebu**

Fiscal year 2014

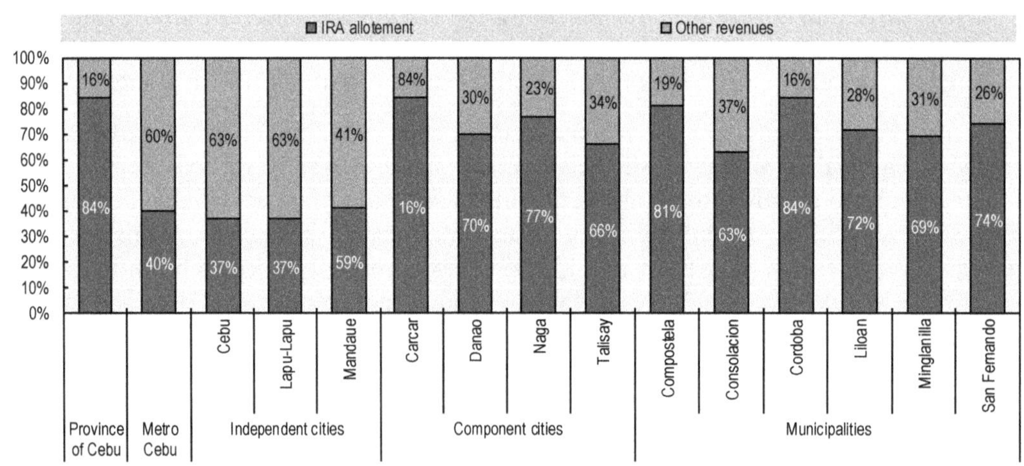

Notes: Inter-local transfers and grants/aids were excluded from the figure due to their very minor share of revenues in each category. Data for "Metro Cebu" is a weighted average. IRA allotment refers to the share of revenues of local governments from the Philippines national government.

Source: Philippines Department of Finance (n.d.), Department of Finance website, www.dof.gov.ph.

A critical need, however, is to enhance public finance and tailor it to urban green growth objectives. Actions can be taken at both the national and local levels in this regard. First, national governments have a key role to play. Given the large financial capacities of national governments compared to local governments in Southeast Asia, and their weight in local finance, national governments have opportunities in fostering urban green growth. The central government could earmark special funds for green growth-related activities. In Indonesia, the Special Allocation Fund is supposed to deliver earmarked funding to subnational governments, but the allocation in practice remains quite general, similar to the General Allocation Fund (OECD, 2016b). Prioritising the allocation of the Special Allocation Fund towards green growth objectives can only be effective if the national government adopts a clearer national green growth strategy that details well the role to be played by local governments, so that such funds be used efficiently and coherently across territories by cities, and in line with national strategies. This would encourage local governments to spend more on green growth purposes. Half of the expenditures (49.5%) of the city of Bandung in 2014 was spent on employee expenditure.[6] Environmental projects only accounted for 3% of direct expenditures and it is difficult to know to what extent some other direct expenditure, such as public works, contributed to green growth. Similar recommendations could be made in the other ASEAN-5 countries. In Viet Nam, the good planning co-ordination between green growth plans at the national and local levels could be enhanced by such financial channels. In the Philippines, the LGUs are currently required to set aside no less than 20% of their Internal Revenue Allotment for development projects as directed by the Local Government Code, including 5% for disaster mitigation and a further 3% on other areas deemed as national priorities (OECD, 2015e). However, the efficiency of such a measure seems questionable and shows the benefits of outreach and collaboration between national and local governments for greater impact.

The use of direct transfers earmarked for infrastructure is practiced in India through the Jawaharlal Nehru Urban Renewal Mission, whose aim is to develop infrastructure in Indian cities. It provides co-financing for cities to improve efficiency in urban infrastructure and service delivery and to promote transparency, accountability and public participation. The programme's success can be attributed to national leadership accompanied by financing, a demand-driven approach, capacity building and peer-to-peer learning in local government (Ellis and Roberts, 2016; Matsumoto and Nuttall, 2014). Southeast Asian countries could replicate such a mechanism for infrastructure that demonstrates its contribution to green growth objectives.

Direct financial channels could also be unlocked at the national level to stimulate specific green growth initiatives at the local level and respond to local willingness to foster green growth. In Sweden, a national programme (KLIMP) provides local governments of all sizes financial support to manage greenhouse gas emissions and adapt to climate change. Local governments can apply for national subsidies that can be used to promote local investment to reduce emissions and improve energy efficiency and independence. Examples of funded municipal activities include removing disincentives for individuals to reduce emissions, such as eliminating free parking, and subsidising the cost of retrofitting filling stations to add a pump to supply renewable biofuels (Corfee-Morlot et al., 2009). This could also be achieved in Southeast Asian countries, especially to support metropolitan-wide forms of management.

Local governments should improve tax collection and increase fees and charges in green growth sectors

Local governments in Southeast Asia also have a critical role to play, even though their financial capacities are currently limited. They should first improve the efficiency of the tax collection system, which in many cases is far from being optimised. Total tax revenues in 2013 only represented 13% of Indonesia's GDP, while this share is around 34% on average in OECD countries (OECD, 2015a). The Bangkok Metropolitan Administration, for instance, faces significant challenges in collecting the building and land tax, and the land development tax, partly because capacities are lacking to map and collect data on land use and to periodically reappreciate the value of properties in the city of Bangkok. In the Philippines, only 73% of the real property tax was actually collected on average in 2013. There is also an urgent need to update the rate of such taxes. In Thailand, the rate of the building and land tax for commercial buildings is regulated by national legislation and has been kept at 12.5% for years despite requests from local governments to raise it (OECD, 2015b). In many cities and municipalities of the Philippines, property tax rates are also outdated and sometimes based on calculations dating back before 2000. Only 28 provinces out of a total of 80 have updated schedule of market values (Philippines Department of Finance, n.d.). OECD (2013b) advised that a first step for municipalities to strengthen their property tax collections would be to set up cadastres and carry out a comprehensive review of cadastral values to restore the tax base. In Mexico, a new programme to update cadastres (Programa de Modernización Catastral) has been set up by the National Institute of Statistics and Geography with the financial support of the development bank BANOBRAS. This has successfully contributed to updating the cadastre of 11 municipalities and increased their property tax collection by an average of 40% (OECD, 2015c).

Another issue faced by local governments is the presence of large numbers of unregistered urban populations. In Bangkok City alone, it is estimated that around 2 million persons are not in official censuses. This impacts local finance as transfers from the national government are partly indexed on the official population living in local governments. The General Allocation Fund in Indonesia, for instance, is partly allocated according to the official number of registered population in the local governments and does not take into account the unregistered population. A similar observation can be made for the value-added tax, the liquor tax and the excise tax in Thailand. Efforts should therefore concentrate on reducing the number of unregistered populations.

More direct efforts can also be made by local governments to raise local finance while encouraging urban green growth. Opportunity lies in raising revenues from fees and charges, in particular. Such a stream of revenues is indeed very low in Southeast Asian cities: it accounts for only 2% of the Bangkok Metropolitan Administration's total revenues, 6% in all of Metro Cebu's LGUs combined and 0.5% in Hai Phong, against 14.9% for subnational governments on average in the OECD area (OECD, 2016g). In the Philippines, fees and charges account for 4.6% of the LGUs' total revenues on average (Philippines Department of Finance, n.d.). Raising more revenues from these sources would help to make urban green growth projects more financially sustainable, but this also represents an opportunity to shape greener behaviours through fiscal policy instruments, as previously discussed in Chapter 2. Developing the abilities of local governments to raise own-source revenues is even preferable to raising the bulk of transfers from the national governments. As observed in the Philippines, the weight of national transfers in local revenues may make local governments dependent on the national government and discourage them from developing streams of locally sourced revenues. For instance, developing taxes on new impervious surfaces could be a tool to guide development in a more sustainable pattern (by discouraging developers to build in risk-sensitive areas) or to recover for the cost of creating flood-resilient infrastructure. Similarly, making a more systemic use of wastewater treatment, public transport, and water supply tariffs and charges helps to raise more revenue while increasing the sustainability of green utility systems. Solid waste collection or wastewater fees also often do not cover sufficiently for the investment and operation cost of such urban utility systems in Southeast Asian cities. Development charges and land-value capture tools are also potentially powerful economic instruments to be considered and currently not in use. Water extraction charges, taxes on impervious surfaces, development charges in middle- to high-income areas, and land-value capture tools along public transport networks are all instruments that could help to raise local finance and guide the development of Southeast Asian cities towards green growth.

In many cases, increasing fees and charges will require a certain level of autonomy of local governments in applying and modifying tax rates, a power which is generally in the hands of the national governments in Southeast Asia. In green growth-related sectors where local governments have been given extended responsibilities (in Indonesia and the Philippines, for instance, following decentralisation laws), giving more autonomy to local governments to perceive taxes and fees may bring high benefits, as it should enable local utilities to recover costs more easily and increase the sustainability of utility systems in the long term. In Viet Nam, the Law on Fees and Charges adopted by the national government in 2015 gives local authorities more autonomy in managing such financial instruments and goes in this direction.

The metropolitan dimension of public finance for urban green growth

Local governments in Southeast Asia should also pay attention to the metropolitan dimension of financing urban green growth projects. As explained above, metropolitan thinking, forms of governance and urban projects may bring high benefits in green growth-related sectors, rather than secluded projects that do not consider the functional area of urban utilities and systems. Several obstacles, however, prevent harmonised metropolitan projects, especially in the absence of strong metropolitan co-ordination mechanisms. The different status of local governments within a single metropolitan area may result in significant inequalities in autonomy and financial resources across cities and municipalities: in Metro Cebu, for instance, the three independent cities (Cebu City, Lapu-Lapu and Mandaue) are much more autonomous as the Internal Revenue Allotment only accounts for 29% of their total revenues, while it accounts for 68% of that of the component cities and municipalities of Metro Cebu. Indeed, Cebu City, Lapu-Lapu and Mandaue have much more capacities and power to manage local taxes and charges, and the revenue per inhabitant is higher than in all other LGUs, except Liloan municipality (Figure 3.3). In the Bangkok Metropolitan Region, the powers of the city of Bangkok, which has the status of a province, are much different from the adjacent municipalities within the provinces of the BMR.

The discrepancies in financial resources may result in inequalities in terms of infrastructure quality, and eventually in the economic and environmental performance of local governments within the same metropolitan areas. In addition, in terms of investment, metropolitan co-operation tends not be encouraged: in the Philippines for instance, two LGUs cannot take out a loan together. Given the horizontal fragmentation of local governments in many metropolitan areas and the need to develop infrastructure across the whole region (e.g. water, transport), this is a critical obstacle to finance urban green growth. In Metro Cebu, the creation of the Metro Cebu Development Authority (MCDA) should, however, go hand-in-hand with the establishment of a Mega Cebu Investment Board, which should be entitled to borrow from banks and on markets to make the necessary investment to carry out the functions devolved by the Local

Government Code. If implemented, the success of such initiatives should be carefully analysed and lessons drawn for other metropolitan areas in Southeast Asia.

Figure 3.3. **Revenue per inhabitant in local government units of Metro Cebu**

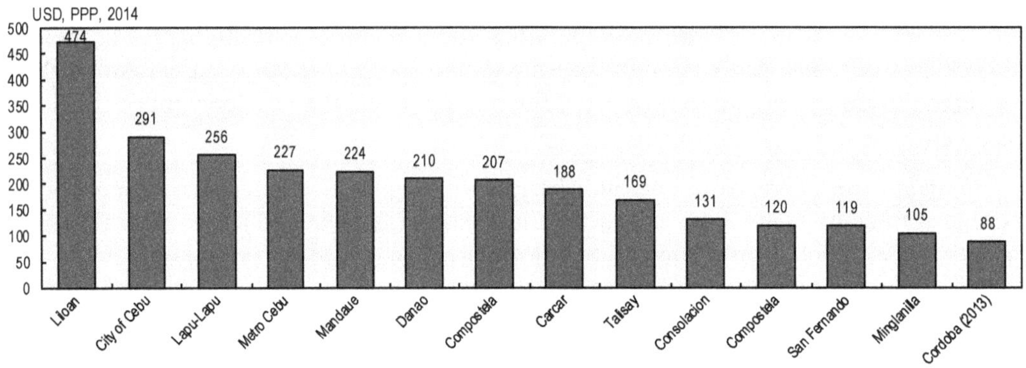

Source: Philippines Department of Finance (n.d.), Department of Finance website, www.dof.gov.ph.

Finally, in addition to presenting opportunities for local governments, fees and charges are also a critical opportunity to raise revenues for metropolitan governance entities. Indeed, solid waste, water and transport infrastructure typically have a metropolitan dimension, as explained above, and operation and application of fees is the responsibility of metropolitan governments in many OECD metropolitan areas. For instance, Metro Vancouver's revenues are mostly built through water sales (37%), sewer levy (29%) and solid waste tipping fee (12%). Similarly, 43% of Area Metropolitana Barcelona's budget is built through the waste management tax and the mobility tax, and 13% from PPPs for water supply and night bus service.

Creating a public investment framework for urban green growth

Urban green growth requires a significant amount of public investment across levels of government. Both the national and subnational levels have a role to play in enhancing public finance for urban green growth. Local governments need funding tools, capacity building in terms of effective public investment, and planning professionals need a working knowledge of how to prioritise and implement the plans they develop. In addition, the reliance of local governments on national grants and subsidies indicates a real need for a more robust funding strategy and understanding of how to successfully achieve integrated public investment across levels of government in Southeast Asia. In this context, creating a more effective public investment framework is crucial (Box 3.7).

The challenges in attracting private finance in green growth opportunity areas

Barriers to foreign direct investment should be loosened in green growth opportunity areas

Governments should not only seek to enhance public finance and increase public investment for urban green growth, but also facilitate foreign and domestic private investment in the green growth opportunity areas. Generally speaking, foreign direct investment (FDI) still remains low in low- and middle-income countries of Southeast Asia. FDI per capita was at USD 380 in Malaysia in 2012-13, far above that of Thailand

(USD 177), Viet Nam (USD 95), Indonesia (USD 76) and the Philippines (USD 36). In comparison, FDI per capita in Singapore and Hong Kong, China was USD 11 660 and USD 10 557 (Figure 3.4). The low FDI attractiveness of ASEAN-5 countries can be associated to the high restrictions they impose on foreign investment: indeed, the high FDI Regulatory Restrictiveness Index of Southeast Asian countries is strongly correlated to the low stocks of FDI: the Philippines shows the highest FDI Regulatory Restrictiveness Index and the lowest FDI stocks of the region, expressed as a percentage of GDP (Figure 3.5).

Box 3.7. **OECD Recommendation of the Council on Effective Public Investment Across Levels of Government**

In 2014, the OECD adopted the *Recommendation of the Council on Effective Public Investment Across Levels of Government*. Recommendations are not legally binding, but practice accords them great moral force as representing the political will of member countries.

Local governments undertook 58.8% of total public investment in 2014 throughout the OECD area in terms of volume. Variations across countries are important, as subnational public investment ranges from 12% in Chile to 95.4% in Canada. More effective public investment has a critical role to play to address inequalities, rebuild trust, restore growth and enhance well-being. The impact of public investment depends to a significant extent on how governments manage this shared competence across levels of government. Effective public investment requires substantial co-ordination across levels of government to bridge information, policy or fiscal gaps that may occur, as well as critical governance capacities at different levels to design and implement public investment projects.

The purpose of these principles is to help governments assess the strengths and weaknesses of their public investment capacity in a multi-level governance perspective and set priorities for improvement. An Implementation Toolkit provides guidance with details for all countries and is available at: www.oecd.org/effective-public-investment-toolkit.

Source: OECD (2014b), *Recommendation of the Council on Effective Public Investment Across Levels of Government*, www.oecd.org/gov/regional-policy/Principles-Public-Investment.pdf.

Figure 3.4. **Foreign direct investment per capita in emerging Asian countries**

USD, 2012-13 average

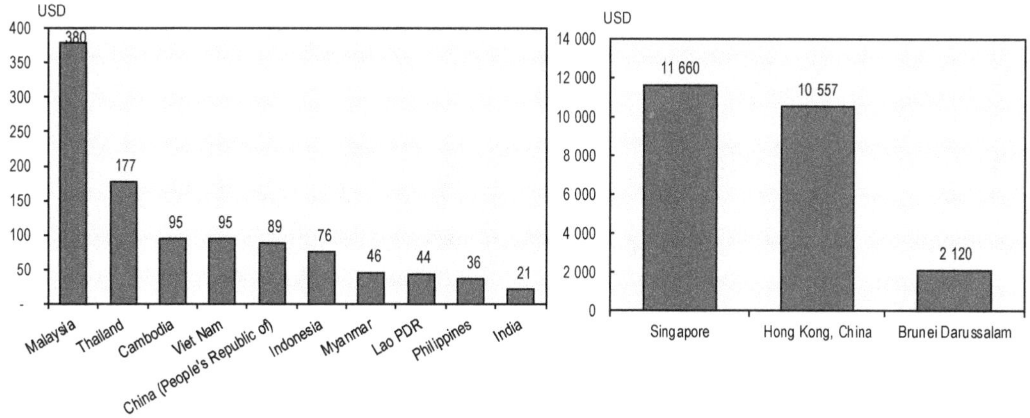

Source: OECD (2014c), "Southeast Asia policy investment perspectives", www.oecd.org/development/se-asia-investment-policy-perspectives.htm.

Figure 3.5. **FDI Index scores vs. foreign direct investment stocks as a share of GDP in ASEAN-9 member countries**

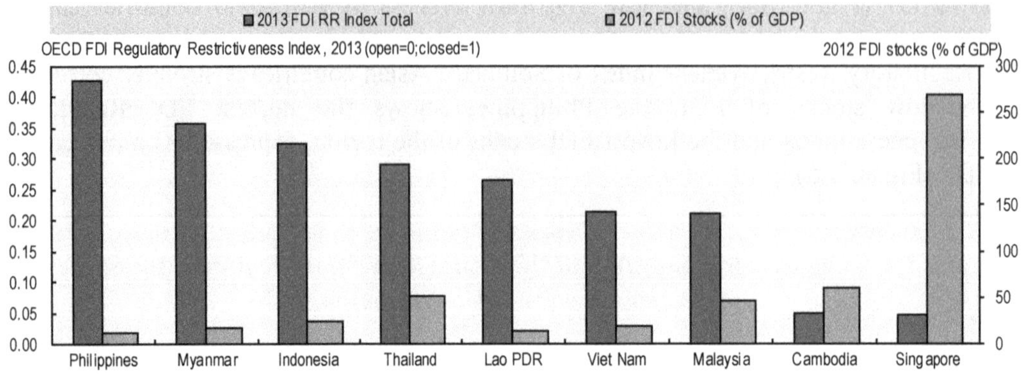

Source: OECD (2014c), "Southeast Asia policy investment perspectives", www.oecd.org/development/se-asia-investment-policy-perspectives.htm.

The national governments in Southeast Asia should consider loosening such restrictions in critical green growth sectors such as transport and energy. In the Philippines, for instance, the Constitution restricts ownership in the land and transport sectors to Filipinos and Filipino companies: foreign investors can only own up to 40% of land or transport companies, and only where leases are permitted (OECD, 2014c). While this could be seen as a means to avoid speculation on land from foreign companies, as it has happened in Iskandar Malaysia, this does not prevent domestic speculation or poor urban planning and management. In the transport sector, such restrictions are problematic to develop public transport networks; currently, the domestic market for public transport, in particular mass transit, is weak and inefficient, and the restrictions prevent the necessary investment that such infrastructure requires. Likewise, Indonesia's difficulties in attracting FDI can be explained by disincentives such as limited infrastructure, and complicated and time-consuming investment procedures (Salim, 2014). One major constraint for foreign investors is that the Foreign Investment Law requires foreign investment to be approved by the Indonesia Investment Co-ordinating Board (Badan Kordinasi Penanaman Modal) and that the share of foreign ownership is restricted in some sectors, in particular in transport services, energy and mineral resources, agriculture, forestry, maritime and fisheries, finance and banking, and education (UNEP, 2015). The national governments have a critical role in addressing these issues and stimulating FDI in urban areas.

In parallel, national governments should take measures to encourage green urban infrastructure. Only 1.4% of total lending by 29 major banks in Indonesia was considered to be "green" in 2013, according to a survey of Bank Indonesia (UNEP, 2015).[7] This accounted for about USD 1 billion. The main sectors benefiting from green financing in 2012 were mini hydropower (26.1% of green financing), geothermal (25.7%), environmentally efficient machineries (19.6%) and sustainable agriculture (19.5%) (UNEP, 2015). The government of Indonesia has, however, made remarkable efforts recently in terms of design innovations in financial markets to encourage green lending and investment, which can therefore be expected to increase significantly in the coming years. One of the flagship policies in this regard, and which is very innovative for a developing country, was the creation of the SRI-KEHATI Index and the SRI-KEHATI-ETF, which are sustainability ratings for the stock markets. The Ministry of Finance is also considering green weighting for capital requirements, which could significantly encourage green finance (UNEP, 2015). Another policy with potentially high impact is the development of the Roadmap for Sustainable Finance in Indonesia by the Ministry of Finance, which may include a binding regulatory framework for green finance which could include the establishment of compulsory environmental and social management systems and reporting in both capital and stock markets (UNEP, 2015). Other countries in Southeast Asia could consider developing similar green finance mechanisms.

Strengthening subnational capacities for public-private partnerships

Public-private partnerships (PPPs) represent further opportunities to involve the private sector in financing urban infrastructure. PPPs provide a tremendous opportunity to leverage private sector innovation and capability towards meeting the public interest. As demonstrated in Cebu by FDR Integrated Resource Recovery Management Inc., which was originally a construction company but is now diversified and providing waste management services for local governments, PPPs are effective not only for infrastructure (design/build/operate), but also for service agreements. This company entered into 20-25 year agreements with local government units in order to collect, process and treat non-hazardous solid waste from households, commercial and industrial sectors (OECD, 2016c).

Generally speaking, PPPs are poorly used in Southeast Asia, but the policy context in the region tends to be increasingly favourable to this type of public procurement. In the Philippines, in 2010, a new emphasis placed on PPPs was identified as a key component of an overall growth strategy by the national government and was translated into critical organisational and legal reforms to promote PPPs. The Department of Trade and Industry of the National Economic and Development Authority is now composed of a unit specifically dedicated to PPP management, the Public-Private-Partnership Centre. These changes have been fruitful: prior to 2010, the Philippines had limited experience with PPPs, with only six solicited projects being completed in the period 1992-2010. Since 2010, nine PPPs have been tendered and awarded and a further 14 are at an advanced stage in the development pipeline (OECD, 2015f). In Indonesia, by the turn of the 2010 decade, the national government also made PPP a strategic instrument for rail construction and power generation. Complex issues such as defining the PPP policy and legal framework, identifying a project pipeline, setting up PPP expertise units and developing concepts to guide projects have been undertaken at the national level (OECD, 2012). The number of PPPs in 2010-12 was the highest in the West Java Province, mainly in the forms of concessions.

Most PPP projects are undertaken by national governments. For instance, in Cebu, the extension and upgrading of the Mactan-Cebu International Airport (the second largest airport in the country and hub of the southern regions) is a priority PPP project of the central government, undertaken with GMR Megawide Cebu Airport Corporation, with financial support of the Asian Development Bank.[8] Likewise, only two cities in Indonesia have successfully implemented PPPs: Tangerang (project on water supply) and Makassar (project on sewerage). The city of Bandung is an example of a city with strong willingness to develop PPPs at the local level. The Bandung Light Rail Transit/LRT (ready to offer project) and the Integrated Gedebage Multipurpose Terminal (Railway) (prospective project) are two PPPs in development. The current Mayor of the city of Bandung has erected PPP projects as the new approach of financing urban development. A list of 91 projects, with total capital requirement of around USD 6 billion, has been prepared by the current local administration, including flagship projects such as the construction of cable cars and a light rail transit. This strategy aims to circumvent the lack of local government budget.

In order to make most use of PPPs, subnational governments need to develop capacities to design them, especially in green growth opportunity areas. Local governments in Southeast Asia critically lack capacities to implement PPPs effectively and in a short period of time. While they can deliver value for money, they can also be dangerous for fiscal sustainability and require complex procurement, administrative and legal procedures, as well as skills. Problems associated with attempts to lead PPPs by local governments were illustrated in Surabaya City, Indonesia. It took the local government several years to complete a feasibility study and to make the proposal commercially viable, even with the support of a consultant agency.[9] The case studies have revealed the following obstacles that need to be addressed in priority:

- The difficulty in identifying projects with high potential for cost recovery, such as commercial and industrial development. The lack of cost recovery is particularly problematic for urban PPPs as the transport, solid waste and water sectors are sectors with potentially high infrastructure costs but with a low return on investment due to low fees, charges and tariffs, as explained previously.
- The technical challenge of PPPs and the limited timeframe of the local policy leaders and chief executives to complete their projects. In particular, assessing the value for money of a project – compared to a traditional public procurement scenario – may be difficult, as it results from a combination of factors such as risk transfer, output-base specifications, performance measurement and incentives, competition in and for the market, private sector management expertise, and the benefits for end users and society as a whole (OECD, 2012).
- The inability of many local governments to borrow has particularly hindered public investment at the local level and prevented them from spending and borrowing for PPPs, which can especially be observed in the Philippines.
- The difficulty to undertake PPPs across jurisdictions at the metropolitan level in order to match investment with the right geographical scale. There is a lack of incentives and regulations to tackle the inability of two or more local governments to enter into a binding contract with private sector actors.

National governments must take an active role in building capacities to develop PPPs at the subnational level. In Indonesia, for instance, any government contracting agency, including subnational authorities, willing to set up a PPP will likely need a government guarantee or fiscal support, and in this perspective needs to comply with three specific presidential regulations[10] to be submitted to the Ministry of Finance. Unfortunately, the process has been dogged by the lack of co-ordination between the government contracting agencies and the two main ministries involved in PPP procedures: the Ministry of Finance and Bappenas. In particular, government contracting agencies, including subnational authorities, develop projects in isolation, and the proposals often fall short of the requirement of the Ministry of Finance and therefore do not qualify for government guarantee and fiscal support and as a result are abandoned or delayed (OECD, 2012). There is no assistance either to subnational authorities from the Ministry of Finance's Risk Management Unit or Indonesia Infrastructure Guarantee Fund in putting together the feasibility studies (OECD, 2012). Bappenas' PPP Central Unit is supposed to assist government contracting agencies in developing their PPP projects but is under-capacitated (OECD, 2012). Similarly, there is no financial mechanism, such as in the form of grants, to support local feasibility studies and bidding processes undertaken by subnational authorities. The recent creation of a PPP unit under the Ministry of Finance is a timely reform. This national PPP unit – or by default the current national agencies in charge – should work closely with Bandung City and the future BMA co-ordinating body to realise the expected PPPs in green infrastructure. Local governments in particular need support from the start of the PPP projects, i.e. the planning phase to the next steps, i.e. feasibility study, tender preparation, bidding and contract signing (OECD, 2012).

In the Philippines, the national government is now advocating the mainstreaming of PPPs at the local level through the PPP Centre's Capacity Building Programme for Local Government Units, created in 2013. The Internship Programme and Partnerships with selected Local Capacity Building Institutions has also been created with the aim to provide assistance to LGU-PPP programmes and projects (KPMG, 2015). The PPP Centre has promoted the PPP initiative and invited expressions of interest from the LGUs, provided training for LGU officials, produced a comprehensive three volume PPP Manual[11] and engaged with a few LGUs seeking advice and internships to help develop PPP proposals (OECD, 2015f). The centre is also working on the creation of PPP subcommittees in local government councils, to "assist in the formulation of action plans and strategies to the implementation of PPP programmes and projects" (PPP Centre, 2012). The PPP Manual defines the types of projects eligible for PPPs at the LGU level. Sectors related to green growth include the environment and solid waste management, land use (land reclamation and dredging), transport, and water and sanitation. Nonetheless, the PPP Centre's initiatives at the LGU level are very recent and have not yet resulted in tangible achievements, except in Tanauan City (OECD, 2015f). Still, very few LGUs show interest in PPPs.

Metropolitan forms of government, in this perspective, can be instrumental in facilitating PPPs. They represent an opportune level of governance to explore PPPs because of the dispersal of risk and ability to pool resources among its constituent local governments. OECD (2015f) indeed recommends that alliances of LGUs in the Philippines be given a legal status to carry out joint PPP projects. In the future, it will be critical to develop PPP projects in green growth opportunity areas that will spread over or involve multiple jurisdictions (BRT, metro system, drainage and recycling facilities, etc.). Likewise, by comprising cities and smaller municipalities, metropolitan forms of government should help to integrate municipalities with lower tax authority and borrowing capacities into metropolitan projects with the private sector. In parallel, such metropolitan authorities should work with each local government to explore options to raise cost recovery capacities in the critical green growth opportunity areas mentioned above, by raising charges and fees for environmental services.

Enhancing the impact of official development finance on urban green growth

Indonesia and Viet Nam are the largest recipients of official development finance in Southeast Asia

International co-operation plays a non-negligible role in the development of Southeast Asian countries. One of the forms it takes is official development finance (ODF), comprising official development assistance (ODA) and non-concessional other official flows (OOF),[12] such as the Clean Technology Fund and the Climate Investment Fund. Between 2002 and 2014, Indonesia and Viet Nam have been the top two recipients of ODF in Southeast Asia, with respectively an aggregated USD 80 billion and USD 68.5 billion committed from donors. Thailand and Malaysia, as the most advanced economies of the region, only received limited amounts of ODF: over the same period, USD 8.7 billion and USD 4.8 billion were committed to these two countries, respectively. The Philippines received around USD 29.5 billion.

Not all official development finance committed to Southeast Asia benefits (urban) green growth, however. As a matter of fact, among all funds committed to ASEAN-5 countries, only 23.2% of all ODF between 2002 and 2014 (USD 44.3 billion out of a total of USD 191.4 billion) targeted either or simultaneously environment, climate change mitigation, climate change adaption, biodiversity and desertification objectives (i.e. the objectives set by the Rio Conventions).[13] Viet Nam is the largest recipient of environment-related ODF over this period, with around USD 20.3 billion, against USD 14.6 billion for Indonesia (Figure 3.6).

Figure 3.6. **Total official development finance committed to selected ASEAN countries**

USD billion, constant 2014 prices, 2002-14 aggregated

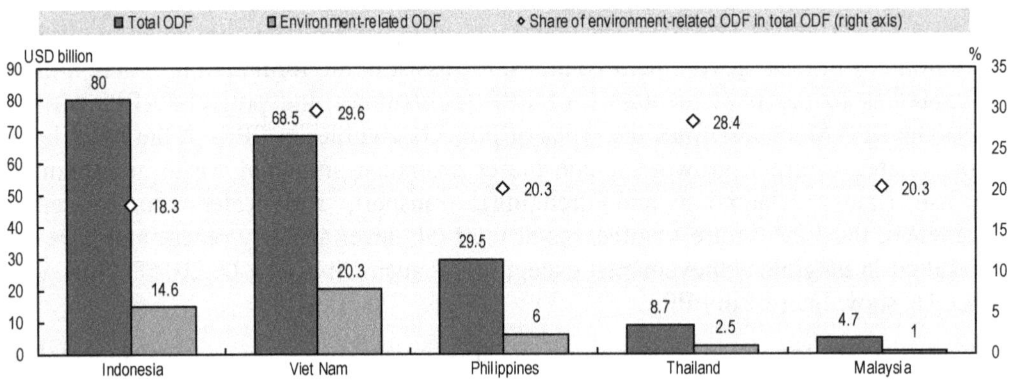

Note: ODF: official development finance.

Source: OECD (2016a), "Aid activities targeting global environmental objectives", *DAC Creditor Reporting System* (database), https://stats.oecd.org/Index.aspx?DataSetCode=RIOMARKERS.

Both amounts of total ODF and environment-related ODF committed to ASEAN-5 countries have increased over time. Total ODF in ASEAN-5 countries increased from USD 8 billion in 2002 to USD 15.9 billion in 2014, with a peak at USD 22.3 billion in 2009. The growth was mostly born by OOF, which increased from USD 1 billion in 2002 to USD 7.9 billion in 2014; meanwhile, ODA grew from USD 7 billion in 2002 to USD 7.9 billion in 2014. Indonesia, in particular, and to some extent the Philippines have received large amounts of OOF in comparison to ODA. Likewise, total amounts of environment-related ODF committed to ASEAN-5 countries have (unsteadily) increased over time, from USD 1.5 billion in 2002 to USD 4.1 billion in 2014, and from 18.9% to 25.6% of total ODF (Figure 3.7).

Environment-related official development finance to cities has been unsteady and mainly targeted capital cities

Among ODF committed for environmental purposes in ASEAN-5 countries, around 37.2% (in terms of funds) can be clearly identified as targeting cities in 2002-14, against 16.1% to rural areas. However, a significant number of projects, accounting for 46.7% of total ODF over this period, cannot be identified as either "urban" or "rural". This is due to the nature of some projects which are not always place-based (e.g. education), the lack of geographical details given in the description of projects in the Credit Reporting System database, or the wide coverage of some projects that encompass both urban and rural areas. Thailand and Malaysia are the top two recipients of ODF targeting cities as a share of total environment-related ODF (81.3% and 78.2% of total ODF in 2002-14, respectively) but this is mainly due to a handful of single commitments financing massive infrastructure projects, in particular the mass transit development project in Bangkok and the Pahang-Selangor Water Tunnel project in Kuala Lumpur. Viet Nam is the top recipient of urban ODF among ASEAN-5 countries (in terms of total environmental funds), with an aggregated USD 8.3 billion in 2002-14 (41.5% of total environment-related ODF).

Figure 3.7. **Total official development finance and environment-related finance committed to ASEAN-5 countries**

USD billion, constant 2014 prices, 2002-14

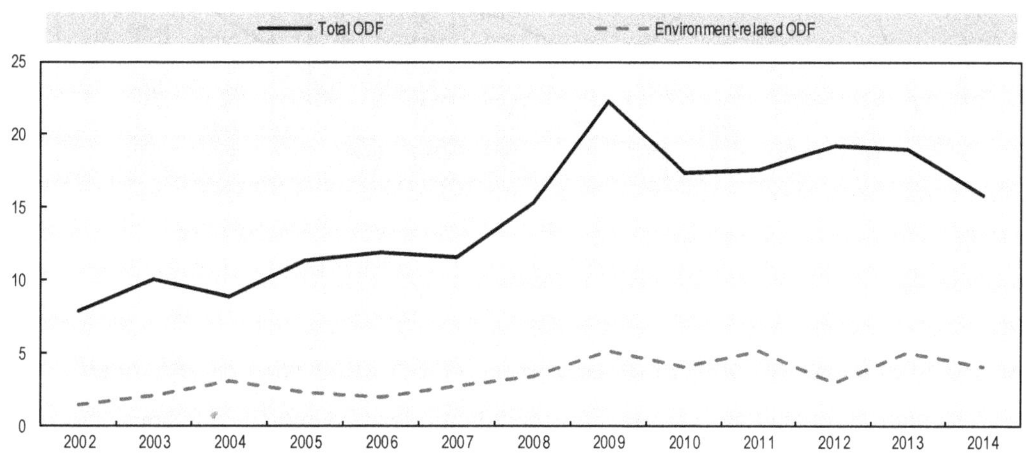

Note: ODF: official development finance.

Source: OECD (2016a), "Aid activities targeting global environmental objectives", *DAC Creditor Reporting System* (database), https://stats.oecd.org/Index.aspx?DataSetCode=RIOMARKERS.

ODF committed to ASEAN-5 cities increased from USD 0.2 billion in 2002 to USD 1.1 billion in 2014, but the progression was very unsteady. The share of urban ODF in total ODF tends to be dependent on the commitment of single large projects such as the two mentioned previously. There is no clear progression of urban ODF as a share of total ODF over this period: it increased from 11.9% to 21.9% of total ODF, but peaks were reached in 2004 (57.8% of total ODF) and 2013 (56.1% of total ODF) (Figure 3.8).

Capital cities concentrated 40.1% of environment-related ODF committed to cities in ASEAN-5 countries in 2002-14, although they concentrated only 15.9% of the total urban population. Kuala Lumpur and Bangkok have even received 98.5% and 98.6% of total environment-related ODF committed to cities in their respective countries, for the reasons mentioned previously. Ha Noi, Manila and Jakarta received 20.9%, 68.9% and 20.8% of total environment-related ODF committed to cities in their respective countries. Ho Chi Minh City is the only exception, as it concentrated 25.1% of environment-related ODF committed to Vietnamese cities: the amount is higher than in the capital city Hanoi, but Ho Chi Minh City is the most populated city of Viet Nam. Together, Ha Noi and Ho Chi Minh City account for 46.1% of environment-related ODF committed to

Vietnamese cities. In comparison, secondary cities are "left behind", or are not the object of major targeted projects supported by international aid: Hai Phong, Iskandar Malaysia, Bandung and Metro Cebu received 2% (USD 500 million), 0% (USD 0.4 million), 0% (USD 10 million) and 0.2% (USD 12 million) of environment-related ODF committed to cities in their respective countries.

Figure 3.8. **Urban and rural official development finance committed for environmental purposes in ASEAN-5 countries**

USD million, constant 2014 prices, 2002-14

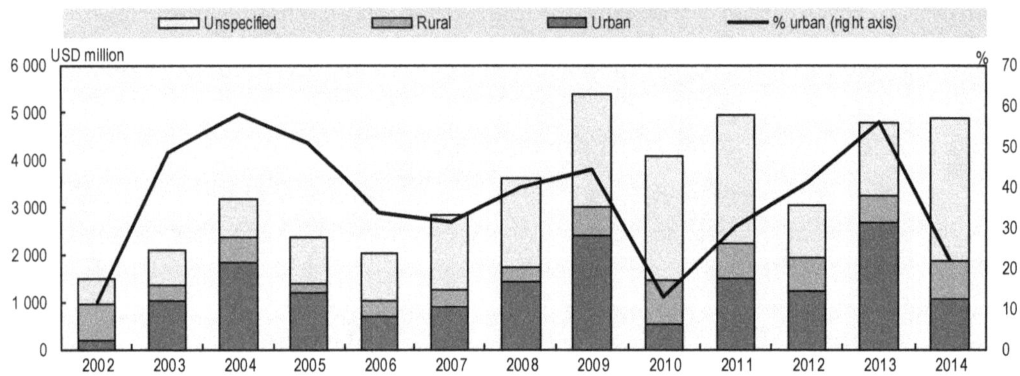

Source: OECD (2016a), "Aid activities targeting global environmental objectives", *DAC Creditor Reporting System* (database), https://stats.oecd.org/Index.aspx?DataSetCode=RIOMARKERS.

Access to official development finance in secondary cities must be enhanced

The high share of ODF committed to capital cities can be explained to some extent by their population size and the share in the country's economy, but it remains disproportionate. The proximity of the national government is a critical factor benefiting capital cities. As a matter of fact, Hai Phong is likely to have benefited from a higher share of ODF compared to other secondary cities of the region thanks to the strong involvement of the national government in some urban projects, in particular the construction of port infrastructure, which accounted for 43% of the funds received by Hai Phong between 2002 and 2014. The modernisation of Hai Phong port – the second seaport of the country – is a pillar of the Ministry of Construction's Viet Nam Seaport Master Plan 2020 and is directly driven by the central government. National governments in ASEAN-5 countries are indeed the channel of ODF, even when they target specific cities. In Indonesia, for instance, local governments are not allowed to contract direct loans from foreign donors. To obtain additional funding, local governments are allowed to borrow from the central government, other local governments, domestic banks or financial institutions, and from the public through municipal bonds (Law 33/2004). They can therefore receive donor support, but only with a two-step loan (or sub-loan agreement), which is complicated as it needs the approval of the central government. The ability of cities, and in particular secondary cities, to access ODF is therefore very restricted in Southeast Asia. In Thailand, cities need to receive recommendations from the Office of Natural Resources and Environmental Policy and Planning (Ministry of Natural Resources and Environment) or the Thai government before applying for grants. In the Philippines, although the 1991 Local Government Code allows the LGUs to directly propose projects and negotiate grants with foreign donor agencies, international lending institutions tend to require guarantees of the national government, and the LGUs are not allowed to use private commercial banks as depositary institutions, among other issues (Brillantes, Llanto and Alonzo, 2010).

In addition, the capacity of local and national governments to process ODF effectively is often lacking. For instance, the French Development Agency plans to commit funds to the development of a viaduct and the removing of an intersection grade crossing obstructing the traffic of the light rail transit in the Bandung Metropolitan Area. However, to date the project has experienced delays due to issues of co-ordination between the Ministry of Finance, the operator (PT KAI) and the Bandung Metropolitan Area, and no disbursement has been made yet. In the Philippines, local authorities in Cebu were unable to benefit from a loan within the Clean Development Mechanism scheme from a German bank because of the lack of capacity of local authorities in Cebu to propose a good project and a lack of capacity of the Land Bank of the Philippines to review the submitted proposals from the LGUs. Generally speaking, the LGUs in the Philippines do not have sufficient technical capacity to prepare feasibility studies, access or manage ODF (Brillantes, Llanto and Alonzo, 2010).

Access to ODF in ASEAN-5 cities must therefore be enhanced to increase the impact of foreign development aid on urban green growth. While the national government should seek more aggressively for ODF – especially because they are called to increase substantially in the post-COP21 era – it should also play a critical role in ensuring that local governments outside capital cities benefit more concretely from these sources of finance. This is all the more important as national governments generally are the contact points of international financial schemes application, as mentioned previously. It is therefore important that local authorities and the national government work hand in hand to propose concrete, well-designed projects and programmes to international funds and donor organisations, to optimise all large cities' chances of getting financial and technical support for urban green growth. International donors should also try to concentrate more efforts on secondary cities. The national government could further communicate with cities and the relevant ministries to raise awareness and share lessons on how to apply for finance from bilateral donors and also the range of funds available, such as Climate Investment Fund, the Adaptation Fund, the Green Climate Fund and the Global Environment Facility. A potential effective measure could be to allow local governments – especially major cities like Bandung with strong financial health – to contract loans directly.

Another option to involve cities more directly in ODF management is to set up local investment funds for sustainable urban development. It could be an opportunity to attract more easily official development finance in cities, but also to give local governments a larger role in co-ordinating international finance to achieve green growth objectives. Such a local mechanism has already been set up in Ho Chi Minh City and a few other cities in Viet Nam such as Can Tho and Da Nang. The French Development Agency has been the main international donor providing support to these local investment funds, and has channelled funds for projects in the health, education, housing, urban development and environment sectors.[14] For some projects, however, these local investment funds will need to collaborate effectively with the national government. Regional railway development (where the national government has authority), for instance, largely falls under the authority of the state, but has a strong local dimension. Nonetheless, in the solid waste and flood resilience sectors, for instance, the local government is less dependent on the national government and such a local investment fund could be convenient, especially considering that these two sectors have not been much targeted by ODF (Figure 3.9).

Projects need to contribute to green growth more comprehensively

Among environment-related ODF committed to ASEAN-5 cities, 43.4% were committed to transport projects (USD 7.4 billion, accounting for 13.1% of projects), 30.5% to water supply and sanitation projects (USD 5.2 billion, accounting for 30.2% of projects) and 11.8% to energy projects (USD 2 billion, accounting for 4.8% of projects) (Figure 3.9). While ODF has contributed to diverse sectors, projects are often undertaken in silos and lack a comprehensive vision.

Figure 3.9. **Official development finance committed for environmental purposes in ASEAN-5 cities**

Constant 2014 prices, 2002-14

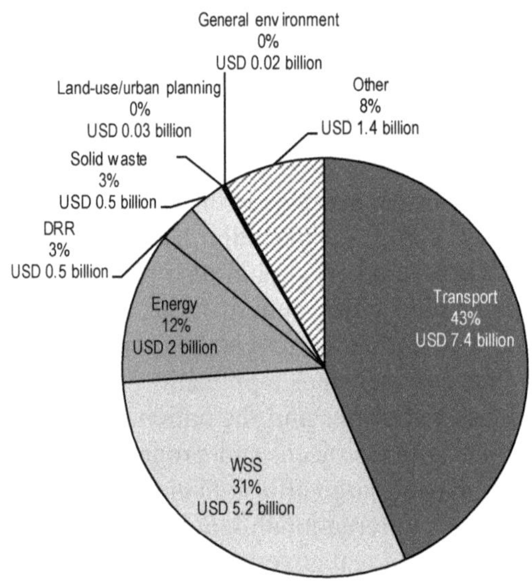

Source: OECD (2016a), "Aid activities targeting global environmental objectives", *DAC Creditor Reporting System* (database), https://stats.oecd.org/Index.aspx?DataSetCode=RIOMARKERS.

Many projects are indeed undertaken by sector, with no sustainability vision, and not embedded in long-term sustainable local development plans. In Hai Phong, only two projects contributed to transport development in the city, and focused on the construction of roads and bridges within the framework of port development. No funding was committed to develop complementary and low-carbon transport modes or related urban development projects. The construction of the international Port of Lach Huyen will generate a surge in cargo volumes in the Port of Hai Phong, and will therefore require higher capacity and more efficient hinterland connections to move goods and containers from the port to warehouses and dry ports, and from the hinterland to the port. The Port of Hai Phong already suffers from inefficient hinterland connections, including railways and waterways, and the construction of more roads and bridges will not solve these issues (OECD, 2016d). The increase in cargo volumes generated by the new port may even exacerbate these issues. Only a significant development of railways and waterway connections can efficiently increase the competitiveness of the port in the long term, and multi-modal transport should therefore be viewed as the necessary complement to other infrastructure projects undertaken in the city. Similarly, the growth of the port may create environmental externalities (e.g. air emissions, oil spills, loss of biodiversity) that should be addressed early on. ODF for the port should therefore be presented as a comprehensive package for developing the port's activities, including its hinterland connections and its environmental performance. The lack of comprehensiveness in international activities and funding in Hai Phong reflects broader trends in the country. Much of the focus of international co-operation projects in Viet Nam has been placed on development, with no particular consideration so far for green growth. As in Hai Phong, most of the past activities with international partners on transport have financed the construction of bridges, expressways and roads, while low-carbon transport modes have not yet been sufficiently taken into consideration. For instance, between 2010 and 2012, around 25% of ODA in Viet Nam targeted the transport sector, among which around 70% was disbursed for road improvements (Darko, Manh Hai and Whitley, 2015).

In this perspective, it is critical that donors and all levels of government involved in a project financed through ODF ensure that each project contributes to a long-term sustainability vision. In the transport, energy, solid waste and water sectors, in particular, the impact of each project on green growth should be carefully evaluated. In addition, synergies and complementarities across green growth opportunity areas should be sought. Chapter 2 provides some examples of such complementarities which can be an inspiration for cities and donors.

Official development finance projects must acknowledge the metropolitan dimension of urban green growth

Finally, some ODF projects tend to focus on core cities in an urban agglomeration and ignore the metropolitan dimension of urban populations, economies and infrastructure. In the Bangkok Metropolitan Region, most projects have focused on the city of Bangkok and not adjacent provinces, and there is no major metropolitan-wide project supported by ODF. A similar issue is found in Metro Cebu: the current fragmentation of the LGUs within the same metropolitan area makes metropolitan-wide projects hard to design, agree on and implement. An example of this problem is the current development of the bus rapid transit system supported by the French Development Agency and the World Bank. The BRT is only being designed and implemented in Cebu City, as discussed previously.

In the perspective of local investment funds and cities having more autonomy in contracting loans from foreign donors, metropolitan forms of governments can have a critical role to play. The future Metro Cebu Development Authority, for instance, would be an appropriate scale of governance in managing ODF for Cebu's urban areas. As mentioned previously, some urban systems which present green growth opportunities, such as transport, water supply and sanitation, flood management and solid waste, extend beyond historic cities' boundaries and have a strong metropolitan dimension. Giving such metropolitan authorities responsibilities in contracting loans and managing ODF would help to use such funds at the appropriate scale and raise their impact. It could also help to use such funds in a more comprehensive way and make sure they contribute to the long-term sustainability of the metropolitan areas. The same observations can be made to the IRDA and the future co-ordinating body of Bandung Metropolitan Area, and could be applied to the context of the Bangkok Metropolitan Region.

Southeast Asian cities need to improve their capacities to produce and collect data on green growth

Southeast Asian cities must collect green growth indicators more consistently

Despite substantial evidence presented in Chapter 1 on the need to green Southeast Asian cities' growth, much effort remains to be made on producing and collecting data related to green growth in cities of the region. The following types of data issues are often encountered:

- The absence of data: many cities do not possess basic statistical information such as CO_2 emissions and commuting data. Table 3.3 lists the main critical data gaps in most of the five case study cities. Generally, some data are available at the national level, but not at that of cities (e.g. energy consumption); in some cases the data are missing at both the national and local levels (e.g. employment and GDP output in the environmental goods and services sector). A critical issue, in addition, is the absence of data at the metropolitan level. A lot of data are available in one municipality – usually more data are available in core cities – but not in other municipalities of a same metropolitan area. For instance, in the Bangkok Metropolitan Region and Metro Cebu area, data on CO_2 emissions are only available in Bangkok City and Cebu City, respectively. OECD cities face similar issues: not all cities, for example, possess data on employment and GDP output in the environmental goods and services sector. However, the absence of data also includes more basic information in the case of Southeast Asian cities, such as total population.
- The lack of time-series data: when data are available it is often for one point in time. This does not allow for an assessment of the evolution of the socio-economic and environmental performance of cities over the past years. This is particularly critical as Southeast Asian cities are urbanising fast and much change is observed in short periods of time. Similarly, Southeast Asian cities lack statistical projections on their performance in all key green growth-related sectors, such as water consumption. This is all the more important, again, considering the speed of change in these cities. Establishing such projections would help to assess the future impact of continued urbanisation and economic growth on natural resources consumption and motorisation in business-as-usual scenarios, for instance.
- The reliability of data: the method employed to calculate some data could be improved. For instance, air quality measurement is often taken in one or a few spots in the city, at one point in time, while frequent measurements in many locations of the city would provide more accurate data. Likewise, some indicators may be difficult to measure (e.g. percentage of households at risk of floods).

The lack of (reliable) data on sectors that are critical opportunity areas for green growth is a major governance challenge for Southeast Asian cities. This is mainly due to lack of capacities in local administrations to collect and produce the data, and a lack of support from national and regional governments to assist the collection process in these sectors. The lack of acknowledgement of the importance of green growth also creates difficulties in unlocking resources to produce such statistics. The causes of such issues are therefore both institutional and political, and in the case of more technical data, a skill issue. The data gaps are obstacles to green growth in Southeast Asia, by generating:

Table 3.3. **Main green growth data gaps in the five case study cities**

Sector	Data
Social	– Unregistered population – Slum population – Gini coefficient
Economic	– Employment and GDP output in the green industry/environmental goods and services sector – Unemployment – Size of the informal economy
Land use	– Recent land-use map – Location of slums
Transport	– Commuting by trips and distance – Modal split (including walking and cycling)
Solid waste	– Coverage of the solid waste collection system – Solid waste recycled by industries and informal "scavengers"
Water	– Water consumption – Sources of water supply for households and industries – Share of households equipped with salubrious septic tanks – Quality of rivers and other water bodies – Quality of drainage infrastructure
Energy	– Final energy consumption in households, industries and businesses and by type of energy (here mainly electricity, and heating if appropriate) – CO_2 emissions – Renewable energy production potential
Other	– $PM_{2.5}$ concentrations in the ambient air – Health impact of air pollution – Vulnerability to natural disasters by urban area – Status of major fauna and flora species (including coastal mangrove)

Source: Authors.

- Difficulties to assess accurately the socio-economic and environmental trends of fast urbanisation and economic growth in Southeast Asian cities.
- Difficulties to compare cities' performance across a single metropolitan area, across provinces/states and across cities of different countries. Comparing cities' performance is, however, often difficult anyway: for instance, comparing water consumption per capita or renewable energy supply as a share of total energy consumption may be misleading if the cities at focus have very different geographical and climate contexts. Comparisons should be restrained to comparing cities with similar characteristics as much as possible.
- A lack of incentives for policy makers, at the national, regional and local levels, as well as for donors, to put urban green growth on their agenda, owing to a lack of statistical evidence. Similarly, this creates a lack of incentives to invest in the opportunity areas for green growth (e.g. there is less incentive to invest in urban public transport if the long-term environmental and economic benefits of such a system in comparison to private motorised transport are unknown). Conversely, the lack of data may result in ineffective and wasteful public investment, if not target the core problems.
- Lower attractiveness to invest in green growth opportunity areas for private investors. Poor visibility on the performance of existing utility systems is likely to discourage private investors. The lack of knowledge on the number of households equipped with salubrious septic tanks, for instance, would represent a risk for private investors, as they would not be able to assess the investment needed to fix existing infrastructure and develop new ones.

- Finally, the lack of data at the metropolitan scale is a missed opportunity to justify the needs for metropolitan forms of governance, which is so critical for green growth, as demonstrated at the beginning of this chapter.

Developing metropolitan capacities to collect green growth indicators

A set of green growth indicators is proposed in Annex C. It is inspired by two existing sets of green growth indicators developed by the OECD, but is adapted to fit the context of Southeast Asian cities:

- *Green Growth in Cities* (OECD, 2013a) provided indicators to assess green growth in OECD cities. A similar structure is provided in Annex C, mainly dividing indicators by sector (e.g. land use, transport, solid waste, etc.). A distinction between core and complementary indicators is also replicated. However, the proposed set of indicators does not follow a pressure-state-response approach, which was initially developed by the OECD (OECD, 1994). Specific indicators for Southeast Asian cities were also added, such as population living in informal settlements and estimated economic damage from natural disasters. More practical indicators than those in *Green Growth in Cities* have also been chosen, to take into account the data availability issues and core development challenges faced by Southeast Asian cities.
- *Green Growth Indicators 2014* (OECD, 2014a) provides a set of indicators to assess green growth at the national level in OECD countries. Indicators are grouped into five main categories: 1) the socio-economic context and characteristics of growth; 2) the environmental and resource productivity of growth; 3) the natural asset base; 4) the environmental dimension of quality of life; and 5) economic opportunities and policy responses. The proposed set of indicators for Southeast Asian cities in Annex C places greater emphasis on the natural asset base and the environmental dimension of quality of life. This is due to the magnitude of environmental degradation and well-being issues stemming from the rapid urbanisation and economic growth context in Southeast Asia. The proposed set of indicators also places less emphasis on the environmental and resource productivity of growth, which is a more advanced assessment tool, due to the lack of data in Southeast Asian cities and the difficulty to obtain such indicators at the city level. The most basic indicators are nonetheless included and metropolitan regions should progressively equip themselves with the capacities to produce significant data in this category. Economic opportunities and policy responses are also minimised in the proposed set of indicators for Southeast Asian cities, because green growth is largely absent from national and local policies – for instance, there are no identifiable R&D and patents in the green growth sector – and because such "response" indicators are not always reliable (i.e. an environment-related tax may have been created in a city but not be implemented or have very limited impact). The present volume, however, presents some complementary indicators which can help local and national governments in Southeast Asia assess their "response" to green growth bottlenecks.

Overall, the proposed set of indicators for green growth in Southeast Asian cities in Annex C presents the following characteristics:

- It contains 39 indicators in total, which is significantly lower than in the aforementioned OECD indicator frameworks. The purpose is to make the set of indicators more user-friendly and to encourage policy makers in Southeast Asia to concentrate efforts on the most critical data. The list provided does not exclude local and national governments to go more in depth in each sector and expand some sections on their own, especially if some indicators show a low performance in a specific area. Out of the 39 indicators, 12 are marked as core indicators and 27 are complementary indicators. Local and national governments should focus on these 12 indicators, and then expand to the other 27 if possible.

- The 39 indicators are grouped into 10 categories: social, economic, general environment, opportunity areas for green growth (land use, transport, energy, water, and sanitation and solid waste), environmental and resource productivity, and policy responses.
- Indicative benchmarks are proposed for each indicator, while none were given in *Green Growth in Cities* and *Green Growth Indicators 2014*. The benchmarks are based on international standards, trends observed in Southeast Asian cities as presented in Chapter 1, or other expert sources on sustainable cities in developing countries (e.g. the Inter-American Development Bank). The goal is to guide policy makers and give them a reference of performance, so that they can more easily interpret the data they collect.

Southeast Asian cities must to develop their capacities to collect such data, and monitor progress on a regular basis. The increase in revenues observed in the region provides opportunities for local governments to concentrate more resources for data collection in each relevant department corresponding to the sections constituting the set of indicators in Annex C. An alternative solution would be to concentrate such resources in a statistical department which could co-ordinate between relevant departments, which would have the advantage of centralising the data in one unique department. The national governments should also directly assist local governments in collecting the data, especially where the methodology is more technical. Capacity-building programmes and financial channels could be created in this regard as a means of vertical co-operation between the national and local governments.

It is also critical to establish such capacities not only in each municipality or at the metropolitan level, so that the green growth performance is not only known for isolated municipalities, but also for the entire urban region. Local governments should take the example of the Iskandar Malaysia Development Authority, which is developing the Iskandar Malaysia Urban Observatory to tackle the data availability issues encountered in this region. The Iskandar Malaysia Urban Observatory is one of the catalytic projects of the Comprehensive Development Plan ii and consists of:

- A Central Data Centre as the focal point to collate, update, analyse, manage and disseminate data and information about Iskandar Malaysia.
- A Knowledge Hub that will improve the region-wide evidence base of urban knowledge about Iskandar Malaysia Economic Region. It will also be the physical repository of all documents related to urban planning such as local plans, state structure plans and other studies.
- A Monitoring and Assessment Centre that will monitor the progress of the Iskandar Malaysia Economic Region in implementing the Comprehensive Development Plan ii as well as its urban status and trends. It will undertake "development impact assessments" periodically to ensure sustainability.

- A Technical Services Division to develop tools and methods to monitor programmes and provide capacity-building efforts to implement policies at the local level.

Central and local governments in Southeast Asia could also take the Gauteng City-Region Observatory (GCRO) as an example. It was established in 2008 as a partnership between the University of Johannesburg, the University of the Witwatersrand, Johannesburg and the Gauteng provincial government, with local government in Gauteng also represented on the GCRO Board. Its objective is to build strategic intelligence to better plan, manage and govern the city-region through improved data, analysis and reflective evaluation on its opportunities and challenges.[15] The GCRO is a good example of stakeholder engagement, in particular universities. Setting up such partnerships could be an efficient solution to circumvent the capacity issues of local governments in Southeast Asia. A city like Bandung, for instance, possesses more than 80 higher education establishments whose contribution to produce data on green growth could be much enhanced (OECD, 2016b).

Enhancing data collection through digital technologies

Smart city tools offer opportunities to increase local governments' capacities to collect data in green growth-related sectors. A largely shared understanding of the concept of smart city is a city monitored through information and communication technology (ICT) and digital technologies, the general idea being that enhanced real-time data, automated utility systems and digital communication tools will increase the provision of urban services (e.g. transport, energy, water) and governance in a way that is cost-effective and accountable. The ability of modern technologies to remotely undertake complex measuring and transmit information on a real-time basis in particular offers new opportunities to governments facing technical, human and financial capacity issues to increase their understanding of their cities.

Smart city devices can help collect data in different ways: in some cases, the smart device itself can collect the data, such as smart metres for household water and electricity consumption, or mobile phones providing mobility patterns through GPS. In Bangkok, for instance, sensors placed along water gates provide real-time data on water levels in the city, enabling the local government to control more efficiently flood resilience infrastructure. In other cases, smart devices can help to create more legible information from existing data: it is the case, for instance, of GIS software mapping that uses information collected on-the-ground. The range of benefits of smart city tools for data collection that have been developed so far is listed in Table 3.4. Southeast Asian cities could get some inspiration from these examples, mostly found in OECD cities; some cities in the region have already started to develop smart city tools, such as Bandung City under the leadership of Mayor Ridwan Kamil. A range of tools are currently under development in the capital city of West Java, including the Bandung Command Centre, a recent but promising initiative that already helps to collect data on some urban systems and directly from local communities (Box 2.6). While some improvements remain to be made on the Bandung Command Centre, in particular targeting more directly green growth data and co-ordinating better between existing departments of the local administration, this initiative can be an inspiration for developing Southeast Asian cities.

Table 3.4. **Main types of data collected by smart devices**

Sector	Type of data (general)	Data collected by Bandung
General environment	– Air pollution sensors – Greenhouse gas emissions sensors – Weather forecast sensors	– Humidity, temperature sensors – CO_2 and CO emissions sensors – Air pollution sensors (in development)
Energy	– Energy consumption in households (sensor) – Power outage in the electricity grid (smart meters)	not available
Water	– Water consumption in households (sensor) – Water quality (sensor) – Water levels and pressure in canals/rivers and pumps/gates (sensors) – Weather forecast modelling – Water flow patterns (simulation tools) – Water infrastructure condition (pipelines, dikes, gates, etc.) (sensors, GIS) – Sewer overflow (sensors) – Sea-level rise map (GIS)	– Digitalisation of clean water disaster reports
Transport	– Transport users (smart cards) – Traffic situation (CCTV and sensors) – Parking congestion (electronic ticketing) – Automatic detection of traffic event (CCTV) – Traffic violation (radars) – Mobility patterns (mobile data) – Bridge and road condition (sensors, GIS, mobile apps, CCTV) – Real-time transport schedule (Tokyo)	– Traffic situation (CCTV) – Parking congestion – Detection of traffic event (CCTV)
Solid waste	– Solid waste amounts (sensors in garbage cans/trucks/landfills) – Location of garbage trucks (GPS) – Location of garbage in the city (mobile apps, sensors)	– Location of garbage trucks and efficiency of the collection system (GPS) – Digitalisation of reports on cleanliness
Land use	– Vulnerability mapping (GIS software)	not available
Governance	– Data on citizens	– Tax records (e.g. parking tax)
Others	– Earthquake detection – Direct inputs from citizens (all sectors) – Mobile phone usage[1] – Ambulance turn-around times (computer software) – Emergency needs (mobile phones)	– Inputs from citizens – Emergency need (mobile application) – Digitalisation of land inventory and cadastral data

Note: 1. This could reveal need for public Wi-Fi spots, www.atelier.net/en/trends/articles/manycities-maps-urban-residents-daily-lives-produce-smarter-insights_437558?banner=1#ptlink.fid=23829&isc=1&did=bookmark.02e229d5ce938f892eaba8e6d031dffeb798e5b6&ctp=article.

Source: Author.

A critical measure that Southeast Asian cities could take to encourage knowledge and research on the city, and the development of smart devices to collect data, would be to create an open data website to facilitate access to information for city staff as well as researchers, citizens and the private sector. The Open Data website of New York City, for instance, displays a great quantity of datasets in a range of sectors, such as GIS maps of building footprints, maps of the projections of the impacts of sea-level rise on urban land, street tree census, time-series water consumption data, bicycle parking, demographic statistics, etc.[16] It is also an example of how digital tools can facilitate access to data and spur innovation and research. Southeast Asian cities could adopt a similar strategy to make data more easily accessible to companies and universities and broaden the use of smart city tools to the diffusion of knowledge. In addition, it would support smart open government and transparency, and reinforce public trust.

Mobilising local communities and research capacities to foster urban green growth

Raising public awareness and tackling capacity issues by involving local communities

Southeast Asian cities need to consider more systematically involving local communities to foster urban green growth. Given the burden placed on local governments, as demonstrated in Chapter 1, community-based approaches can be a pragmatic solution to cope with the lack of capacities and resources, to enhance social inclusion (especially for unregistered urban poor), and to raise public awareness on sustainable urban development and the role to be played by the civil society in this regard. Such approaches can be applied to all opportunity areas for green growth.

Several cities in the ASEAN-5 region are already promoting community involvement and outreach through community-based initiatives. In Indonesia, the city of Bandung has erected community enhancement as one strategic pillar of development and elaborated this vision in "Bandung Collaborative Society". Some existing initiatives include the creation of biopores and biodigesters meant to alleviate solid waste issues; street cleaning volunteering; the setup of Bandung City Creative Forum, a platform of exchange and innovation amongst communities; and advisory groups to the local government, constituted by the civil society (Box 3.8). In Metro Cebu, some LGUs are making use of the *purok* system, a micro-structure of a barangay[17] that promotes empowerment of communities and effective governance at the sub-village level (urban or rural). This system was first set up in the Comodes Island and later used in Liloan municipality. The scorecard developed by the Metro Cebu Development Co-ordination Board (MCDCB) to assess the LGUs' governance performance tends to indicate that LGUs using this system perform better than those that are not.

The most promising areas for community involvement, according to existing initiatives at the city level in Southeast Asia, are solid waste management and climate change adaptation. The city of Surabaya has been a pioneer in large-scale community involvement for solid waste management in the recent years. Under the leadership of Mayor Tri Rismaharini, communities have been formally organised around leaders being contact points for the municipality, and who have helped to steer community efforts towards solid waste management goals. The success of the initiative has been significant, as Surabaya is now considered one of the cleanest Indonesian cities. Likewise, an initiative of the Thailand Institute of Packaging and Recycling Management for Sustainable Environment to create recycling centres – called "Zero-Baht shops" – in communities has begun to improve solid waste collection and recycling in a few locations in Thailand, including in Bangkok City. The example of Bangkok is particularly interesting as it has formalised the contribution of informal waste pickers, in particular by providing social benefits (Box 3.8).

Community-based approaches have also proven to have positive impacts on urban resilience. Managing floods, for instance, can be enhanced by involving local communities in preparedness, prevention and response activities. The major floods that hit Bangkok in 2011 showed that the help of volunteers can be a decisive element to ensure the resilience of a city to such a climatic event (OECD, 2015b). Aspects of preparedness and prevention are equally important. Communities can contribute, for instance, by developing rainwater storage devices at the household level to ease the pressure on aquifers and avoid runoff during the storm. In Bandung City, the biopores initiative has similar objectives. Community involvement and public awareness are also critical to react efficiently during a major climatic or geological event and avoid panic from lack of preparedness.

Box 3.8. Community-involvement initiatives in Bangkok, Bandung and Surabaya

Zero-Baht shop: Community-based recycling in Thailand

A "Zero-Baht shop" is a cash-free barter system that allows the trade of recycled materials in communities for necessities, goods and services.

The system works as follows: 1) community members collect recyclables; 2) they separate the collected recyclables by type and bring them to a "Zero-Baht shop"; 3) the recyclables are weighed; 4) the community members receive an invoice from a member of the shop's staff; 5) they bring the invoice to the shop and exchange it for goods and services of the same value, or deposit it into a "bank" as savings; 6) the collected recyclables are sold to junk collectors; 7) the income is used to create a welfare fund and provide services to community members.

Through the system, low-income community members are officially registered as formal garbage collectors and separated from informal waste pickers. They are also able to receive some social support (such as medical care, support for funeral services, etc.) as community members. Overall, the system helps to formalise the informal sector, to promote recycling and alleviate poverty.

In 2006, the Thailand Institute of Packaging and Recycling Management for Sustainable Environment established, with the Federation of Thai Industries, the concept and continued expansion of the network of Zero-Baht shops. They can send a consultant to communities and organisations interested in the establishment of Zero-Baht shops. As of 2013, 12 Zero-Baht shops were in operation. The Thailand Institute of Packaging and Recycling Management for Sustainable Environment also organised the "Zero-Baht Shop Mobile," as a showcase of the project to communities, educational institutes and governmental agencies.

Bandung: The fast growth of community involvement initiatives

In Bandung, one of the visions developed by Mayor Ridwan Kamil is to build a collaborative society where community-based development is seen as an internal decentralisation process to manage the city more effectively (City of Bandung, 2015). The following community engagement initiatives are particularly remarkable:

- The mayor has created eight advisory groups on eight different topics (smart city, public policy, law, creative economy, environment, green building, cultural heritage, arts), mainly constituted by citizens of Bandung City. This is a very innovative idea to encourage public participation and raise public awareness on some critical issues.
- Some community-based solid waste management systems are in place in the city. The city is planning to set up biodigesters – waste decomposition machines – in addition to existing waste composting facilities, as residents seem already well-aware of the necessity of having organic waste services. The organic fertilizer from biodigesters has been used for urban farming and stocks for the citizens. Informal waste pickers also play an important role in the solid waste collection process (Tarigan et al., 2015). An interesting – although punctual – initiative also took place in April 2015, when the city called for volunteers to help clean up the Asia Afrika Street, in preparation of the 60th Asia-Africa Conference commemoration. Thousands of residents answered the call and participated in an effective collection process, showing the potential contribution of communities when mobilised effectively by the local government. More generally, the Pick Up the Trash Movement was launched by the municipality in June 2014 to encourage garbage collection three days a week (City of Bandung, 2015), and the Clean Cikapundung River programme launched in 2010 is meant to encourage community participation in cleaning up river banks from improperly disposed solid waste, and in reintroducing fingerlings to restore river ecosystems.

Box 3.8. Community-involvement initiatives in Bangkok, Bandung and Surabaya (*continued*)

- The city of Bandung has recently set up an innovative system to build the city's resilience to flash floods: the biopores. Biopores are community-based or household-based holes dug in the ground and meant to absorb water in times of heavy rain, thereby reducing runoff in the city and flood risk. In addition, organic waste can be added to the hole to make compost. Currently, there are 350 biopores in Bandung City and the city targets to install 120 biopores in each of the 9 561 neighbourhood units (*Rukun Tetangga*) of the city (Tarigan et al., 2015).
- An urban farming programme has been kicked off in every district, at the initiative of the mayor, to increase food security and encourage community participation in the city's sustainability. Increasing the amounts of green/agricultural spaces in the city can also have positive benefits on flood resilience by increasing the urban environment's absorption capacity. On the same topic, the Bandung Agri-Market is held every month and aims to promote locally grown food.

Surabaya's community involvement for solid waste management

Surabaya is the capital of the East Java Province and the second largest city in Indonesia. Rapid and uncontrolled urbanisation resulted in a range of environmental issues in the city by the mid-2000s, including solid waste pollution due to unsorted garbage and open waste disposal.

To address these problems, the city of Surabaya engaged into an ambitious solid waste management programme based on community involvement. The creation of a waste bank and 24 composting houses in the city were two important measures taken by the municipality, but raising public awareness was the keystone of the programme. It was carried out through community education programmes on waste management. These programmes promoted the use of simple and appropriate technologies at the household level, such as the Takakura Box. The programme insisted on how to sort out organic waste and other procedures of waste management.

In order to facilitate implementation, 420 environmental facilitators were appointed and trained by the local government. They were recruited from community leaders, the younger generation and cadres of the Family Welfare Programme. Their role is to further raise awareness of the population about the need to preserve the environment and drop habits that result in local pollution, such as open waste dumping. The environmental facilitators also trained environmental cadres at a lower level in the whole city. The city of Surabaya has gradually expanded training of facilitators and provided aid supplies and finance to support their community activities. Environmental cadres operate at a lower level than the facilitators, but carry the same functions of raising awareness among urban residents. They come from diverse backgrounds (e.g. students, office workers) and each accompanies a group of ten houses. Around 28 000 cadres were recorded in 2012, which represents significant manpower for the local government to implement on the ground its solid waste management principles.

In addition, the city of Surabaya was assisted by a network of non-governmental organisations to disseminate the new solid waste management techniques, and were integrated into the city administration (Office of Cleanliness and Gardens of Surabaya).

Sources: TIPMSE (2014), presentation at the Bangkok Knowledge Sharing Workshop on Urban Green Growth in Dynamic Asia, 6-7 August, Bangkok; APEKSI (2012), *Best Practices of Indonesian Cities*.

Efforts to mobilise local communities should be continued in all Southeast Asian cities. Often, their contribution or their importance in the city's life is widely acknowledged but remains poorly assessed and organised. A first need is therefore to better identify and organise such communities. In Bandung, for instance, while city administrators often speak of the importance of local communities, it remains very unclear what they refer to. For instance, in its vision "Bandung Collaborative Society", the city of Bandung mentions the presence of more than 5 000 communities in the city, but does not detail what they are (people often vaguely refer to them as loose groups of people united by family ties, urban areas and social activities or interests). The municipality should therefore undertake a cumbersome, but nonetheless useful, process of listing the main communities, and identify those which could support green growth objectives by area of opportunity or by area. A concrete example are waste scavengers, who are participating in the waste collection process but whose role in waste recovering activities has not been well recognised (Damanhari et al., 2009), although the Environmental Management Agency of Bandung City is currently considering developing strategies to collaborate with them. In total, around 800 scavengers – mostly volunteers organised by local communities and universities – support the waste collection system in the city, by bringing waste to the 151 transfer stations scattered in the Bandung Metropolitan Area. However, there is no benefit mechanism in place, and therefore no strong incentive to ensure large-scale community support in the long term.

An option for local governments in order to mobilise more effectively local communities could be to create a co-ordination unit for civil society organisations (CSOs) to encourage citizens' participation, assist in community actions and manage mechanisms of dialogue. A CSO co-ordinating mechanism could be particularly helpful given the large (and growing) size of many cities in the region, the local authorities' lack of resources, and the many potential contributions of local communities. It could help set up tools to receive feedback from citizens, such as letterboxes and newsletters, regular neighbourhood meetings, information kiosks and management software, and simple updates and analytical reports. To encourage consultation with citizens on an informal and permanent basis, this unit could offer open office hours, giving citizens regular opportunities to meet and talk to decision makers. Advisory committees like those in Denmark and Poland, composed of representatives of community interests, could ensure broad representation and provide a forum for ongoing consultation (OECD, 2015b). Slum representatives should be part of all these participatory processes, including urban planning. Such a co-ordination unit for CSOs would be a critical instrument to foster social innovation. In Bandung City, the Bandung Creative City Forum was set up in 2008 by individuals and communities (including the current mayor) to develop creativity and social innovation in local communities. The Bandung Creative City Forum works around four main programmes, including a community festival, participation of local residents in light infrastructure projects in urban villages, teaching opportunities for communities and an international workshop for innovative urban solutions.[18]

Fostering innovation and data production with research establishments

Academic institutions and research centres are critical partners that can help to foster urban green growth in Southeast Asia. They can contribute to spur green technology innovation (e.g. energy, water resources management, smart city tools) but also directly assist local governments and bring their capacities to achieve green growth goals. The Bangkok Metropolitan Administration University, for instance, works in close co-operation with the Institute of Metropolitan Development. It has designed programmes and courses whose objective is to carry out research and increase the understanding of urban development and management from a science and engineering perspective. It is worth noting that these programmes involve the private sector in their curriculum in a substantive way. The BMA has also co-operated with the Thai Environment Institute to conduct research on community-based solid waste management and environmental protection to study the different ways to cope with these issues. The BMA also contracted

Kasetsart University as a consultant for waste disposal, as well as to develop a master plan for the handling of waste. It will be used to increase the impact of the "3Rs" (reduce, reuse and recycle) strategy introduced by the BMA. The Metro Cebu Development Co-ordinating Board is also closely interacting with and composed of members of local universities, such as the University of San Carlos, and of research centres.

Iskandar Malaysia and Bandung also possess reputed higher education establishments. The Universiti Teknologi Malaysia has been a strategic partner of the IRDA over the past several years. It was the lead institution in developing the Low Carbon Society Blueprint, one of the most important policy guidelines in Iskandar Malaysia, which encouraged green growth. The Universiti Teknologi Malaysia is also leading the Iskandar Malaysia Regional Centre of Expertise on Education for Sustainable Development, with important responsibilities to raise public awareness about sustainable development. In 2014, Bandung counted 78 higher education establishments (including colleges and universities), giving it great potential to become a world-class knowledge-based city. Many of these institutions – in particular the Institute of Technology Bandung – are amongst the best in Indonesia and attract many talented people from across the country (Tarigan et al., 2015). Also, the proportion of the population having achieved a higher educational level is high in the city of Bandung, compared to general trends in West Java Province (OECD, 2016b). The university has contributed to some projects related to green growth with Bandung City, in particular the smart city vision.

The contribution of universities and research centres to green growth can be enhanced. In particular, they can support local governments' efforts to collect data. Cities should identify the most appropriate institutions in each opportunity area to outsource some data research and analysis. They could take some inspiration from Metro Vancouver, which has created an overall Memoranda of Understanding with several local universities and research institutes to improve existing knowledge on the dynamics characterising the metropolitan area. An interesting option would be to create Metropolitan Observatories for Green Growth, as recommended previously, jointly with local universities so that their contribution is well organised. The Gauteng City-Region Observatory offers a good example in this regard. In the future, more ambitious research projects such as the City Science MIT MediaLab could be created and developed in Southeast Asian cities to undertake advanced urban analytics.[19]

The contribution of local universities in each green growth opportunity area should also be explored and organised beyond data collection. Hai Phong, for instance, hosts the Viet Nam Maritime University, offering a range of specialised education, with 34 bachelor degrees, 11 masters and 8 doctoral programmes. Its Vocational College develops specific skills, with a strong focus on shipbuilding and ship crew training. Around 12 000 to 15 000 students are enrolled in this programme, including 2 000 in a special international co-operation section.[20] However, the programmes of the Viet Nam Maritime University are not much tailored to green growth objectives, although Hai Phong hosts the second largest seaport of the country and faces competitiveness and environmental issues. The university's courses, in this regard, could be more oriented towards environmental performance, and it could work further in collaboration with maritime industries and government agencies to measure air pollution, consider on-shore power supply, enhance bunkering activities, etc.

In general, systematic forms of communication and convening strategies could be set up between public authorities and local universities. Although created in a different context, an institution such as the Alliance for Regional Development in the Chicago Tri-State Region in the United States could also be a model for Southeast Asian cities. It was set up in order to effectively engage different types of stakeholders across the entire metropolitan region (extending beyond state boundaries) working together toward a set of common goals. It includes academic institutions, such as the Illinois Institute of Technology, the Gateway Technical College, the University of Wisconsin at Milwaukee, South Metropolitan Higher Education Consortium, and other academic institutions which interact with planning agencies/commissions and other public bodies in the Chicago Metropolitan Area.

Conclusion

The success of cities and national governments in achieving urban green growth in Southeast Asia will largely depend on their capacity to address governance obstacles. The benefits of green growth plans and policies in opportunity areas indeed can only be realised and maximised if the proper institutional setups, co-ordination, resources, skills and knowledge are in place. Otherwise, cities and national governments will continue to meet significant implementation issues and to waste resources. Table 3.5 summarises the main governance obstacles and recommendations to enable green growth in Southeast Asian cities.

Table 3.5. **Main governance observations and recommendations in Southeast Asia**

Aspect of governance	Strengths observed in Southeast Asia	Issues encountered in Southeast Asia	Recommendations
Vertical co-ordination	– Decentralisation reforms since the 1990s have empowered cities (Indonesia, the Philippines and Thailand) – Growing recognition of urban issues	– Lack of national policy framework in water, solid waste, smart cities and green growth – Failures to translate national plans at the local level – Failures to implement local plans	– Recognise the role of cities in national plans – National governments should engage further in outreach and build capacities at the local level
Metropolitan governance	– Metropolitan governance initiatives have emerged in a few places (e.g. Iskandar Malaysia, Metro Cebu, Metro Manila, Greater Jakarta, Bandung Metropolitan Area)	– Overall too few metro governance initiatives despite increasing co-ordination needs due to decentralisation – Lack of impact of existing metropolitan initiatives – Little public awareness about the benefits of metropolitan governance	– Apply the OECD's functional urban area methodology to find appropriate scale of action – Build metropolitan forms of governance and plan for green growth – Ensure support and involvement of the national government for vertical co-ordination
Financing	– Substantial (but still insufficient) growth in local own-source revenues – Increasing amounts of environmental-related official development finance (ODF) to cities (but not in proportion)	– Missed opportunities to raise local revenues (property taxes, fees and charges) – Lack of financial support from national governments to develop urban infrastructure – Lack of private investment in green growth opportunity areas – Low amounts of environment-related ODF delivered to secondary cities – Lack of effectiveness of ODF and poor integration in long-term plans	– Update property tax values – Raise fees and charges in green growth opportunity areas (wastewater treatment, solid waste collection, etc.) – Earmark national funds for urban green growth projects – Develop strategies and regulations to facilitate public-private partnerships at the subnational level, in particular at the metropolitan level – Ease regulations for cities' direct access to ODF and create local investment funds – Embed ODF in broader and long-term urban sustainability visions

Table 3.5. **Main governance observations and recommendations in Southeast Asia** (*continued*)

Aspect of governance	Strengths observed in Southeast Asia	Issues encountered in Southeast Asia	Recommendations
Data collection		– Absence of many basic data – Absence of centralised databases for green growth at the local level – Lack of reliability of data – Absence of metropolitan data and co-ordination between local governments	– Collect urban green growth indicators following Annex C – Develop technical capacities and direct resources to collect data at the metropolitan level – Make greater use of ICT
Stakeholder engagement	– Some cities have developed strategies to mobilise communities (e.g. Bangkok, Bandung, Surabaya, Liloan in Metro Cebu) – Some cities possess valuable research and higher education resources (e.g. Iskandar Malaysia, Bandung)	– Overall local communities are not always recognised as strategic resources in cities and do not contribute to green growth objectives – Lack of co-operation between local governments and universities and research institutes in green growth opportunity areas	– List and formalise local communities – Develop community involvement strategies in the solid waste and urban resilience sectors – Develop frameworks of co-operation (e.g. Memorandum of Understanding) with local universities and mobilise their resources and skills to collect data and design projects on urban green growth

Notes

1. Local government units in the Philippines refer to all subnational levels of governments: provinces, cities, municipalities and barangays.

2. Infrastructure development remains very unequal across Indonesian provinces, generally speaking. The *OECD Economic Survey of Indonesia* (2016f) provides more detailed information and comparison across provinces.

3. One of the consequences of the decentralisation reforms was the blossoming of local government units. Between 1999 and 2015 the number of provinces increased from 26 to 34, the number of regencies/cities by 55%, districts by 77% and villages by 20% to over 83 000 (OECD, 2016a).

4. The Jabodetabekpunjur Development Cooperation Board (*Badan Kerjasama Pembangunan Jabodetabekpunjur*), comprising DKI Jakarta and the regencies of Bogor, Tangerang and Bekasi, was established in1975.

5. Transfers from the national government in Viet Nam are partially indexed on the capacity of local governments to raise revenues.

6. In Indonesia, personnel expenditure accounted for 47% of all regency/city expenditure, up from 31% in 2009. This is mainly financed by the General Allocation Fund: half is indeed used to cover wages and salaries in regencies and cities (OECD, 2016a).

7. "Green" lending was defined in this survey as lending contributing to renewables, sustainable agriculture, green industry and eco-tourism.

8. In December 2014, the Board of the Asian Development Bank approved a direct loan of USD 75 million to the GMR Megawide Cebu Airport Corporation (SPV).

9. Eventually, the PPP project was not carried out, due to a change in national political agenda.

10. Presidential Regulations 67/2005, 13/2010 and 56/2011.

11. Volume 1 is entitled *Understanding PPP Concepts & Framework*; Volume 2 is entitled *Development of PPP projects for Local Government Units* and Volume 3 is entitled *Utilising LGU Project Templates and Bid Documents*.

12. Other official flows (OOF) are defined as official sector transactions that do not meet official development assistance (ODA) criteria. OOF include: grants to developing countries for representational or essentially commercial purposes; official bilateral transactions intended to promote development, but having a grant element of less than 25%; and, official bilateral transactions, whatever their grant element, that are primarily export-facilitating in purpose. This category includes, by definition: export credits extended directly to an aid recipient by an official agency or institution (official direct export credits); the net acquisition by governments and central monetary institutions of securities issued by multilateral development banks at market terms; subsidies (grants) to the private sector to soften its credits to developing countries; and, funds in support of private investment. OOF is measured in million USD constant prices, using 2014 as the base year.

13. Bilateral ODA activities targeting environmental objectives can be identified in a dataset accessible through the OECD statistical website and from the Creditor Reporting System database. This dataset contains commitment data on aid in support of environmental sustainability and aid targeting the objectives of the Rio Conventions (biodiversity, climate change mitigation, climate change adaptation and desertification). Multilateral ODA activities targeting environmental objectives can be identified in the Creditor Reporting System database accessible through the OECD statistical website. The main approach to identifying projects committed to urban areas was based on a word search of their purpose name (e.g. "urban development and management"). For all other projects whose purpose name did not make it possible to determine whether the project was urban, the "urban" character was identified by examining each project description. Similarly, the main element used to identify projects committed to rural areas was their purpose name ("rural development"). A second step, if the purpose name was not conclusive, was to look at the titles and a short description of the projects. Agricultural, fishery and forestry projects were classified as rural. The remaining rural projects were identified based on their long description. Unspecified projects refer to all other projects, with no detailed description, no details on the geographical scope or inconclusive geographical scope.

14. See: Agence Française de Développement (2015).

15. http://www.gcro.ac.za.

16. https://nycopendata.socrata.com.

17. A barangay is the smallest unit of government in the Philippines.

18. www.gsef-net.org/en/node/337 (accessed 16 September 2016).

19. https://sap.mit.edu/article/standard/city-science-initiative-media-lab (accessed 5 January 2016).

20. See: VMU Vocational College website, http://eng.vimaru.edu.vn/faculty-staff/vmu-vocational-college.vmu-0 (accessed 30 March 2016).

References

ADEREE (2012), "Stratégie territoriale en matière de développement énergétique durable: Proposition Cadre 2012-2014", Agence Nationale pour le Développement des Energies Renouvelables et de l'Efficacité Energétique.

Agence Française de Développement (2015), "Projets d'appui aux fonds urbains", www.afd.fr/home/pays/asie/geo-asie/afd-vietnam/cac-du-an-cua-afd-tai-viet-nam/phat-trien-o-thi/projets-d-appui-aux-fonds-urbains (accessed 18 June 2016).

APEKSI (2012), *Best Practices of Indonesian Cities*, 8th Edition, Jakarta, Indonesia.

Brillantes Jr., A.B., G.M. Llanto and R.P. Alonzo (2010), "LGU access to official development assistance (ODA): Status, issues, and concerns", *PIDS Discussion Paper Series*, No. 2010-10, Philippines Institute of Development Studies, Manila, http://dirp4.pids.gov.ph/ris/dps/pidsdps1010.pdf.

Chaudhuri, S. and A. Taylor (2013), "Indonesia economic quarterly FY13: Compilation of the July 2012, October 2012, December 2012 and March 2013 Indonesia economic quarterly reports", World Bank Group, Washington, DC, May, http://documents.worldbank.org/curated/en/517101468042884934/Indonesia-economic-quarterly-FY13-compilation-of-the-July-2012-October-2012-December-2012-and-March-2013-Indonesia-economic-quarterly-reports.

City of Bandung (2015), "Smart bdg City", a presentation by Mayor of Bandung at the fourth OECD Knowledge Sharing Workshop, May, Bandung, Indonesia.

City of Bandung (2014), *Low Carbon City Planning in Bandung*, www.iges.or.jp/isap/2014/PDF/pl11/pl11_07_ayu%20sukenjah.pdf (accessed 15 February 2016).

City of Vancouver (2016), "Regional Context Statement", http://vancouver.ca/home-property-development/regional-context-statement.aspx (accessed 28 October 2016).

Corfee-Morlot, J. et al. (2009), "Cities and climate change: Harnessing the potential for local action", in: *Competitive Cities and Climate Change: OECD Conference Proceedings, Milan, Italy, 9-10 October 2008*, OECD, Paris, www1.oecd.org/gov/regional-policy/50594939.pdf.

Damanhari, E. et al. (2009), "Evaluation of municipal solid waste flow in the Bandung Metropolitan Area, Indonesia", *Journal of Material Cycles and Waste Management*, Vol. 11/3, pp. 270-276, http://dx.doi.org/10.1007/s10163-009-0241-9.

Darko, E., N. Manh Hai and S. Whitley (2015), "Mapping current incentives and investment in Viet Nam's transport sector: Informing private climate finance", Working Paper No. 417, Overseas Development Institute, London, https://www.odi.org/sites/odi.org.uk/files/odi-assets/publications-opinion-files/9692.pdf.

Ellis, P. and M. Roberts (2016), *Leveraging Urbanisation in South Asia: Managing Spatial Transformation for Prosperity and Livability*, World Bank Group, Washington, DC, https://openknowledge.worldbank.org/handle/10986/22549.

Firman, T. (2009), "Decentralisation reform and local-government proliferation in Indonesia: Towards a fragmentation of regional development", *Review of Urban & Regional Development Studies*, Vol. 21, No. 2/3, pp. 143-157, http://dx.doi.org/10.1111/j.1467-940X.2010.00165.x.

Government of Malaysia (2007), Iskandar Malaysia Development Authority Act.

Government of Viet Nam (2014), *National Action Plan on Green Growth for Period 2014-2020.*

Government of Viet Nam (2012), *Viet Nam National Green Growth Strategy for the Period 2011-2020, with a Vision to 2050*, https://www.giz.de/en/downloads/VietNam-GreenGrowth-Strategy.pdf.

Green Growth Best Practice (n.d.), Green Growth Best Practice website, www.ggbp.org.

IGES and City of Kawasaki (2015), "Feasibility study on FY2014 large-scale JCM project for realizing low-carbon development in Asia: Developing a low carbon society under collaboration between Bandung City and Kawasaki City", Institute for Global Environmental strategies, Japan Environmental Sanitation Center, Kawasaki City, Japan, https://www.env.go.jp/earth/coop/lowcarbon-asia/english/project/data/EN_IDN_2014_03.pdf.

JICA and MCDCB (2015), *The Roadmap Study for Sustainable Urban Development in Metro Cebu*, Japan International Cooperation Agency and Metro Cebu Development and Coordinating Board, Cebu, Philippines.

Korea Telecom (2015), "Korea Telecom and its role in smart city development", presented at SSC Workshop ITU-TRAI.

KPMG (2015), "Infrastructure in-depth: Philippines", 2015 Investment Guide, R.G. Manabat & Co., www.kpmg.com/Global/en/IssuesAndInsights/ArticlesPublications/Documents/infrastructure-in-depth-philippines.pdf.

Laquian, A.A. (2011), "The planning and governance of Asia's mega-urban regions", Population Distribution, Urbanization, Internal Migration and Development, UN Department of Economic and Social Affairs, Population Division, New York.

Matsumoto, T. and C. Nuttall (2014), "Integrating subnational action", in: *Green Growth in Practice: Lessons from Country Experiences*. www.ggbp.org/report/best-practice-report/integrating-subnational-action (accessed 20 August 2016).

MLIT (2015), *An Overview of Spatial Policy in ASEAN and European Countries*, Ministry of Land, Infrastructure, Transport and Tourism, Japan, www.mlit.go.jp/kokudokeikaku/international/spw/general/malaysia/index_e.html (accessed 2 September 2015).

OECD (2016a), "Aid activities targeting global environmental objectives", *DAC Creditor Reporting System* (database), https://stats.oecd.org/Index.aspx?DataSetCode=RIOMARKERS (accessed 26 February 2016).

OECD (2016b), *Green Growth in Bandung, Indonesia*, OECD Publishing, Paris, http://dx.doi.org/10.1787/9789264264113-en.

OECD (2016c), *Green Growth in Cebu, the Philippines*, OECD Publishing, Paris, forthcoming.

OECD (2016d), *Green Growth in Hai Phong, Viet Nam*, OECD Publishing, Paris, http://dx.doi.org/10.1787/9789264260207-en.

OECD (2016e), *Green Growth in Iskandar Malaysia, Malaysia*, OECD Publishing, Paris, forthcoming.

OECD (2016f), *OECD Economic Surveys: Indonesia 2016*, OECD Publishing, Paris, http://dx.doi.org/10.1787/eco_surveys-idn-2016-en.

OECD (2016g), "Subnational governments in OECD countries: Key data", brochure, OECD, Paris, www.oecd.org/gov/regional-policy/Subnational-governments-in-OECD-Countries-Key-Data-2015.pdf.

OECD (2015a), *Governing the City*, OECD Publishing, Paris, http://dx.doi.org/10.1787/9789264226500-en.

OECD (2015b), *Green Growth in Bangkok, Thailand*, OECD Publishing, Paris, http://dx.doi.org/10.1787/9789264237087-en.

OECD (2015c), *OECD Urban Policy Reviews: Mexico 2015: Transforming Urban Policy and Housing Finance*, OECD Publishing, Paris, http://dx.doi.org/10.1787/9789264227293-en.

OECD (2015d), *Revenue Statistics in Asian Countries, Trends in Indonesia, Malaysia and the Philippines*, OECD Publishing, Paris, http://dx.doi.org/10.1787/9789264234277-en.

OECD (2015e), *The Metropolitan Century: Understanding Urbanisation and its Consequences*, OECD Publishing, Paris, http://dx.doi.org/10.1787/9789264228733-en.

OECD (2015f), "The Philippine PPP Framework and Programme", an OECD Review in Collaboration with the Government of the Philippines and the Department of Trade Affairs of Australia.

OECD (2014a), *Green Growth Indicators 2014*, OECD Publishing, Paris, http://dx.doi.org/10.1787/9789264202030-en.

OECD (2014b), *Recommendation of the Council on Effective Public Investment Across Levels of Government*, OECD, Paris, www.oecd.org/gov/regional-policy/Principles-Public-Investment.pdf.

OECD (2014c), "Southeast Asia investment policy perspectives", OECD, Paris, www.oecd.org/development/se-asia-investment-policy-perspectives.htm.

OECD (2013a), *Green Growth in Cities*, OECD Publishing, Paris, http://dx.doi.org/10.1787/9789264195325-en.

OECD (2013b), *OECD Economic Surveys: Mexico 2013*, OECD Publishing, Paris, http://dx.doi.org/10.1787/eco_surveys-mex-2013-en.

OECD (2012), *OECD Reviews of Regulatory Reform: Indonesia 2012: Strengthening Co-ordination and Connecting Markets*, OECD Publishing, Paris, http://dx.doi.org/10.1787/9789264173637-en.

OECD (1994), *Environmental Indicators*, OECD Core Set, OECD Publishing, Paris.

Patunru, A.A. and E.A. Rahman (2014), "Local governance and development outcomes", in: Hill, H. (ed.), Regional Dynamics in a Decentralized Indonesia, Institute of Southeast Asian Studies, Singapore, pp. 156-85.

Philippines Department of Finance (2015), "LGU taxation and revenue practices", Bureau of Local Government Finance, Manila, http://blgf.gov.ph/wp-content/uploads/2015/11/LGU-Taxation-and-Revenue-Practices-October-2015.pdf.

Philippines Department of Finance (n.d.), Department of Finance website, www.dof.gov.ph.

PPP Centre (2012), *Developing Public-Private Partnerships in Local Infrastructure and Development Projects: A PPP Manual for LGUs, Volume 1: Understanding PPP Concepts & Framework*, Public-Private Partnership Center, Quezon City, Philippines, https://ppp.gov.ph/wp-content/uploads/2012/07/PPP-Manual-for-LGUs-Volume-1.pdf.

Ratanawaraha, A. (2010), "Regulatory and governance issues in controlling urban development in the Bangkok Metropolitan Region", paper presented at the International Workshop on Sustainable City Region, 24-25 February, Tainan, Chinese Taipei.

Salim, Z. (2014), "Indonesia's ways to sustainable economic growth and development", in: Looney, R. (ed.), *Handbook of Emerging Economies*, Routledge, Oxford and New York, pp. 265-286.

Tarigan, A.K.M. et al. (2015), "Bandung City, Indonesia", *Cities*, Vol. 50, pp. 100-110, http://dx.doi.org/10.1016/j.cities.2015.09.005.

TIPMSE (2014), presentation at the Bangkok Knowledge Sharing Workshop on Urban Green Growth in Dynamic Asia, 6-7 August, Bangkok.

UNESCAP and UNHabitat (2015), The State of Asian and Pacific Cities 2015: Urban transformations, Shifting from quantity to quality, http://unhabitat.org/books/the-state-of-asian-and-pacific-cities-2015 (Accessed 7 November, 2016).

UNEP (2015), "Towards a sustainable financing system in Indonesia", in partnership with IFC and AsRIA, Geneva.

UTM Low Carbon Asia Research Centre (2013), *Iskandar Malaysia Low Carbon Society Blueprint 2025*, Johor Bahru, Malaysia.

Annex A. Profiles of the case study cities

Bangkok, Thailand

Spatial definition of the study

As a functional economy, defined by settlement patterns and human activity rather than by administrative frontiers, Bangkok extends far beyond the city of Bangkok, the capital city of Thailand, to the Bangkok Metropolitan Region (BMR) and beyond. The BMR consists of the city of Bangkok and five adjacent provinces (Nakhon Pathom, Nonthaburi, Pathum Thani, Samut Prakan and Samut Sakhon), encompassing 7 761.50 km² (Figure A.1). The BMR is the unit of analysis in this study, although some analyses cover only the city of Bangkok due to limited data availability.

There is no metropolitan government to administer the BMR. The city is governed by the Bangkok Metropolitan Administration (BMA), and does not belong to any province; it has a status of special local authority. It is subdivided into 50 districts, which are further subdivided into 169 sub-districts.

Figure A.1. **Map of the Bangkok Metropolitan Region**

Source: OECD, based on Global Administrative Areas (n.d.), *GADM Database of Global Administrative Areas*, www.gadm.org.

Policy context

In 2010, the BMR was home to an estimated 14.5 million people, including unregistered migrant workers and commuters from surrounding provinces, and accounted for just over 20% of the national population. However, it generated 44.2% of the national gross domestic product (GDP) in 2012, more than double its population share (Table A.1). The economy is increasingly driven by the services sector, but manufacturing activities continue to expand on its outskirts and beyond to the east.

Table A.1. **Key statistics for the Bangkok Metropolitan Region**

Item	Unit		Year
Land size	Km²	7 761.50	
Population	Million	14.5	2010
% growth rate	%	3.75	2000-10
% of national population	%	22	2010
GDP	Billions USD	443.3	2012
GDP per capita	USD	29 540	2012
GDP growth rate	%	3.1	2005-12
Contribution to national GDP	%	44.20	2012
Unemployment rate	%	1.	2015
GINI coefficient		0.451	2013

The BMR faces several challenges to its long-term growth, including the lack of a highly qualified labour force to drive urban green growth and a rising Gini coefficient, with growing social inequality between the rich and poor. More than 2 million people live in urban slums, many of them without adequate housing, potable water, wastewater treatment, solid waste collection, and with poor access to public transport services to commute to work, school or other services.

The BMR faces several critical environmental challenges undermining its long-term economic growth and residents' quality of life. The transport sector offers the most important opportunity for green growth. The number of privately owned vehicles has doubled over the past ten years. This has contributed to debilitating traffic congestion, resulting in lost productivity and reduced quality of life for residents and commuters, worsening air pollution with its attendant health costs, and half of all Bangkok's greenhouse gas emissions and high concentrations of particulate matter.

The energy sector is the second most important area of opportunity that could facilitate a shift away from "brown" development toward a "green" growth model. This cross-cutting lever also affects other sectors, such as transport and buildings. Electricity consumption has increased faster than population growth, especially in the residential and service sectors, but improved energy efficiency in buildings and homes offers great promise. Energy production in Thailand still depends heavily on fossil fuels, accounting for 76% of final energy consumption in 2013, while renewable energy alternatives only accounted for 11%. Renewable energy sources are developing quickly in the country, and the BMR has considerable potential in the solar and waste-to-energy sectors.

The BMR is at high risk of floods in the rainy season, which have caused great economic, social and environmental damage in the past. The metropolis is highly exposed to floods given its topography, location and sprawling urban development. At the same time, it is highly vulnerable to future flooding or other threats. Building greater resilience to such risks is critical to achieve green growth in the BMR.

Wastewater and solid waste management also present serious challenges and opportunities. Only 46% of wastewater generated in the city of Bangkok is treated; untreated water is discharged into soils, drainage systems, canals, rivers and even directly into the Gulf of Thailand. This contaminates the environment and poses serious public health risks, especially during disasters. About 10 000 tonnes of municipal waste are collected every day in the city. As much as 87% of collected municipal solid waste is disposed of in sanitary landfills, while recycling activities, which are undertaken at the community level and by the private sector, are still very limited.

Major green growth initiatives

The Bangkok Metropolitan Region (BMR) is making strides to decarbonise its transport sector. Its mass transit network now extends to a 25.3-kilometre elevated rail system (BTS SkyTrain), a 21-kilometre underground train network (mass rapid transport) and an 18.5-kilometre Airport Rail Link. Multiple extensions are planned and under construction on all three systems. The city of Bangkok recently announced plans to extend Pun-Pun, the city's first bicycle-sharing programme, from 500 to 10 000 bicycles and to connect it to the BTS, mass rapid transport and Airport Rail Link stations. Nonetheless, Bangkok's mass transit project fell short of its target listed in the BMA Action Plan on Global Warming Mitigation (2007-12), reaching only 20% of projected CO_2 reductions. This was due to a great extent to delays in the public transit investments.

With regards to buildings, Bangkok City has deployed and is using actively floor area ratio and open space ratio bonuses to encourage more efficient energy use in buildings. The city of Bangkok continues to invest in the construction of a central system of wastewater collection and treatment. The city is currently considering introducing fees for wastewater, which would be a big leap for financing wastewater treatment. It also started solid waste separation at the community level in 2010, and composting at the community level is conducted in 42 out of 50 communities. The first waste-to-energy plant in the city of Bangkok has just started its operations in the Nongkhem district. It can incinerate 300 tonnes per day and generate 8 megawatts of electricity, although the treatment capacity only accounts for about 3% of the total solid waste generated in the city. Thailand has an active green labelling programme. In the energy sector, the Label Number Five, a nation-wide energy efficiency labelling system for electric appliances, is widely known and used for most of major electric appliances, such as air conditioners and refrigerators.

Governance context

The absence of metropolitan governance for the BMR and therefore a lack of horizontal co-operation among its constituent provinces are observed, particularly in land use and flood management. The city of Bangkok has designed ambitious climate change action plans, but they do not include other provinces of the BMR. While the city publishes the Statistical Profile of the BMA annually and has developed key performance indicators, data are lacking at the BMR level to assess the BMR's green growth performance. Local finances at present are heavily dependent on transfers and grants from the national government, and own-source revenues are not sufficiently developed. Fees and charges only accounted for 2% of the BMA's total revenue in 2012. In terms of official development finance (ODF), Thailand was only the fourth recipient among the ASEAN-5 countries, but its capital Bangkok nonetheless benefited from substantial financial support, at around USD 2.4 billion over the period 2002-14, in particular to expand the mass transit system. This represents almost the entirety (99%) of ODF committed for environmental purpose to Thai cities. However, such aid has only targeted the city of Bangkok and not surrounding areas within the BMR.

Table A.2. **Core green growth indicators for Bangkok**

Item	Unit		Year
Population living in informal settlements, as a share of total urban population	%	14	2014
Urban dwellers living under the poverty threshold, as a percentage of total urban population	%	1.06	2013
Air pollution (annual average concentration of $PM_{2.5}$)	$\mu g/m^3$	25	2015
Air pollution (annual average concentration of PM_{10})	$\mu g/m^3$	50	2015
Biochemical oxygen demand (BOD) in rivers and lakes	mg/L	not available	
Transport modal share in commuting (cars, motorcycles, taxi, bus, metro, tram, bicycle, pedestrian)	%	57	2011
Electricity consumption in households, per capita	toe/dwelling	6 MWH	2012
Proportion of total energy derived from renewable energy sources (RES) as a share of total city energy consumption (in TJ; compared to benchmark of 20% (links to EU target))	%	not available	
Total water consumption per capita	L/day/capita	211	2008
Non-revenue water	%	26.76	2012
Percentage of residential and commercial wastewater that is treated according to applicable national standards	%	45.8	2012
Total solid waste generation per capita	Kg/year/capita	640	2013
Proportion of municipal solid waste that is sorted and recycled	tonnes/day	3 005.30	2013

Table A.3. **Major urban green growth initiatives in Bangkok**

Areas	Initiatives
General	– Bangkok 2020 (2009), Bangkok 2032 – BMA Action Plan on Global Warming Mitigation (2007-12) – Master Plan on Climate Change (2013-23)
Land use and transport	– Bangkok Comprehensive Plan 2013 – Mass transit network (BTS SkyTrain, mass rapid transport, Airport Rail Link)
Buildings	– Thailand Rating Energy and Environment System (TREES)
Waste	– Solid waste separation programme at the community level (2010) – Composting at the community level (conducted in 42 out of 50 communities) – Supporting community projects such as the "Zero-Baht shops" – Waste-to-energy plant in the Nongkhem district (first of this kind)
Water	– Investment in wastewater treatment plants – "Metropole Watch" programme
Green industry	– Thai Green Label Scheme (1994) – National Green Label Programme, including Label Number Five, a nation-wide energy efficiency labelling system for electric appliances – Carbon Reduction Label/Carbon Footprint Label – Green public procurement

Iskandar Malaysia, Malaysia

Spatial definition of the study

Iskandar Malaysia is located on the southern tip of the Malay Peninsula along the Strait of Johor and in close proximity to the South China Sea and the Straits of Malacca. It incorporates the Johor Bahru administrative district and the sub-districts (*Mukim*) of Jeram Batu, Serkat, Sungai Karang and Kukup Island (located in Ayer Masin) within the Pontian administrative district. Roughly three times the size of Singapore, Iskandar Malaysia covers an area of 2 217 km² with 64 kilometres of coastline. Iskandar Malaysia is the unit of analysis in this case study.

Figure A.2. **Map of Iskandar Malaysia**

Source: Iskandar Regional Development Authority (2015), "Answers to the OECD case study questionnaire", internal document, unpublished.

Policy context

Iskandar Malaysia is an emerging urban region located in southern Peninsular Malaysia. It is the fastest growing metropolitan area in Malaysia and comprises a population of 1.8 million spread across five local government areas and a territory of 2 217 km², roughly 2.5 times the size of Singapore. It is anticipated that a young and multi-ethnically diverse population of more than 3 million people will be living in Iskandar Malaysia by 2025, a 50% increase in population in the next ten years. Iskandar Malaysia is home to a prosperous and expanding urban economy. Between 2005 and 2013, Iskandar Malaysia's gross regional product almost doubled in absolute terms. During the same time period, the economy has enjoyed annualised GRP growth of 8.3%. Economic growth in Iskandar Malaysia has been stronger than that of neighbouring cities, such as Kuala Lumpur, Bangkok and Singapore, and Iskandar Malaysia's contribution to both state and national GDP is rising. Yet, Iskandar Malaysia's per capita GRP of USD 20 940 remains less than half that of the Federal Territory of Kuala Lumpur.

Iskandar Malaysia's growth is supported by strong foreign direct investment (FDI). As of 2013, more than a third of the accumulated investment of USD 42 billion (MYR 131.64 billion) had been committed by foreign investors. Singapore in particular is a major source of FDI and an important partner to the region's continued economic development. Iskandar Malaysia's major industries, which have received significant FDI, are manufacturing, petrochemical refineries and food processing. The service industry has also grown fast.

Table A.4. **Key statistics for Iskandar Malaysia**

Item	Unit		Year
Land size	Km²	2 217	
Population	Million	1.9	2014
% growth rate	%	3.70	2005-13
% of national population	%	6.4	2010
GDP	Millions USD	not available	
GDP per capita	USD	20 940	
GDP growth rate	%	8.30	2005-13
Contribution to national GDP	%	6.30	2013
Unemployment rate	%	2.8	2013
GINI coefficient		not available	

Iskandar Malaysia's three ports (Tanjung Pelepas, Johor Bahru and Tanjung Langsat) are progressively expanding in size to handle increasing cargo volumes and ever-larger cargo ships. Economic growth and port activities have also resulted in the fast development of associated industrial activities, including shipyards and boat repair support services, and other harbour and port facility services. Iskandar Malaysia is endowed with natural assets of high conservation value. However, its green growth prospects may be destabilised by soaring resource consumption. Urban areas increased by 53.5% between 2000 and 2010 (an annual growth rate of 6.7%), from around 271 km² to 416 km², to a large extent driven by the booming housing market in Iskandar Malaysia. Agricultural land has declined by half, and natural areas by 10% since 2005. The generation of municipal solid waste in Iskandar Malaysia stood at 2 100 tonnes per day in 2015. Although almost three-quarters of Malaysia's municipal solid waste generated is organic or paper, less than 10% is composted or recycled. There is great potential for Iskandar Malaysia to convert this waste stream into a renewable energy resource through enhanced municipal solid waste management practices. Insufficient sewerage management also endangers the water quality of local river systems and residents' health. Four of Peninsular Malaysia's seven most polluted rivers are found within Iskandar Malaysia.

Iskandar Malaysia is rapidly becoming a car-dependent society. Air pollution and an expanding fleet of private motor vehicles characterise its green growth challenges. By 2025, the number of registered vehicles is projected to increase from 500 to 800 per 1 000 inhabitants, or more than 3 million units. While accessibility to public transport is already relatively low, at 39%, it is forecast to decline further to 14% by 2025 under a business-as-usual scenario. Between 2000 and 2015, CO_2 emissions increased fourfold in absolute terms and doubled on a per capita basis. Severe air pollution events carry long-term health risks. Car-dependent infrastructure is not only difficult to adapt or circumvent in the future, but it directly and powerfully 'locks-in' the future growth trajectory of the local community, the economy and environment.

Major green growth initiatives

Iskandar Malaysia is identified as one of Malaysia's key development areas by the National Development Strategy. The Comprehensive Development Plan ii 2014-25 (CDP-ii), released in 2016 following the first Comprehensive Development Plan 2006-25 (CDP), sets out Iskandar Malaysia's path towards green growth. It is a statutory document and incorporates a comprehensive framework of physical, economic and social development strategies. The Low Carbon Society Blueprint for Iskandar Malaysia 2025, launched in 2012, is one of the first comprehensive green growth strategy at a subnational level in an ASEAN country. It aims to reduce Iskandar Malaysia's carbon intensity by 58% by 2025 (over 2005 levels). It incorporates a comprehensive set of 12 actions across 3 major sectors with a total of 281 programme proposals.

Public transport is recognised as a key driver of economic growth as well as a critical means by which to reduce air pollution and greenhouse gas emissions in Iskandar Malaysia. The Transportation Blueprint 2010-2030 aims to increase the public transport modal split from 15% to 50%, reduce the motorisation index down to 300 cars per 1 000 inhabitants, sustain greenhouse gas emissions at 2010 levels, ease congestion, and increase density from 20 inhabitants per acre to 60 inhabitants per acre. The first phase of a bus rapid transit (BRT) system is expected to be ready by 2020. The BRT project is expected to cover about 90% of Iskandar after its three-phase deployment. A light rail transit system is also underway.

In 2014, Iskandar Malaysia achieved the recognition of being invited as one of the partnering cities for the Global Energy Efficiency Accelerator Platform, a flagship programme for the Sustainable Energy for All (SE4ALL) initiative. Iskandar Malaysia will use this platform to learn about the experiences of other cities and share its own with other international cities, as well as develop further instruments to further improve energy efficiency.

On water, the city is embarking on the Segget River Restoration Project, a symbolic initiative that demonstrates its commitment to clean its rivers and enhance the attractiveness of Johor Bahru's urban centre. The river has long been buried under roadways and has been an obstacle to private investments, detracting from the attractiveness of the area and well-being of nearby residents due to its high level of pollution and the foul smell generated. Its renewal will also boost the local economy through the provision of some public urban amenities alongside the river.

The Green Economy Guidelines manuals, published in 2014 by the IRDA, intend to urge the private sector to begin taking actions to "green" their operations and facilities. They provide a checklist that businesses can adopt to address areas of procurement, operations and supply chain management in order to minimise their impact on the environment.

Governance context

The Iskandar Regional Development Authority (IRDA) was established as a statutory body in 2007 and is the regional planning authority for the Iskandar Malaysia Economic Region. The IRDA is a joint state and federal government initiative to co-ordinate development and foster economic growth in this strategic region. The IRDA has been critically contributing to the development of Iskandar Malaysia through the creation of comprehensive development plans and blueprints. Despite strong initiatives from the federal government, implementation by the subnational governments has been a challenge. In addition, there is a lack of engaging citizens, civil society and the private sector in fostering urban green growth policies and activities.

National policy strategies such as the 11th Malaysia Plan also do not place much emphasis on the role of subnational government agencies and wider stakeholders to foster green growth.

In terms of financing, many private actors are investing in the real estate market, manufacturing, and in particular port facilities, but policy options to encourage further private investment in infrastructure for green growth are further needed. This is all the more important because Malaysia does not benefit from substantial amounts of ODF as a higher middle-income country.

Table A.5. **Core green growth indicators for Iskandar Malaysia**

Item	Unit		Year
Population living in informal settlements, as a share of total urban population	%	not available	
Urban dwellers living under the poverty threshold, as a percentage of total urban population	%	0.42	2011
Air pollution (annual average concentration of $PM_{2.5}$)	µg/m³	not available	
Air pollution (annual average concentration of PM_{10})	µg/m³	not available	
Biochemical oxygen demand (BOD) in rivers and lakes	mg/L	not available	
Transport modal share in commuting (cars, motorcycles, taxi, bus, metro, tram, bicycle, pedestrian)	%	22	2015
Electricity consumption in households, per capita	toe/dwelling	2	
Proportion of total energy derived from renewable energy sources as a share of total city energy consumption (in TJ; compared to benchmark of 20% (links to EU target))	%	not available	
Total water consumption per capita	L/day/capita	798 million	
Non-revenue water	%	24%	2010
Percentage of residential and commercial wastewater that is treated according to applicable national standards	%	not available	
Total solid waste generation per capita	Kg/year/capita	1.11	
Proportion of municipal solid waste that is sorted and recycled	%	2%	2015

Table A.6. **Major urban green growth initiatives in Iskandar Malaysia**

Areas	Initiatives
General	– Comprehensive Development Plan ii 2014-25 (CDP-ii) – Low Carbon Society Blueprint for Iskandar Malaysia 2025 (LCSBIM)
Land use and transport	– Transportation Blueprint 2010-2030 for Iskandar Malaysia – Bus Rapid Transit (BRT), light rail transit system
Energy	– Global Energy Efficiency Accelerator Platform (GEEAP)/Sustainable Energy for All (SE4ALL) Initiative
Building	– Malaysian Green Building Index
Water	– Segget River Restoration Project
Green industry	– Green Economy Guidelines manuals

Bandung, Indonesia

Spatial definition of the study

Bandung is located in the central-west interior of the island of Java, about 140 kilometres south-east of the Indonesian capital, Jakarta. The Bandung Metropolitan Area (*Cekungan Bandung*, as it is widely known) covers a mountainous and elevated area of 3 488 km². Bandung City, located at the centre of this metropolitan area, is the capital of West Java Province.

Bandung's economic activities extend beyond the administrative borders of Bandung City and encompass a much larger urban agglomeration. The Bandung Metropolitan Area (BMA) boundary identified in the West Java Province Spatial Plan is the principal analytical unit of this report. On some occasions where data for the metropolitan area are not available, the analysis only takes Bandung City into account.

The BMA was first designated a National Strategic Area (PKN) by the National Spatial Plan, Government Regulation No. 26 of 2008. It includes two city (*Kota*) and two regency (*Kabupaten*) municipalities: Bandung City (*Kota Bandung*) and Cimahi City (*Kota Cimahi*), and Bandung Regency (*Kabupaten Bandung*) and West Bandung Regency (*Kabupaten Bandung Barat*), as well as a part of Sumedang Regency (*Kabupaten Sumedang*), which incorporates five neighbouring sub-districts: Jatinangor, Cimanggung, Tanjungsari, Sukasari and Pamulihan (Figure A.3).

Figure A.3. **Map of the Bandung Metropolitan Area**

Source: Bandung City (2016), "Answers to the OECD case study questionnaire", internal document, unpublished.

Policy context

The BMA's population is 8.6 million, the most populous Indonesian metropolitan area after Jakarta. It has been growing faster than comparable Indonesian cities, at 1.9% annually between 2000 and 2010. Recent population growth has primarily been concentrated in outlying districts. The BMA's population is expected to reach 9.1 million by 2020, when the population of the Jakarta-Bandung urban corridor is projected to be 40 million.

The BMA, and particularly Bandung City, have benefited from robust economic growth more rapid than the Indonesian average and commensurate with that of other Indonesian metropolitan areas. Between 2002 and 2012, the BMA's GRP doubled in size, averaging 6.6% annual growth. However, the BMA's per capita GRP of USD 7 490 is less than one-quarter of that of the Jakarta Metropolitan Area (USD 32 013) and is only marginally higher than Indonesia's per capita GDP (USD 7 475).

Table A.7. **Key statistics for the Bandung Metropolitan Area**

Item	Unit		Year
Land size	Km²	3 392.27	
Population	Million	8 603 524	2015
% growth rate	%	1.94%	2000-10
% of national population	%	3%	
GDP	Billions USD	54.81	2012
GDP per capita	USD	7 490	2012
GDP growth rate	%	6.6	2002-12
Contribution to national GDP	%	3.10%	2012
Unemployment rate	%	8.4	2014
GINI coefficient		0.4	2014

The BMA's economic growth is underpinned by a burgeoning tertiary sector and is supported by strong local demand for services, even though the manufacturing industry remains the largest employer. Bandung's urban environment and high quality of life lie at the heart of its economic competitiveness relative to other large Indonesian cities such as Jakarta. However, inequality has risen sharply. This is demonstrated by a rising Gini co-efficient and overall numbers of people living in poverty, as well as those enduring and high unemployment.

By and large, changing land-use patterns and a growing population have severely strained local infrastructure and the provision of basic urban services, such as transport, water management and municipal solid waste (MSW). The number of vehicles increased by more than 400% between 2004 and 2014 which has contributed to severe traffic congestion and high air pollution. Limited sanitation and poor water service coverage have resulted in negative environmental externalities, such as decreasing groundwater levels, land subsidence and high levels of pollution in the local rivers that meet the city's water needs. Less than half of the BMA's households have access to piped water services. The existing wastewater treatment in Bojongsoang (IPAL) has the capacity to serve a population of only 500 000, while the BMA's total population is 8.6 million. The volume of MSW produced has almost doubled to 56 909 cubic metres daily. Furthermore, the BMA faces several acute disaster risks, primarily related to flooding and seismic activity. Flooding, in particular, has been exacerbated partly due to the reduction of permeable surfaces for water infiltration in the built environment.

Major green growth initiatives

Under its "Better Urban Mobility 2031" plan, Bandung City is working on plans to construct public transport infrastructure. The centrepiece of the vision is a new seven-line light rail transit system. Bandung's Blue Skies programme initiated by the Ministry of Forestry and the Environment promotes low-emission vehicles by awarding a certificate to cars that meet certain emission standards. Bandung City has also announced that a green building certificate will be a requirement, not simply a recommendation, as it was previously, for obtaining a city building permit (*Izin Mendirikan Bangunan*, or IMB).

Although a new national target seeks to increase the share of renewable energy to 23% of the primary national energy mix by 2025, subnational governments including Bandung do not appear to be actively working toward this target. Solar energy presents a highly promising and practical option. Nonetheless, encouraging feed-in-tariff mechanisms could create relatively favourable market conditions. On municipal solid waste, Bandung City's Low-Carbon City Plan includes a target to reduce the proportion of waste going to landfill from 69% to 25% between 2013 and 2018, and proposes two key measures to achieve this goal: promotion of the "3Rs" and waste-to-energy (Bandung City, 2014). Planning is under way to build a waste-to-energy incinerator in the BMA after a 2016 Presidential Decree (No. 18). Bandung City has also recently drawn up a plan to introduce bio-digesters to generate gas and fertiliser supported by the city of Kawasaki, Japan. A local community initiative Waste Bank (Bank Sampah) also aims to collect non-organic waste (plastic, bottles, etc.) for recycling and organic waste to compost from households (Salim, 2013).

Bandung aims to become a model for smart cities in Indonesia and the developing world. The intent is to use information and communication technologies and innovation to manage the city's development. The Bandung Command Centre, the flagship smart city project, collects data on traffic and violations, emergency needs and the location of public utility vehicles. Collecting input from citizens on a range of issues through social media helps identify problems and react to them more rapidly.

Table A.8. **Core green growth indicators for the Bandung Metropolitan Area**

Item	Unit		Year
Population living in informal settlements, as a share of total urban population	%	5	
Urban dwellers living under the poverty threshold, as a percentage of total urban population	%	8	
Air pollution (annual average concentration of $PM_{2.5}$)	µg/m3	not available	
Air pollution (annual average concentration of PM_{10})	µg/m3	not available	
Biochemical oxygen demand (BOD) in rivers and lakes	mg/L	not available	
Transport modal share in commuting (cars, motorcycles, taxi, bus, metro, tram, bicycle, pedestrian)	%	not available	
Electricity consumption in households, per capita	toe/dwelling	not available	
Proportion of total energy derived from RES as a share of total city energy consumption (in TJ; compared to benchmark of 20% (links to EU target))	%	not available	
Total water consumption per capita	L/day/capita	not available	
Non-revenue water	%	50	2014
Percentage of residential and commercial wastewater that is treated according to applicable national standards	%	not available	
Total solid waste generation per capita	Kg/year/capita	325	2014
Proportion of municipal solid waste that is sorted and recycled	%	not available	

Governance context

Indonesia's decentralisation reforms since the late 1990s have empowered local governments, but they still lack critical capacities and resources to undertake their assigned responsibilities. The national government directs development through plans and regulatory mechanisms, but not sufficiently through capacity building and outreach. Decentralisation has also resulted in fragmented development at the local level, which in the BMA has translated into uncoordinated management of transport, solid waste and floods. The establishment of a BMA co-ordinating body (currently in progress) should help address these co-ordination issues. In terms of finance, Bandung City's budget has significantly increased over the past six years, in particular thanks to rising amounts of local own revenue. The budget, however, remains low compared to the increasing investment needs for urban green growth. Its revenue from tariffs and fees is limited. However, there is an ambitious local strategy to rely on public-private partnerships (PPPs). Indonesia is the top recipient of ODF in the whole Southeast Asian region, but the benefits to Bandung's green growth has been almost non-existent. Co-ordination with the central government is not always efficient and local governments cannot directly contract loans from donor agencies.

Table A.9. **Major urban green growth initiatives in Bandung**

Areas	Initiatives
General	– BMA-wide master plan (by the West Java governor's law) in 2015 including sectoral plans on water and solid waste – Bandung City's Medium-term Development Plan (2014-19)
Land use and transport	– Green City Master Plan (25% of land for public space; 15% of land for green open space) – Urban farming – "Better Urban Mobility 2031" Plan, including new seven-line light rail transit system – Blue Sky programme (awarding a certificate to cars that meet certain emission standards) – Bike sharing, free school bus services, car sharing, car emissions testing – Increase of city's parking tax
Water	– Revitalising the Citarum River Basin
Waste	– Bandung City's Low-carbon City Plan (target to reduce the proportion of waste going to landfill to 25% between 2013 and 2018; promoting 3Rs and waste-to energy) – Waste-to-energy incinerator/bio-digesters – Waste Bank (*Bank Sampah*)
Building and housing	– Green building certificate (linked with a mandatory building permit) – Upgrading informal settlements
Energy	– National Energy Policy (in 2014 Regulation No. 79): a target for new and renewable energy to contribute 23% to the national energy primary mix in 2025 – National feed-in-tariff system, Energy Security Fund – Bandung City's low-carbon society initiative (targeting a 20% reduction in energy use) – Campaigns to encourage compact fluorescent lightbulbs (CFLs)/light-emitting diodes (LEDs)
Smart cities	– Bandung Command Centre

Hai Phong, Viet Nam

Spatial definition of the study

With 1.96 million inhabitants, Hai Phong is the third-largest urban area in Viet Nam. Hai Phong's city government has the status of a province, along with the other four large cities in Viet Nam (Ha Noi, Ho Chi Minh City, Can Tho and Da Nang). Hai Phong is divided into 15 administrative units (7 urban districts, 6 rural districts and 2 island districts) (Figure A.4). The unit of analysis in this report is Hai Phong City.

Policy context

Hai Phong is the third-largest urban area in Viet Nam, with 1.96 million inhabitants, after the two largest cities (Ha Noi and Ho Chi Minh City). Rural-urban migration in Hai Phong has occurred at a rapid rate, with the proportion of the urban population increasing from 34% to 47% between 2000 and 2015, although its population dynamics have been increasingly determined by movements from and to other provinces in Viet Nam.

Hai Phong is located in a key economic area of Viet Nam, the Red River Delta, where important logistical activity and almost 50% of the country's rice production is concentrated. Hai Phong is an important node in the Eastern Economic Corridor of the Greater Mekong Subregion. Hai Phong's port provides Ha Noi and the hinterlands of northern Viet Nam as well as southern China with access to goods and services.

Figure A.4. **Map of Hai Phong City by district**

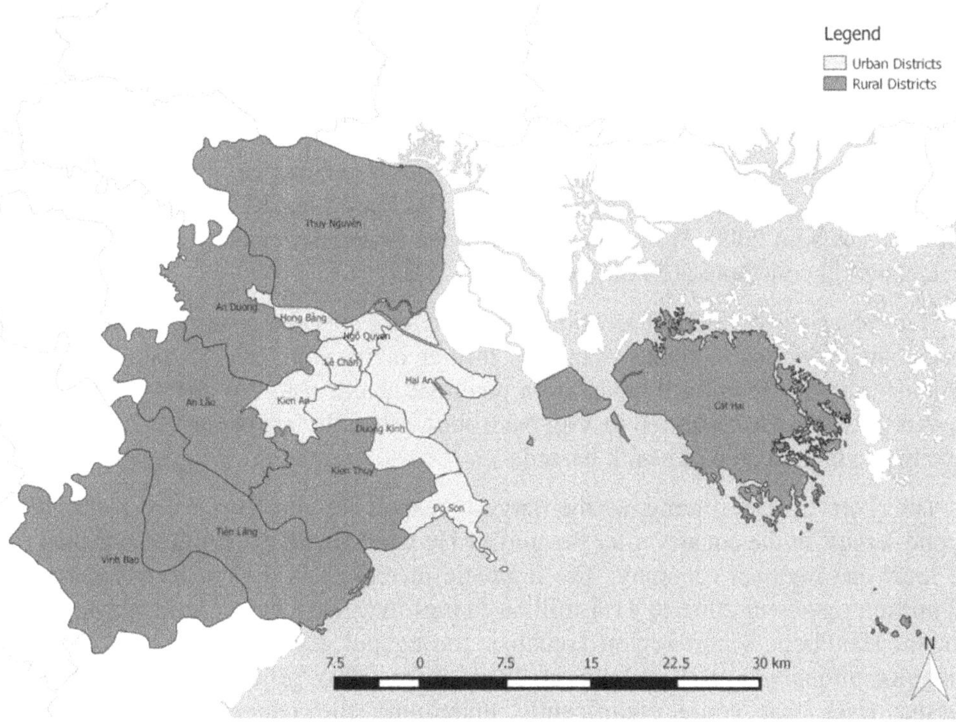

Source: Based on Schneider, A. et al. (2015), "A new urban landscape in East-Southeast Asia, 2000-2010", http://iopscience.iop.org/article/10.1088/1748-9326/10/3/034002/meta;jsessionid=9D6988DCBDEE4E3E5D505D371111AE88.c2.iopscience.cld.iop.org.

Table A.10. **Key statistics for Hai Phong**

Item	Unit		year
Land size	Km²	1 527	
Population	Million	1.96	2015
% growth rate	%	1	2000-10
% of national population	%	2	2015
GDP	Millions USD	3.969	2015
GDP per capita	USD	3 940	2015
GDP growth rate	%	8.91	2010-15
Contribution to national GDP	%	not available	
Unemployment rate	%	3.89	2015
GINI coefficient		0.353	2015

Economic growth measured by gross domestic product (GDP) between 2010 and 2015 increased annually at an average of 8.91%. GDP per capita in 2015 was USD 3 940, 2.5 times higher than in 2010, and grew at a rate of 20% annually during the period. Hai Phong has benefited from the fact that more than 60% of the population is of working age. The industry and service sectors are becoming increasingly important, to the detriment of agriculture, forestry and aquaculture. Changes in the economic structure have been accompanied by a steady increase in the literacy rate (to 90% in 2015) and in the share of workers with a high-level education (12% of the total labour force in 2015). Rapidly increasing levels of personal income have helped to significantly reduce poverty. While unemployment in Hai Phong remains low, it has been on an upward trend in the last few years.

Rapid urbanisation and economic growth have increased the need for sustainable management of resources. Electricity use is expected to increase almost threefold between 2013 and 2020. The increase in private motorised vehicles has resulted in severe congestion, and transport-related deaths from PM_{10} emissions are expected to double between 2007 and 2020 if no action is taken. The availability of surface water is threatened by industrial plants and urban areas that discharge untreated wastewater into lakes and rivers. Hai Phong has no municipal wastewater treatment facilities at present. Poor surface water quality in the city poses serious environmental and public health hazards. Domestic waste generated in Hai Phong in 2025 is expected to be four times the levels in 2000. Waste management is a first-order priority; industrial waste, in particular, will constitute 60% of total waste in 2025.

Hai Phong's geographical location leaves the city exposed to natural hazards such as storms and typhoons. Climate change is further increasing risks of natural disaster, in particular coastal flooding. Floods are a potential health risk. An analysis conducted by the World Health Organization in Viet Nam shows that climate change is likely to expose the city to a high degree of health hazards.

The Port of Hai Phong is the largest seaport in northern Viet Nam, and the second-largest in the country after the port of Ho Chi Minh City. It plays a critical role in the local and regional economy. The dramatic increase in cargo in recent years – from 7.7 million tonnes in 2002 to 41.4 million tonnes in 2014 – has contributed to the city's growth. Hai Phong's port region container throughput accounted for 25% of the total container throughput in Viet Nam in 2014. It has also generated environmental and disaster risks that could significantly undermine the entire city's economic and environmental performance if they are not urgently addressed. Maritime and inland cargo traffic result in the emission of pollutants such as CO, SO_2, NO_x, particulate matter and also dust. Levels of PM_{10} in Hoang Dieu, Chua Ve and Tan Vu terminals are on average 142 $\mu g/m^3$, 136 $\mu g/m^3$ and 141 $\mu g/m^3$, respectively. In addition, an estimated 3 000-5 000 tonnes of waste oil spilled during regular bunkering operations are generated in the port annually, only 20% to 30% of which is collected. Furthermore, several studies have reported significant loss of biodiversity due to low seawater quality and sedimentation, and handling of contaminated masses during dredging activities present further environmental risks. This is of great concern, as Hai Phong is located in an estuary with valuable and sensitive ecosystems of mangrove forests, coral reefs, seagrass and aquaculture.

Major green growth initiatives

The Hai Phong Green Growth Strategy Action Plan was adopted in 2014, based on the National Green Growth Strategy and the National Action Plan on Green Growth for the period 2014-20. This action plan aims to green urban areas, green industry, green the environment and transform Hai Phong into a "green port city", by taking advantage of the historical port city and setting up a modern, competitive and eco-friendly green port system. In 2015, the city also produced the Green Growth Promotion Plan to identify tangible projects to implement the Action Plan.

A priority for Hai Phong and for Viet Nam is to increase energy efficiency in manufacturing. The central government has standards, targets and a programme (Master Plan 7). At the city level, the Hai Phong Green Growth Strategy for Industry in 2020 (with the target for 2030) formulates a vision for modernising industry and encourages energy-effective production. Based on this plan, the city will help the 120 casting companies that use coal to transform their manufacturing process. The city is already supporting firms in energy auditing and has provided consulting solutions to save energy. According to the Energy Conservation and Cleaner Production Centre of Hai Phong City, the energy audit activities have saved a total of 50.3 million kWh per year, equivalent in monetary terms to more than USD 3.03 million (VDN 64 billion) and a reduction in carbon emissions of 42 000 tons per year (ECCH, 2014).

With the increasing demand for water, Hai Phong continues to invest in water treatment plants and distribution systems to ensure stable water supply from local water resources. For wastewater, the city is now constructing the first large-scale wastewater treatment plant in Vinh Niem Ward, Le Chan district, with a daily capacity of 36 000 m^3. More plants are planned in three districts (Hong Bang, Hai An, Ngo Quyen). With regards to municipal solid waste, the priority for Hai Phong is to separate recyclable materials at source. Currently, even though several composting facilities at landfill sites have been experimented with, many non-compostable materials are mixed in, which makes it difficult to produce good-quality compost (for use as fertiliser), despite the fact that a high proportion of waste generated is organic. At present, three urban districts are undertaking a waste separation pilot project (2014-18) namely, Lam Son, Tran Nguyen Han and An Duong.

Hai Phong has been exploring renewable energy options. To increase the proportion of its energy sourced from sustainable sources, use of biomass electricity is expected to rise from 0.6% in 2020 to 1.1% in 2030 (City of Hai Phong, 2015). In addition, the city is promoting solar hot water heaters and providing financial support to citizens purchasing new solar energy appliances. The city is also implementing pilot projects using solar batteries for public lighting and traffic lights (City of Hai Phong, 2015).

Governance context

Hai Phong's green growth will depend to a large extent on the effectiveness of its governance structure. In Viet Nam, the national government has a key role in providing suitable legal and policy frameworks and support for investments to ensure that Hai Phong achieves its green growth goals. The central government in this regard has been actively promoting green growth, recognising the role cities can play. Green growth also requires cross-sectoral planning to tackle issues comprehensively. Close co-ordination between the Port Authority and Hai Phong's city government is critical for achieving green growth targets and better public investment in the particular context of this city. However, port activities are not covered in depth in the Hai Phong Green

Growth Promotion Plan, despite the vision of this strategic document to transform the city into a "green port city". Hai Phong's green growth action plan may also be constrained by the lack of financial resources, although own-source revenues have soared in recent years, thanks to rising customs revenues. The use of charges and fees, which can foster green growth, is extremely limited (accounting for only 0.5% of Hai Phong's total budget in 2013). Strategies to involve the private sector, such as PPPs, are also under-developed. Finally, Viet Nam is the second top recipient of ODF in Southeast Asia, with around USD 70 billion between 2002 and 2014. Hai Phong has received around USD 500 million over this period, for the development of the port primarily. However, such projects have not come as comprehensive development packages and the port's hinterland connections and environmental performance have been largely left out.

Table A.11. **Core green growth indicators for Hai Phong**

Item	Unit		Year
Population living in informal settlements, as a share of total urban population	%	not available	
Urban dwellers living under the poverty threshold, as a percentage of total urban population	%	1.53	2015
Air pollution (annual average concentration of $PM_{2.5}$)	µg/m³	not available	
Air pollution (annual average concentration of PM_{10})	µg/m³	not available	
Biochemical oxygen demand (BOD) in rivers and lakes	mg/L	4.8	2009
Transport modal share in commuting (cars, motorcycles, taxi, bus, metro, tram, bicycle, pedestrian)	%	not available	
Electricity consumption in households, per capita	toe/dwelling	not available	
Proportion of total energy derived from RES as a share of total city energy consumption (in TJ; compared to benchmark of 20% (links to EU target))	%	not available	
Total water consumption per capita	L/day/capita	110	2013
Non-revenue water	%	13.7%	2013
Percentage of residential and commercial wastewater that is treated according to applicable national standards	%	not available	
Total solid waste generation per capita	Kg/year/capita	474.5	2015
Proportion of municipal solid waste that is sorted and recycled	%	10	2013

Table A.12. **Major urban green growth initiatives in Hai Phong**

Areas	Initiatives
General	– Green Growth Strategy Action Plan (2014)/Green Growth Promotion Plan (2015) – Hai Phong Socio-Economic Development Master Plan
Port	– Hai Phong Port Master Plan
Waste	– Master plan of medical waste treatment for the period of 2011-15, with orientations towards 2020
Buildings	– Viet Nam Clean Energy Program: Program: Energy Efficiency Promotion in the Building Sector" (four-year pilot programme supported by USAID)
Land use and transport	– National Urban Master Plan/Hi Phong's City Master Plan – Pilot projects using solar batteries for public lighting and traffic lights
Water	– Water supply system expansion investment (additional daily capacity of 175 000 m³) – Wastewater treatment plant in Vinh Niem Ward, Le Chan district (the first large-scale plant with a daily capacity of 36 000 m³)
Green industry	– Green Growth Strategy for Industry in 2020 (with the target for 2030) – 11 vocational colleges, 10 vocational high schools and 24 job centres in Hai Phong
Energy	– Financial support to citizens purchasing new solar-energy appliances

Cebu, Philippines

Spatial definition of the study

The Metropolitan Area of Cebu (Metro Cebu) is located on the central-eastern flank of Cebu Island and covers an area of 1 163 m² (Figure A.5). It extends along a narrow 70-kilometre coastal strip of territory which is sandwiched between rugged mountain ranges that traverse the island's north-south spine and the Strait of Cebu. The City of Cebu lies at the centre of this metropolitan area and is the capital of the Province of Cebu, which is largely focused on the Island of Cebu, and covers an area of 4 944 km².

Metro Cebu as delineated by the Metro Cebu Development and Coordinating Board (MCDCB) is the primary unit of analysis. In situations where information pertaining to the metropolitan area is unavailable, the study utilises data covering the Province of Cebu, the Central Visayas Region, the City of Cebu and the other highly urbanised cities located in Metro Cebu. Metro Cebu is comprised of 13 different local government units (LGU): three highly urbanised cities (City of Cebu, City of Mandaue and City of Lapu-Lapu); four component cities (City of Carcar, City of Danao, City of Naga and City of Talisay); and six municipalities (Municipality of Compostela, Municipality of Consolacion, Municipality of Cordova, Municipality of Liloan, Municipality of Minglanilla and Municipality of San Fernando).

Figure A.5. **Map of Metro Cebu by local government unit**

Source: Global Administrative Boundaries (2016), www.gadm.org/country.

Table A.13. **Key statistics for Metro Cebu**

Item	Unit		Year
Land size	Km²	1 163	
Population	Million	2.8	
% growth rate	%	2.63	2000-15
% of national population	%	3	2015
GDP	Billions USD	16.4	2012
GDP per capita	USD	5 084	2012
GDP growth rate	%	not available	
Contribution to national GDP	%	not available	
Unemployment rate	%	35	
Gini coefficient		not available	

Policy context

Metro Cebu is home to 2.8 million people and is the most populous Filipino city after Metro Manila (13 million). It is growing faster than comparable Filipino cities, 2.8% annually between 2000 and 2010, and the population growth has been fastest in peripheral local government units. It is anticipated that Metro Cebu's population will reach 3.8 million people by 2030. The demographic structure of Metro Cebu remains young and it has benefited from significant expansion of the working-age population.

Cebu has achieved remarkable economic growth that is faster than the national average and stronger than Metro Manila. Between 2010 and 2014, the GRP of the Central Visayas Region averaged 8.1% annual growth, underpinned by the rapid expansion of the secondary sector. Metro Cebu is recognised as the primary economic centre of the Central Visayas Region. By 2030, Metro Cebu's GRP will 71% share of the regional economy (as opposed to 56% in 2012). Metro Cebu's estimated per capita GRP of USD 5 084 (PHP 69 700) still remains slightly less than one-third of Metro Manila's (USD 14 816) and only marginally higher than the Philippines' per capita GDP (USD 4 765).

Unplanned land-use patterns and a growing population have severely strained local infrastructure and the provision of basic urban services, such as transport, energy, water management and municipal solid waste. Similarly, developments have led to encroachments on environmentally critical areas such as watersheds. Vehicle numbers almost doubled between 2003 and 2010, contributing to worsening traffic congestion and high air pollution levels. Limited sanitation and water service coverage is leading to negative environmental externalities, such as pollution and salinity intrusion in groundwater, which are placing great stress on the metropolitan area. Less than half of Metro Cebu's households have access to piped water services. The volume of municipal solid waste produced daily has rapidly increased.

Water security is a cornerstone of urban green growth strategies in Cebu. The Province of Cebu, and in particular Metro Cebu, area face great water challenges, including increasing water demand in a context of diminishing resources, relative inefficiency of the water distribution network, and suboptimal coverage of the water supply and sanitation infrastructure, leading to quality issues in surface and ground water. Projected total water demand in the Metro Cebu area is expected to almost triple by 2040; the non-revenue water rate is high at 25%; only 49.9% of water used for other purposes than drinking is supplied through pipe connections; and 80% of grey water receives no treatment.

Metro Cebu is exposed to acute disaster risks. It regularly experiences flooding, especially during the wet season from June to November and annual tropical storms. In 2013, Cebu City experienced a magnitude 7.2 earthquake which affected 870 000 people and damaged nearly 1 000 houses, local infrastructure and community facilities.

Major green growth initiatives

The Metro Cebu Development and Coordinating Board (MCDCB) is responsible for metro wide planning and development. The harmonisation of the land use plans of the 13 LGUs falls within its mandate. In 2012, the MCDCB, supported by the Japanese International Cooperation Agency, initiated a project which includes the "Metro Cebu Vision 2050" and "Roadmap Study for Sustainable Urban Development". The primary focus of the initiative has been the production of a blueprint to guide the city's sustainable economic development. Land use is also a critical pillar and it is expected that Vision 2050 will be interpreted into the official comprehensive land use plans in each of Metro Cebu's 13 LGUs and subsequently into their zoning ordinances.

Revitalising Cebu's downtown area by making more land available for development and improving connectivity will be essential to Metro Cebu's economy. The green loop and colon revitalisation project are vital for the transformation of the city. The focus of the green loop on a pedestrian-dominated and transit-oriented corridor across the four cities of Cebu, Mandaue, Lapu-Lapu and Cordova is a laudable step towards achieving green growth objectives. One of the first large public investments in "green" infrastructure in Cebu will be the Cebu bus rapid transit project, which is currently underway. This is in line with Mega Cebu Vision 2050 which hopes to ensure accessible and efficient movement through an integrated and sustainable system. The Cebu-Cordova bridge, a third bridge to link the southern section of Mactan with Cebu City, is planned to relieve the traffic on the two existing bridges whilst providing connectivity for traffic from the south of Metro Cebu.

In addressing the solid waste management challenges, Cebu promotes the "No segregation, No collection" policy that requires residents in Metro Cebu to segregate their household waste in conformity with international practice. Every barangay should have a materials recovery facility for final sorting, segregation composting and recycling. Yet as at 2011, out of 349 barangays, only 101 (29%) had operational materials recovery facilities. Besides, innovative practices are being piloted in various LGUs for waste management such as vermicomposting and biogas digesting.

In terms of greening industry, the Promotion of Green Economic Development project began in 2013. It is a joint initiative of the Department of Trade and Industry's Regional Operations Group and the GIZ and aims to improve the competiveness of micro, small and medium enterprises to enable the adoption of climate-smart and environmentally friendly approaches in their value chain. Some economic zones in Metro Cebu such as the Cebu Business Park have shown a greater green potential through their solid waste management practices, sewage treatment, green gas emission management and lighting system.

Governance context

In the Philippines, as in other Southeast Asian countries, significant gaps are observed between national policy objectives and concrete actions taken by subnational governments on the ground. Despite decentralisation reforms, there is a capacity constraint at the national level, an over-reliance on regulatory approaches rather than outreach, collaboration and capacity building between the national and local governments. In terms of metropolitan governance, the Metro Cebu Development and Coordinating Board (MCDCB) is a promising initiative, a consortium of the 13 LGUs of Metro Cebu, regional line agencies of the national government, private sector representatives and civil society organisations. It is expected to be converted into the Mega Cebu Development Authority (MCDA).

Strategies to unlock and co-ordinate finance for urban green growth will also be critical. There are high discrepancies in the degree of autonomy of the LGUs constituting Metro Cebu, and generally speaking tariffs and user charges are not sufficiently collected (6% of total revenues of Cebu's LGUs on average). In addition, Cebu's LGUs remain very dependent on national government's transfers, but there is no public investment framework for green growth. Finally, similarly to Bandung, very little amounts of ODF have been committed to support green growth objectives in Cebu since 2002, while Manila has concentrated around 69% of total environment-related ODF to cities.

Table A.14. **Core green growth indicators for Metro Cebu**

Item	Unit		Year
Population living in informal settlements, as a share of total urban population	%	not available	
Urban dwellers living under the poverty threshold, as a percentage of total urban population	%	1.53	
Air pollution (annual average concentration of $PM_{2.5}$)	µg/m³	not available	
Air pollution (annual average concentration of PM_{10})	µg/m³	not available	
Biochemical oxygen demand (BOD) in rivers and lakes	mg/L	70	
Transport modal share in commuting (cars, motorcycles, taxi, bus, metro, tram, bicycle, pedestrian)	%	not available	
Electricity consumption in households, per capita	toe/dwelling	not available	
Proportion of total energy derived from RES as a share of total city energy consumption (in TJ; compared to benchmark of 20% (links to EU target))	%	52.89	
Total water consumption per capita	L/day/capita	110	
Non-revenue water	%	25	2013
Percentage of residential and commercial wastewater that is treated according to applicable national standards	%	not available	
Total solid waste generation per capita	Kg/year/capita	159	2015
Proportion of municipal solid waste that is sorted and recycled	%	not available	

Table A.15. **Major urban green growth initiatives in Cebu**

Areas	Initiatives
General	– Metro Cebu Vision 2050/Roadmap Study for Sustainable Urban Development in Metro Cebu
Land use and transport	– Cebu bus rapid transit (BRT) – The green loop and colon revitalization project – Cebu-Cordova bridge
Water	– Improving and developing infrastructure (i.e. dams, reservoirs) and diversify sources of water supply in the long term (proposed in the Roadmap Study)
Waste	– The 2000 Ecological Solid Waste management Act/"No separation, No collection" policy/materials recovery facilities (MRFs) for final sorting, segregation composting and recycling at the Baranguay level – Vermicomposting (Kwarta sa Basura Project) and biogas digesting
Green industry	– Promotion of Green Economic Development Project (ProGED) – Cebu Business Park

References

Bandung City (2016), "Answers to the OECD case study questionnaire", internal document, unpublished.

City of Hai Phong (2015), "Answers to the OECD case study questionnaire", internal document, unpublished.

ECCH (2014a), "Activities of Hai Phong Energy Conservation and Cleaner production Centre associated with green growth and sustainable development", Energy Conservation and Cleaner Production Centre, http://ecchaiphong.gov.vn/defaulte.aspx?pageid=newsdetailsE&catID=6&id=131 (accessed 12 June 2016).

Global Administrative Boundaries (2016), www.gadm.org/country (accessed 9 June 2016).

Global Administrative Areas (n.d.), *GADM Database of Global Administrative Areas*, www.gadm.org (retrieved in May 2015).

Iskandar Regional Development Authority (2015), "Answers to the OECD case study questionnaire", internal document, unpublished.

Schneider, A. et al. (2015), "A new urban landscape in East-Southeast Asia, 2000 2010", *Environmental Research Letters*, Vol. 10/3, http://iopscience.iop.org/article/10.1088/1748-9326/10/3/034002/meta;jsessionid=9D6988DCBDEE4E3E5D505D371111AE88.c2.iopscience.cld.iop.org.

Annex B. The Knowledge-Sharing Platform on Urban Green Growth in Dynamic Asia

Why knowledge sharing?

Outside the jurisdiction of cities, other stakeholders can contribute to fostering urban green growth. The challenges and opportunities presented in this report are shared by many Asian cities and national governments who have an influence on urban policies, and by institutions for development co-operation who provide support to sustainable urban policy making. Despite this urgent agenda, the expertise, knowledge and experience have not sufficiently been shared among these stakeholders.

Knowledge sharing can bring benefits to all the stakeholders through peer learning on an equal footing. Asian cities and national governments, in particular, could mutually learn from different practices, and therefore better address the urgent need to develop urban green growth policies and to implement them. Hearing from other local experiences on successful policy initiatives could provide cities with useful knowledge to take concrete action. In addition, institutions for development co-operation could support cities and countries in dynamic Asia more effectively by sharing their accumulated knowledge and tailoring their own activities based on local specific needs. Knowledge sharing would therefore help to create synergies by assembling fragmented knowledge, and provide new inspiration to pursue and achieve urban green growth.

The OECD Knowledge Sharing Alliance

The OECD Strategy on Development is a corporate endeavour and framework that guides the Organisation's contribution to development. Its overall objective is to strengthen the OECD's contributions to higher and more inclusive growth in the widest array of countries. One of the core elements of the strategy is to strengthen policy dialogue and knowledge sharing to promote continuous learning with partner countries, institutions and other stakeholders with implementation capacity and experience on the ground. To this end, the OECD and some member countries launched the Knowledge Sharing Alliance (KSA) in January 2013. The KSA is open to all countries and, with the support of OECD experts, set up pilots to support continuous consultations.

The KSA aims to leverage the OECD's multi-disciplinary expertise, engage in conversations and mutual learning processes with emerging and developing economies, and increase impact by working closely with multi- and bilateral organisations that have field presence and implementation capacities and/or networks. The objectives of the KSA are threefold:

1. to open the OECD's knowledge, inter-disciplinary policy expertise and peer learning networks to partner countries that seek this access

2. to co-produce knowledge through peer learning
3. to establish feedback loops in order to upgrade the Organisation's knowledge, policy instruments, frameworks and skills.

This will result in better-informed analysis and policy options that are more relevant for countries at different stages of development, are adapted to their contexts and needs, and respond better to the complex challenges of today's rapidly changing global context.

The KSA has a strategic role in promoting and transforming knowledge sharing into action, making it more visible and monitoring progress and lessons learned by all actors involved. It has both a strategic level and an operational level. Several types of knowledge sharing can be used, such as: global forums, country and city level implementation gaps, knowledge exchanges and sharing among clusters of countries and cities, and exchanges of experience and development. All knowledge sharing approaches can make use of a combination of modalities including (global) forum discussions; a web-based platform; country and thematic studies; workshops and seminars; networks (both virtual and real); and partnerships with organisations, think tanks, etc. in developed and developing countries.

The Knowledge-Sharing Platform on Urban Green Growth in Dynamic Asia

In 2013-14, several knowledge-sharing activities and events were conducted under the framework of the project Urban Green Growth in Dynamic Asia, with the support of the OECD Knowledge Sharing Alliance. Throughout these pilot activities, it was confirmed that knowledge sharing is particularly useful to ensure the coherence of different urban green growth initiatives among different actors and to share best practices among cities with similar challenges. It was therefore common consensus to explore further effective options for knowledge sharing on urban green growth. In particular, participants highlighted the importance of engaging in peer learning. Following these preliminary activities, the Urban Green Growth in Dynamic Asia Knowledge-Sharing Platform was set up at the Paris Policy Forum on Urban Green Growth in Dynamic Asia in June 2014. The Knowledge-Sharing Platform is an open, flexible platform articulated around several conferences, peer learning workshops and feedback activities, which all promote policy dialogue on urban green growth. The objectives of the platform are threefold:

1. To facilitate knowledge exchange amongst participating cities (both in dynamic Asia and in the OECD), including city networks, on urban green growth. The goal was to bring together knowledge possessed by each participating city and acquired through their own experience on specific themes, as they may share similar opportunities and challenges.
2. To facilitate knowledge exchange vertically between participating cities and national governments, as both can play complementary roles in fostering urban green growth. This is particularly important because of the development context in dynamic Asia, which tends to emphasise national policies.
3. To facilitate knowledge exchange between cities in dynamic Asia and institutions for development co-operation that support implementation and the OECD. The objective is to learn from the concrete good practices and implementation obstacles Asian cities are facing to achieve urban green growth goals, and the solutions.

The platform's activities were organised around the five case study cities of the project. They included peer learning workshops organised by the five Asian cities of the project and several international conferences organised in Asia and Europe (Table B.1). The five case study cities, and to some extent corresponding national governments and development agencies, participated in each event in order to encourage continuous exchange and pursue the knowledge-sharing activities over several events. The five peer learning workshops constituted the core elements of the platform, as the discussions were concentrated on the policy context in the host city. Each workshop was organised around roundtable discussions and site visits, and focused on a specific topic relevant to the context of the host city. The chosen topics were: flood resilience; urban management under rapid urbanisation; smart cities and green growth; green growth in port cities; and land use, water management and metropolitan governance.

Table B.1. **OECD Knowledge Sharing Workshops and Policy Forums (2013-16)**

Type of activity and title	Date	Location
Consultation workshop Urban Green Growth in Dynamic Asia	May 2013	Stockholm, Sweden
Consultation workshop The Conceptual Framework on Urban Green Growth in Dynamic Asia	February 2014	Bangkok, Thailand
Consultation workshop The Conceptual Framework on Urban Green Growth in Dynamic Asia	March 2014	Jakarta, Indonesia
International conference Policy Forum on Urban Green Growth in Dynamic Asia from Concept to Implementation	June 2014	Paris, France
1st peer learning workshop Urban Green Growth and Climate Change Resilience in Bangkok	August 2014	Bangkok, Thailand
International conference Japan-OECD Policy Forum on Urban Development and Green Growth	October 2014	Tokyo, Japan
2nd peer learning workshop Spatial Development Strategies in Iskandar Malaysia: How to Plan, Manage and Maintain Local Assets Under Rapid Urbanisation?	November 2014	Iskandar Malaysia, Malaysia
3rd peer learning workshop Smart Cities and Green Growth	May 2015	Bandung, Indonesia
4th peer learning workshop Green Growth in Port Cities	June 2015	Hai Phong, Viet Nam
International conference Asia-Pacific Urban Forum (APUF 6)	October 2015	Jakarta, Indonesia
5th peer learning workshop Creating a Sustainable and Resilient Cebu: Land Use, Water and Metropolitan Governance in the Context of Rapid Urbanisation	December 2015	Cebu, Philippines
International conference Green Growth and Sustainable Urban Development (COP21 side event)	December 2015	Paris, France
International conference Green Growth and Sustainable Development Forum (OECD)	November 2016	Paris, France

Source: Authors.

The expected output of the platform has been an increased and shared understanding of what urban green growth entails in the specific local contexts of the participating organisations, and especially in the host cities, which could lead to more effective design and implementation of urban green growth policies. The peer learning workshops and feedbacks were expected to play an important role in integrating fragmented knowledge from the diverse participants and provide output documents promoting concrete actions for the host cities and giving inspirations to all stakeholders. The OECD prepared a discussion paper before each workshop, which was improved afterwards based on the discussions at the event. Each output document from the peer learning workshops informed a special chapter in the five case study reports. The output documents and the case study reports have been shared with the participants and a wider audience, in particular through the community space of the platform hosted by the OECD domain.

Lessons learnt from the Knowledge-Sharing Platform initiative

In terms of policy dialogue, several lessons were learnt from the activities of the Knowledge-Sharing Platform:

- Amongst the three dimensions of knowledge sharing aforementioned, interactions among institutions for development co-operation (e.g. international organisations, development agencies and banks) were the most successful. The need for co-operation and mutual learning between these stakeholders is particularly strong and the knowledge-sharing activities proved to be opportunities for them to discuss their respective projects. These discussions were also beneficial for the OECD, insofar as the studies of the project can inform the activities of development partners; conversely, collaboration with the OECD can result in the implementation of some recommendations contained in the OECD reports.
- The knowledge-sharing activities were opportunities to gather representatives from adjacent municipalities of the same metropolitan region. In the Bandung Metropolitan Area and Bangkok Metropolitan Region, in particular, such interactions are very rare, although the need for horizontal co-operation is strong. Such activities, organised around informal discussions, could be replicated in future knowledge-sharing initiatives as a starting point for more systematic exchange of information and co-operation between such stakeholders.
- In terms of interactions between cities and national governments, the Knowledge-Sharing Platform proved to be less useful. This is partly due to the fact that their relationships in daily operations are more formal in nature, because of the vertical hierarchy. Therefore, the platform could not easily encourage informal and free discussions between representatives of both levels of government.

While the events have proven to be extremely useful to collect information for the case study reports and to build a network of policy makers and experts on urban green growth in Southeast Asia, the following issues need to be carefully addressed if such an initiative is to be replicated in the future:

- The difficulty to assess the impacts of the activities on participants and deliver concrete outputs. In particular, two-day workshops tend to be too short for the host city and participants to share their experiences fully and go in-depth in the discussions. Participants need more time to digest the information and deliver best practices that are tailored to the needs of the host city. The knowledge-sharing activities sometimes only resulted in information sharing from the host city to the guests.
- The language and cultural barriers to knowledge sharing between participants from different countries: finding city staff with good working knowledge of English is not always easy, in particular in countries such as Indonesia, Thailand and Viet Nam, where English is less practiced than in Malaysia and the

Philippines. Likewise, the culture of exchange and open discussions is less strong in some countries than in others, which affects the quality of discussions.

- The difficulty to ensure commitments from the participating cities: although the topics of the workshops are relevant, government officials are often too busy to participate in them, or to prepare well. They are often not able to fund the participants' travel costs as well. It may be difficult to get participants to comment on the output document of the peer learning workshops (or to be actively involved in other activities such as online discussions).

An option to ensure greater impacts of the knowledge-sharing activities could be to tailor the activities further to implementation goals or project collaboration. Cities hosting the knowledge-sharing activities should use the network built during the event to set up more formal collaboration partnerships, use the results of the discussions to improve the quality of their current projects or create new projects based on recommendations made by other cities, national governments and implementation partners. Another option would be to organise follow-up knowledge-sharing activities (after the initial event involving a wide audience) but with a concrete outcome as objective and within a smaller audience. A more limited number of organisations/governments could be invited and work on a specific project related to green growth. This could result, for instance, in more systematic city-to-city collaboration.

Annex C.
Urban green growth indicators for Southeast Asia

Core indicators are written in bold.

Sector	#	Indicator	Unit	Indicative benchmark		
Social	**1**	**Population living in informal settlements, as a share of total urban population**	**%**	<20	20-30	>30
	2	Gini coefficient		<0.3	0.3-0.49	>0.49
	3	Average PISA score in mathematics, reading and science		>470	440-470	<440
Economic	**4**	**Urban dwellers living under the poverty threshold (USD 1.90 a day), as a percentage of total urban population**	%	<7	7-10	>10
	5	Informal employment as a percentage of total employment	%	<20	20-35	>35
	6	Contribution of the local economy to the environmental goods and services sector:[1]				
		– Employment, as a share of total employment	%	>0.6	0.4-0.6	<0.4
		– Gross value added, as a share of total GDP output	%	>1	0.5-1	<0.5
General environment	**7**	**Air pollution**				
		– Annual average concentration of $PM_{2.5}$	**µg/m³**	<10	10-20	>20
		– Annual average concentration of PM_{10}	**µg/m³**	<20	20-50	>50
	8	Annual CO_2 emissions per capita	Tonne/year/capita	<5	5-10	>10
	9	**Biochemical oxygen demand (BOD) in rivers and lakes**	**mg/L**	<2	2-4	>4
	10	Open green space area ratio per 100 000 inhabitants	Hectares	>10	7-10	<7
	11	Mangrove forest preservation, as a share of mangrove forest increase from previous year	%	>0	0	<0
	12	Estimated economic damage from natural disasters (floods, droughts, earthquakes, etc.) as a share of GDP	%	<0.5	0.5-1	>1

Sector	#	Indicator	Unit	Indicative benchmark		
Land-use	13	Population density on urban land	Residents/km^2	7 000-20 000	4 000-7 000; 20 000-25 000	<4 000; >25 000
	14	Sprawl Index	%	>0	0	<0
	15	Share of multi-family houses in total housing units	%	>50	30-50	<30
Transport	**16**	**Transport modal share in commuting (cars, motorcycles, taxi, bus, metro, tram, bicycle, pedestrian)**	**%**	Private transport <30%	Private transport =30-50%	Private transport >50%
	17	Average age of car fleet (total and by type)	Years	<6	6-12	>12
	18	Motorisation rate	Number of vehicles per capita	<0.5	0.5-1	>1
	19	Average travel speed on primary thoroughfares during peak hour	Km/h	>30	15-30	<30
Energy	**20**	**Electricity consumption in households, per capita**	**toe/dwelling**	<0.2	0.2-0.3	>0.4
	21	Average number of electrical interruptions per year, per customer		<10	10-13	>13
	22	Heavy metals emission intensity of manufacturing industries	kg of heavy metals equivalent released per million USD GVA	<0.02	0.02-0.04	>0.04
	23	**Proportion of total energy derived from RES as a share of total city energy consumption (in TJ; compared to benchmark of 20% (links to EU target))**	**%**	>20	10-20	<10
	24	Average share of population undergoing prolonged power outage in case of natural disaster over the past five years	%	<10	10-25	>25
Water and sanitation	25	Percentage of water samples in a year that comply with national potable water quality standards	%	>97	90-97	<90
	26	**Total water consumption per capita**	**L/day/capita**	120-200	60-80 or 150-200	<60; >200
	27	**Non-revenue water**	%	0-20	20-30	>30
	28	Annual average of daily number of hours of continuous water supply per household	%	>20 h/day	12-20 h/day	<12 h/day
	29	**Percentage of residential and commercial wastewater that is treated according to applicable national standards**	**%**	>60	40-60	<40
	30	Percentage of dwellings damaged by the most intense flooding in the last ten years	%	<0.5	0.5-3	>3

Sector	#	Indicator	Unit	Indicative benchmark		
Solid waste	31	**Total solid waste generation per capita**	**Kg/year/capita**	<300	300-400	>400
	32	Share of the population with weekly municipal solid waste collection	%	90-100	80-90	<80
	33	**Proportion of municipal solid waste that is sorted and recycled (total and by type of waste, e.g. paper, glass, batteries, PVC, bottles, metals), including waste handled by informal "scavengers"**	%	>20	10-20	<10
	34	Remaining life of current landfill(s)	Years	>8	5-8	<5
Environmental and resource productivity	35	GDP per unit of energy-related CO_2 emitted	USD per Mt CO_2	>0.5	0.2-0.5	<0.2
	36	Real income per unit of energy-related CO_2 emitted	USD per Mt CO_2	>0.5	0.2-0.5	<0.2
	37	GDP per unit of Total Primary Energy Supply (TPES)	GDP/TPES	>7	4-7	>7
Policy responses (examples)	38	Share of taxes, fees and charges in green growth opportunity areas, in total local revenues	%	>5	2-5	<2
	39	International finance flows of importance to green growth (foreign direct investment, official development assistance, carbon market financing), as a share of total flow in each category	%	>20	10-20	<10

Note: . The environmental goods and services sector is defined activities to measure, control, restore, prevent, treat, minimise, research and sensitise regarding environmental damage to air, water and soil, resource depletion and problems related to waste, noise, biodiversity and landscapes. The definition includes cleaner technologies, goods and services that prevent or minimise pollution and resource-efficient technologies, goods and services that minimise natural resource use (OECD, 2014).

Source: OECD (2014), Green Growth Indicators 2014, OECD Publishing, Paris, http://dx.doi.org/10.1787/9789264202030-en.

ORGANISATION FOR ECONOMIC CO-OPERATION AND DEVELOPMENT

The OECD is a unique forum where governments work together to address the economic, social and environmental challenges of globalisation. The OECD is also at the forefront of efforts to understand and to help governments respond to new developments and concerns, such as corporate governance, the information economy and the challenges of an ageing population. The Organisation provides a setting where governments can compare policy experiences, seek answers to common problems, identify good practice and work to co-ordinate domestic and international policies.

The OECD member countries are: Australia, Austria, Belgium, Canada, Chile, the Czech Republic, Denmark, Estonia, Finland, France, Germany, Greece, Hungary, Iceland, Ireland, Israel, Italy, Japan, Korea, Latvia, Luxembourg, Mexico, the Netherlands, New Zealand, Norway, Poland, Portugal, the Slovak Republic, Slovenia, Spain, Sweden, Switzerland, Turkey, the United Kingdom and the United States. The European Union takes part in the work of the OECD.

OECD Publishing disseminates widely the results of the Organisation's statistics gathering and research on economic, social and environmental issues, as well as the conventions, guidelines and standards agreed by its members.

OECD PUBLISHING, 2, rue André-Pascal, 75775 PARIS CEDEX 16
(04 2016 16 1 P) ISBN 978-92-64-26635-3 – 2016

www.ingramcontent.com/pod-product-compliance
Lightning Source LLC
Chambersburg PA
CBHW061212240926
51846CB00006B/1201
* 9 7 8 9 2 6 4 2 6 6 3 5 3 *